"Two remarkable people writing about a third remarkable man—and full of lessons for the ordinary rest of us. This is a lovely and important book."

—BILL MCKIBBEN, author of *Deep Economy*

"Not many know that *Walden* is not just the product of a brilliant experiment in living: Thoreau spent two years penning six painstaking revisions to arrive at the classic book. In Bill Coperthwaite, Forbes and Whybrow discover a 'Walden' of a man, only to uncover gaps, in him and in themselves, between brilliant solitary achievement and the kind of touch needed to ground and guide a viable community. Many revisions, much pain and forgiveness, and only partial fulfillments follow. But if there is another way to move from our anti-culture into communities ruled by loving intention, I don't know what it is. 'Explore your misunderstandings to your advantage,' advises Zen master Dogen. *A Man Apart* does exactly that. This is a beautifully raw account of loving grief, instructive failure, and steadfast allegiance to an utter planetary necessity: major cultural transformation."

—DAVID JAMES DUNCAN, author of *The River Why* and *The Brothers K*

"What is a good life? The models offered by our celebrity culture are mostly shabby and shallow. To find worthier examples you need to look elsewhere—to books, for example, where you can meet Thoreau, Aldo Leopold, Rachel Carson, Gary Snyder, Barbara Kingsolver, and Wendell Berry, among others. To that lineage of American rebels you can now add Bill Coperthwaite. In this eloquent portrait, Peter Forbes and Helen Whybrow document the search for integrity, wide-ranging competence, and high purpose, not only in Coperthwaite's life, but in their own. This is a wise and beautiful book."

—SCOTT RUSSELL SANDERS, author of *Earth Works: Selected Essays*

"William Coperthwaite was a man of vision and integrity, as well as a personal inspiration to Peter Forbes and Helen Whybrow. His desire to live simply led him to a remote stretch of the Maine shore, where Coperthwaite's commitment to carving wooden bowls and building elegant yurts created human elegance answering to the beauty of his surroundings. Forbes's luminous photographs evoke this aspect of his achievement. Exceptional integrity can sometimes feel rigid or bruising to those whom it also attracts, however. As Emerson once wrote about

Coperthwaite's predecessor Thoreau, 'I'd sooner take an elm tree by the arm.' A great achievement of Forbes and Whybrow in *A Man Apart* is to convey the complexity of this strong-minded life fully and honestly. Such an approach makes their reflections on love, struggle, and grief all the more powerful."

—JOHN ELDER, author of *Reading the Mountains of Home*

"What a rare and important offering. Peter and Helen have given us a deeply honest portrait of a man. We are invited to witness him from above, from beneath, from the side, from within, in his light, in his darkness. This story is about building one last yurt without knowing it's the last; it's about how one solitary man's ethic influenced the lives of many; it's about the complexity, joy, and frustration of friendship. Bill Coperthwaite once said, 'Bite off less than you can chew.' He was right! This book calls out to those of us seeking connection in our modern era. *A Man Apart* left me with the exquisite sense of having traveled somewhere and been transformed because of it."

—MOLLY CARO MAY, author of *The Map of Enough: One Woman's Search for Place*

"This is a terrific book, honestly drafted and beautifully wrought. As it is with yurts, so it is with communities and with books—their lasting strength comes from the integrity of their parts and the genius of their joinery. Deep gratitude to Peter Forbes and Helen Whybrow for their work of grace and love."

—KATHLEEN DEAN MOORE, author of *Wild Comfort*

"In this remarkable and deeply moving book, Peter and Helen tell the story of Bill Coperthwaite, a Maine homesteader, designer, and social thinker whose unique way of life and passionate ideals inspired all who knew him. Beautifully and sensitively told, the story explores the complexities of the relationship between them—the shared ideals, hard realities, disappointments, and joys of intensely interwoven lives. Bill's life—a monumental testament to creativity, brilliance, integrity, and courage—invites the reader to reexamine the profound questions of how each of us chooses to live a life. *A Man Apart* is a riveting and intensely human story—a treasure to be revisited many times."

—OLIVIA AMES HOBLITZELLE, author of *Ten Thousand Joys & Ten Thousand Sorrows: A Couple's Journey Through Alzheimer's*

"A loving tribute to Bill, a wonderful man who inspired all of us with his dedication to indigenous building, natural materials, and, above all else, use of human hands."

—LLOYD KAHN, author of *Shelter* and *Tiny Homes*

A MAN APART

Bill Coperthwaite's
RADICAL EXPERIMENT *in* LIVING

PETER FORBES *and* **HELEN WHYBROW**

PHOTOGRAPHS BY PETER FORBES

Chelsea Green Publishing
White River Junction, Vermont

Unless otherwise noted, all photographs copyright © 2015 by Peter Forbes.
Photograph on page v by Abbie Sewall. Photograph on page 7 by Kenneth Kortmeier. Photographs on pages 104 and 183, *top*, by Courtney Bent. Photographs on pages 139, 147, and 160 from the archives of Bill Coperthwaite. Photograph on page 146 by Nancy Slayton. Photograph on page 238 by Michael Sacca.

"The Long Boat" copyright © 1985 by Stanley Kunitz, from *Passing Through: The Later Poems New and Selected* by Stanley Kunitz. Used by permission of W. W. Norton & Company, Inc.

Developmental Editor: Brianne Goodspeed
Copy Editor: Eileen M. Clawson
Proofreader: Helen Walden
Designer: Melissa Jacobson

Printed in the United States of America.
First printing January, 2015.
10 9 8 7 6 5 4 3 2 1   15 16 17 18 19

Our Commitment to Green Publishing
Chelsea Green sees publishing as a tool for cultural change and ecological stewardship. We strive to align our book manufacturing practices with our editorial mission and to reduce the impact of our business enterprise on the environment. We print our books and catalogs on chlorine-free recycled paper, using vegetable-based inks whenever possible. This book may cost slightly more because it was printed on paper that contains recycled fiber, and we hope you'll agree that it's worth it. Chelsea Green is a member of the Green Press Initiative (www.greenpressinitiative.org), a nonprofit coalition of publishers, manufacturers, and authors working to protect the world's endangered forests and conserve natural resources. *A Man Apart* was printed on paper supplied by RR Donnelley that contains postconsumer recycled fiber.

Library of Congress Cataloging-in-Publication Data is available upon request.

Chelsea Green Publishing
85 North Main Street, Suite 120
White River Junction, VT 05001
(802) 295-6300
www.chelseagreen.com

The Long Boat

When his boat snapped loose
from its mooring, under
the screaking of the gulls,
he tried at first to wave
to his dear ones on shore,
but in the rolling fog
they had already lost their faces.
Too tired even to choose
between jumping and calling,
somehow he felt absolved and free
of his burdens, those mottoes
stamped on his name-tag:
Conscience, ambition, and all
that caring.
He was content to lie down
with the family ghosts
in the slop of his cradle,
buffeted by the storm,
endlessly drifting.
Peace! Peace!
To be rocked by the Infinite!
As if it didn't matter
which way was home;
as if he didn't know
he loved the earth so much
he wanted to stay forever.

—STANLEY KUNITZ

Contents

Preface

Hands built his casket, dug his grave, held his body. Hands paddled him home.

Halfway across the bay those hands, having worked hard to fulfill his last wishes, paused in the chop and swell of the ocean. Six sets of hands in two twenty-foot canoes lashed together with a coffin between them. No one of us orchestrated the pause, and the cold December weather with its wind and threats should have kept us going. But our cold hands on our paddles did pause, as if he were asking us to wait. "Stop right here," he might have said. "I want to remember this. I want to know that I'm truly going home."

Our hands paused three times as we crossed the bay. First as we rounded the point, having finished the most dangerous, open-water part of the journey, when the canoes were facing north toward his homestead. It was then that the sun broke through the clouds and a wind came on our backs, pushing him closer to his resting spot. We had timed the journey to arrive at his tide rip on the slack tide, the easiest, safest time to pass through the narrow opening with such important cargo. Our hands paused again at the mouth of the rip, rocking gently on the swells. We paused a third and final time about a hundred feet from the shore of his homestead, where fires were burning in the early morning light, where his closest friends stood facing us, ready to take him from us. Somehow we knew to pause there in the tidal pond, to let the silence be felt, to let him know his journey was almost over, before our hands took up the paddles again and gently landed him on shore.

This is the story of our relationship to a man whose unusual life and fierce ideals helped us to examine and better understand our own, and this is also an account of the tensions and complexities of mentorship: the opening of one's life to someone else to learn together. This is the story of how we came to be in those two canoes, and it is a story of one man's fifty-year experiment in living on a remote stretch of Maine coast.

William Coperthwaite was a homesteader and social thinker, an architect and designer, decades older than we were, who challenged and encouraged us to do some of the most important things we have done with our lives. He let us down and encouraged us to pick ourselves up again. We loved one another, and we disappointed one another. There are those who knew his influence better and his friendship far longer; we make no claim other than that our relationship to him changed us, so this story is one we are moved to share. And because he made a deep impression on each of us separately, our memoir is in two distinct voices. We tell the story through our different yet interwoven perspectives as two people, standing shoulder to shoulder and looking at this man who occupied the center of our life together. We alternate chapters, beginning and ending with his death. Peter's chapters span this man's lifetime, and Helen's chart an experience of forty days on Bill's wild coastline, accessible only by boat, where we camped and built a home with him, what would turn out to be his last concentric yurt after a lifetime of designing and building that form for which he was well known.

It was building that last concentric yurt, then mourning his unexpected death that became the real work of understanding this generous, radical, brilliant, and complex man. When we set out to write a book, with Bill's help, about his remarkable life and a friendship that spanned a quarter century, we did not expect that we would begin it by lashing his casket across two canoes and paddling him home across the cold December waves. This book—which was conceived as a way of spending more time with Bill as our friendship deepened in his old age, continuing our long apprenticeship to his philosophies of social change and simple living, and honoring all the ways he had influenced and changed us—turned into a journey of writing through our grief. For both of us it became a labor of sadness and love, of searching and revelation. We sought to write a book that reveals the fullness of our understanding, which we could only get to if we were willing to try to see the whole person, the whole relationship, and the whole of ourselves.

—Peter and Helen

Chapter One

THE LAST JOURNEY

—Helen—

Because I could not stop for Death
He kindly stopped for me;
The carriage held but just ourselves
And Immortality.

— EMILY DICKINSON

William Coperthwaite died on November 26, 2013, two days before Thanksgiving. He was driving southwest from his home in Machiasport, Maine, toward Brunswick, to spend the holiday as he always did with his surrogate family, Julie and Tom, their children, and Julie's mother Sonni, who had been a friend of Bill's since his college days in the early 1950s.

When Julie arrived home from work that afternoon she expected to see Bill's car parked on the street near their house. Tom and Sonni were already home and would be there to welcome him. But instead she saw a police cruiser and found an officer waiting for her in the kitchen, her mother sitting down and pale. Bill had been found, his car totaled, along an icy roadside in Washington, Maine, some miles away. It was a single-car accident, without witness, but it appeared that he had died instantly when he spun off the road and impacted an oak tree that was forced through the driver's side door. The roads had been slick that morning, the frozen land glazing to black ice the drizzle of the night prior.

On that dreary cold Tuesday before Thanksgiving, word went
out to all those whom Bill considered family, and soon the calls and
e-mails were flooding in to our farmhouse in Vermont. As one of his
neighbors in Machias once said, "Bill was a hermit who loved people,"
and that day after his death we were reminded how enormous his
circle of friends and admirers really was. We were hosting friends and
family for Thanksgiving at our farm in Vermont, but almost as soon as
the meal was eaten and dishes were done, Peter and I packed up the
leftover turkey and headed for Maine with our nine-year-old daughter,
Wren. Our older daughter, Willow, fifteen, decided to stay home with
relatives and a friend she had invited for the holiday.

We arrived at Bill's on Friday morning, stopping at the Machiasport post office to pick up Bill's mail. The postmistress, Ann, came out,
wanting to hear more about the news. She said they all loved it when
Bill came in, that he was always cracking jokes and that he got the
most interesting collection of mail, all of it sent to "General Delivery."
He was the only person in Machias with neither a street address nor a
post office box. "Our respect for him earned him different treatment,"
Ann said. "He had an arrangement that anyone visiting him could
pick up his mail, and we had lots of locals who would ask if it had been
picked up in a while, because if it hadn't we were apt to get a little
worried about him and go in and check up on things."

We parked in the patch of mossy woods down a rough road where
Bill's car was conspicuously absent and started the long walk in along
his foot trail. We walked over the floating bridge he had made years ago
to cross the beaver pond and meandered through maples and balsam fir.
When we came to the place where the woods open up and the maples are
evenly spaced, with neat piles of firewood stacked among them, I paused,
where normally I would pick up my pace. I could not imagine Bill's home
without Bill, but now there it was, four sweeping curved roofs and four
full circles of windows, gray and silver amid the gray woods and sky.

Peter and I found Bill's friend Kenneth in Bill's woodshop, finishing the top of the rough pine casket that he and Tigger, another close

friend, had made. He was
fastening the pine boards
together with hand-carved
battens, curving at the ends,
the knife marks visible, much
as Bill might have done.

Peter remembered
Bill's showing him where
he wanted to be buried,
just beyond his woodlot in
a grove of maples. Those
of us gathered headed into
the trees, agreed on a place
that was a natural opening
where the ground was less gnarled with tree roots, and with shovels
began to dig. We aligned the head of the grave to the east. Bill's friend
Tim Beal, who owned a sawmill close by and had done much of the
figuring and cutting of boards for Bill's building projects over the
years, was there with his son and brother. We peeled away the duff
of decaying leaves and moss and reindeer lichen, surprisingly soft
despite the season, and made a careful roll of it to the side. Then we
started down through a couple of inches of woodland soil to the thick
gray clay of the ancient seabed. Clay stuck on our boots until we had
small stilts on our feet. It smeared along our jeans and the sleeves of
our rain gear. Slowly we shed our layers as we went deeper into the
ground. All day, chipping with mattocks, then scraping with shovels
at the cold clay, we took turns, others arriving to join, until we had
a perfect rectangle that found bottom on a surprisingly even ledge,
three feet by eight feet, five feet down.

Next morning in the first light six of us carried Bill's two twenty-foot
handmade canoes out of the boathouse and slipped them gently into
the water. In the bottom of each we laid two rafters that we would use

to lash the pine casket across the gunnels for the paddle home. December 1 had dawned cold, with a light icy drizzle. Several of us had lain awake in the night listening to the wind moan over the ocean, worrying that the weather would prevent us from getting across to Duck Cove, but the water in Bill's protected tidal pond looked calm. We would see what we faced in the ocean crossing beyond Johnson Point.

In one boat were Michael, Taz, and I; in the other boat Peter, Dan, and Mike. We spoke little as we headed out across the mill pond, pulling hard through the tide rip, where the water was still rising and flowing in, then hugging the coastline down the reach to Johnson Point and Hobbit Island. A flock of long-tailed ducks, their pointed tail feathers making blades of shadow against the bright ripples of the water, took to flight in front of us. All was gray and silver, from the early morning sky, misting rain, the shifting sea, Michael's paddle dipping and flashing in front of me. We headed due west to Duck Cove. The wind was in our favor with very little chop hitting us broadside: a gift on what can be a difficult crossing when the wind is strong.

As we entered the cove we could see a small huddle of figures on the beach and a black van parked on the dirt road above them. Jennifer, who with long black hair streaked with red dye, long black skirt and coat, and dark lipstick was my very image of an undertaker, stepped down the pebbled beach to greet us. She kept saying, "This is so cool. I've never seen a funeral anything like this." It was hard to know how to respond: This was the peak moment of her profession, this passing of the body, while for the rest of us it was the final moment of something too enormous to absorb. But rather than feeling her enthusiasm inappropriate, I appreciated it. In fulfilling what we knew were Bill's wishes, it was easy to forget how unusual it was to create a funeral that included paddling a body for miles in a handmade casket by canoe catamaran across a stretch of ocean in winter. I felt a little lighter as I paused to consider the audacity of our task.

We lashed the canoes together at the shore, then gathered around her car where Bill's body lay.

Bill's body was enclosed in a shiny black body bag with a tag that read, "Made in China." I think we were all having the same thought: how Bill would have hated that synthetic generic material. We had a Pendleton wool blanket we wanted to wrap around him: the one that he kept on his bed and which was woven with an image from his favorite artist, Inuit painter Kenojuak Ashevak. He always said that her art made him happy; even on the grayest of winter days when his yurt didn't let in much light, he would turn and look at her art on his wall with its deep oranges and yellows and immediately feel a brightening in his mood. We put the blanket inside the casket to line it, then put the pine box and the body bag next to one another on the frozen gravel road.

I was afraid. I had never seen the dead body of someone I loved. When Jennifer opened the body bag I felt my chest heave with a mixture of grief and panic. His head had fallen back, his mouth open and lips slack because his dentures were gone. But when we lifted him from the road and placed him gently on the blanket inside the wooden

box, wrapping him from both sides, it was like picking up an empty
white shell on the beach, unbroken, but no longer animated with what
lived inside. He was naked, vulnerable, elemental. Something broke
free from my heart at that moment; to join with the raw grief I had
been carrying came a sense that Bill's spirit was at peace and among
us, that he was watching us and approving of how we were taking his
body home, how we were working together and loving one another
and bravely picking up the pieces that had fallen. I saw that his body
was unharmed by the accident, and thought about how he had not
had to suffer the indignity of sickness or frailty or the intervention
of hospitals that he so dreaded in old age. It was too soon, but it was
okay. We would all be okay.

We carried the casket to the boats and lashed it firmly to the
crossbeams so that it was parallel and centered between the canoes.
For a long moment we all stood there in silence, as the casket rocked

gently on the waves lapping beneath the boats, the new wood bright against the dark surface of the sea.

Then we pushed off, making our way through the soft salt ice toward the open water. Halfway across the cove Michael flipped a frond of seaweed onto the casket. Small waves stroked the bottom of the box between the boats and once in a while a larger one hit hard and washed over to where I was kneeling, paddling in the center with the casket against my left shoulder. A weak sun came through the clouds and shimmered a straight path east across the water in front of us. We turned up the long finger of water east of Johnson Point, the body of water Bill had named Dickinsons Reach after his favorite poet. We began to see his homeland, dark firs lining the shore. It seemed to me that even the wave-washed rocks and crowds of shoreline trees were bearing witness to the passing of this man, all his loved and known and named things looking back at us as we passed: Hobbit Island, Rosy Ness, Lunch Rock, Moose Snare Cove, Proctors Point.

A strong tailwind pushed us along in surges, our six paddles in sync, no sound but the water breaking and splashing. I sensed more than saw that Dan and Taz, the two men who came closest to being Bill's sons, were standing now as they paddled the stern behind me, as Bill had always done. They stroked the water with Bill's long hand-made paddles, eyes looking into the distance, like raftsmen guiding a riverboat. My breath caught in my throat.

When we came to the tide rip, the passage throat that separates Bill's two-hundred-acre tidal pond from the reach and the open ocean, we paused at the threshold, drifting for a while in silence on the slack tide. Ahead, across the pond, people would be gathering on the beach for his final passing through. A seal came up for a quick glance at us, then dipped his head, and as if his nod were a signal of recognition, we all picked up our paddles. The dark tongue of water delivered us, the sea inside the salt pond suddenly calm.

Soon we could see the smoke and bright smudge of a fire, sad faces, people holding each other in small groups, bundled in the damp cold. We came in and touched the gravel gently with our bows. Almost not a word was spoken as we unlashed the casket and laid it on the beach above the fire. In turns, the twenty or so people gathered to carry him, up past the summer kitchen, across the narrow bridge over the stream, and up the long hill to his home—what he called the Library Yurt. We carried him through the bottom of his yurt where his woodshop and wood supply for the next seven years was curing, then along the trail past the last yurt he built, a little study yurt for his old age, the lumber still bright and the door unfinished, and into the patch of maples to his grave.

For two hours we shared memories. Many addressed their words directly to Bill, looking down at the bright yellow casket in the earth. Mike thanked Bill for always offering him encouragement to try and live a different way, out of the mainstream. Others spoke of his lasting influence on them around the idea of democratic design, of living with intention and grace, of trying to make the world a better place, of his sense of beauty and also his wit. On the casket people placed poems and letters, children laid the drawings they had made for him that morning. Michael read a Dickinson quote: "This world is such a little place, just the red in the sky before the sun rises, so let us keep fast hold of hands, that when the birds begin, none of us is missing."

We packed the thick earth around the coffin, mounding it up until the final layer of peat and moss and decaying leaves. We sat in the smoke and sparks of the fire that we had started behind the grave. The kids poked in the coals with long sticks. We pried the clay from our boots and held our frozen hands over the warm flames. A light rain began to fall.

Chapter Two

SAIL AND ANCHOR

—Peter—

O ne moment the earth was in its normal orbit, chores done, kids asleep, I'm standing by the window of our farmhouse in Vermont taking in the fresh snow, thinking about our families converging for Thanksgiving in two days, and the next moment I'm holding the phone, my universe knocked off its axis, everything spilling over the edge. What did you say? How could he be dead? Is everyone there okay? Then I'm standing by the woodstove telling my wife, Helen, that there's been a car accident, that Bill is dead. I didn't know what to do other than grab her, walk out into the dark, to the top of our pasture, and light a fire in the falling snow, to mark the moment that Bill Coperthwaite died.

Who have the people been in your life who have opened new doors for you, exposed you to new worlds, changed your assumptions, encouraged you to stretch and grow? Who have been the guides in your life who asked you to look hard at yourself and the world around you? Bill is that person for me and my family. He was guided by a force he recognized and honored within himself. He was not confined by culture and certainly not trapped by the satisfactions of a conventional life: the two-week vacations, the security of a salary, health care, the safety and comfort of being part of a system. From the day I first encountered him, twenty years earlier, he asked me to reconsider my life, to discover and pursue my true gifts and how I might give those gifts a form and reality. Standing atop the pasture, fire burning in the dark, snow falling on my shoulders and face, I thought about the many ways my friendship with Bill was made plain and real on our land and in the programs we hosted there: our reliance on beauty to soften and open people to the claims of others, the use of handcrafts to bring different people into relationship, the honoring of manual labor, the power of nature to teach and inspire, the yurts across our landscape. He was everywhere here, and yet now he was dead. He was, at times, both sail and anchor in my life. He was thirty years older than I was, nonconformist, brilliant, visionary, defiant, complex, contradictory, loyal. He made me so angry, and I loved him.

Early the next morning, just as the sun was beginning to show over the Northfield range, black soot still on my hands from the fire the night before, the phone rang again. This time it was Danny Manchester, a fisherman friend from Machias where Bill lived. It was a relief to hear his voice. Just a month before, Danny had taken Wren out lobstering with him for the day, an ocean adventure of their own that she had loved. He and I had shared a few adventures of our own, as well as a respect for this man who was now dead.

Danny was talking fast; there had been state police poking around in town asking about Bill and lots of chatter on the marine radio. A coast guard boat had gone into Mill Pond looking for Bill, and well, he wasn't sure. I could tell that Danny didn't want to finish the thought so I told him that I knew Bill was dead. We both said nothing for a moment. "You and your family meant a whole lot to Bill," I said, feeling myself choke up. Danny offered this: "Everyone out here on the water knew Bill. We all respected him." I imagined this was true, though I also knew that it would have surprised Bill, that he was never sure how he was accepted in the community. "I'm headed up to help bury him, Danny."

We left home for Bill's homestead near Machias, Maine, in late afternoon, timing it so we could pick up our friend, Dan, flying from Seattle to the Bangor airport. We slept there, our number now four, and got up early to finish the trip down the coast. It was a bitter cold morning, and as we drove I considered the challenge of digging a grave in the frozen earth. There was so much else to do when we got there. There would be many others arriving soon to help, and I wanted to get there. We pushed on, tired, emotionally raw and open, everything gray, frozen.

Everything about driving a car, right then, scared me. When the sun made it hard for me to see, or when the tires missed traction for a second, or when a truck passed us, I thought about Bill going about his normal day, driving to Thanksgiving, suddenly turning sideways, shouting out perhaps, hitting the oak tree, lights out. At one point in our journey, we were all talking, laughing even, and I drifted over the line just a bit. Dan's tone changed sharply; he shouted out for me to be careful, making clear what was on all of our minds.

It was surreal, then, to be far from the highway, on much smaller Route 1, just thirty minutes from Bill's homestead, winding through small towns and blueberry barrens, to see an old woman driving toward us and a truck in front of us slowing down as if to make a turn. Is she paying attention? Why is he crossing now? Stop! The sound of impact, steel folding on steel, glass breaking. We felt the vibration, the crash was so close. I pulled our car off the road, glanced at Dan sitting next to me, and we both jumped out and ran back to the twisted cars, the white deflated airbag, the glass and metal on the pavement, the elderly woman crying. I held her in my arms, helped her out of the car to the ground, and looked for the oxygen canister that she was asking for, Dan placing the blue mask over her mouth. When another car pulled over to help, we asked them to call 911 so we could continue on to bury Bill. We drove on in silence, staring forward at the cold, winding road.

I was thinking about how I first met Bill, through Helen Nearing, and how fifteen years ago she, too, had been killed in a car accident. Helen Nearing and her husband, Scott, were organic farming pioneers, respected social thinkers, longtime homesteaders, and evangelists for the back-to-the-land movement. In my early twenties I had read *Living the Good Life*, and it was among the first mighty torques on my heart and mind about how to live my own life. The book asked me questions for a decade as I found my way through a career in politics and into conservation and photography.

Many thousands of people had taken direction and inspiration for their lives from Scott and Helen, who were heroes to me for their social and ecological consciousness. They seemed to see things whole, and that resonated deeply with me. At thirty I was edging closer to Helen Nearing's world and decided to write to her to ask questions about her life, and surprisingly, she wrote back immediately. Her letter grabbed me by the ankle, as she literally did a year later when I was walking past her where she sat on the ground at the outdoor Bread and Puppet Theater. That strong and quick grip was so unexpected from a ninety-year-old woman, and I took her very seriously. Come up and visit, her letter said. And later, after we had come to know one another, she asked me a question that struck at the core of my own sense of service: "Scott and I have done some good with our lives. Will you help me to spread that good when I am gone?"

By then I was thirty-two years old, the youngest regional director of a national conservation organization, and my job was to use the organization's money to buy places of natural significance all over New England that might otherwise lose their nature if turned into houses or strip malls. This organization, Trust for Public Land, had an inspiring start in the early 1970s by helping the Black Panthers to create community gardens in Oakland, California. I saw Helen Nearing's request of me well within this same radical lineage of helping all people to reconnect to the land and to themselves, but many good organizations lose their radicalness as they grow. This work wasn't exactly what the Trust for Public Land did anymore, and I was asking the hard question, why, and what did I want my work to stand for? Engaging the Trust for Public Land in the Nearings' legacy was important to me and valuable for history, I thought, and could be transformative to the organization in helping it to remember its founding history. I asked my colleagues to invest money in protecting the Nearings' homestead, which had inspired so many people to live closer to nature but was a set of radical ideas on a small piece of land. It was far from "majestic nature," like one would see on calendars of conservation groups, but nonetheless a very important story of conservation if conservation also meant people, concepts of justice, and right livelihood.

Only in my older age can I see that the asking of such questions may be the most important work of a young person who cares about an organization. I credit my colleagues at the Trust for Public Land for supporting me and investing a great deal of time and money in helping to launch The Good Life Center, but the process stretched me and pushed me to the margins of that organization. And because I was young and successful and had not yet experienced being marginalized, it all felt too hard. I loved my work as a conservationist, I meant no ill will to my organization, I was a respected and valued leader within it, and yet by following my values and what I thought our work could mean, I began to feel an outsider to it.

Partly because of my respect for the Nearings, I never felt up to the job Helen had given me, and I didn't understand why our lives had collided in such an intimate and important way so late in her years

and so early in mine. I tried to relax into the notion that the universe needed me then to serve her, and I worked diligently to be worthy of Helen's trust. She rewarded me with two gifts: the experience of walking an edge and becoming my own person with my own ideas for what conservation could mean, and the introduction to her friend Bill Coperthwaite in 1993.

I was at Forest Farm, the Nearings' homestead on Cape Rosier, Maine, every month then to work with her on planning the future of her homestead and how to keep their ideas alive after they were gone. Helen was vital and expected to live to age one hundred like Scott, who had died a decade before, and so there seemed no rush to our work. She stopped mid-thought a few times to mention that she wanted me to meet an old friend, a man who lived Down East by the name of Bill. I gathered from her stories that Bill had been one of Scott's most loyal friends in the last years, helping to cut and stack wood and discreetly rounding off the sharp edges of the furniture so Scott wouldn't hurt himself in his increasingly regular falls. In many ways, Helen told me, this Bill was the one person who was most carrying on Scott's life work.

One day that July I drove up the winding dirt road to Forest Farm and was startled to see a freshly painted sixty-foot wooden yacht moored in Orrs Cove, and so it made sense to me that the man nattily dressed in rumpled blue pants and frayed white button-down shirt standing in front of Helen must have come from that yacht. This was Scott Nearing's friend, Bill Coperthwaite. He took my hand in his own larger and more calloused one, smiled wryly and graciously, and rolled out a map of his place two hours farther down the coast. I remember something about a hand-built home, four miles of coastline, no roads, no electricity, and would I come and visit?

Helen laughed at me all that afternoon for thinking that Bill had come to see us in a yacht, but I was months away from understanding why that might be funny. I did visit Bill that Thanksgiving for a week, and upon my return home I walked up to my third-floor flat in Cambridge, dropped my pack in the corner, walked over to the TV, unplugged it, and pushed it into the farthest reaches of my closet. The feeling was a sudden realization that I wanted to be free of something, that my life needed space for more important things to enter. With a surprising ease and grace, given our difference in age and background, our lives connected, and we found that we were thirsty for the same things. Within a year we had spent plenty of time together at his homestead and were dreaming about shared futures.

West of the Bay of Fundy is a place known on maps as Little Kennebec Bay and farther in is Mill Pond, but Bill called the whole territory Dickinsons Reach. No roads, just a 1.5-mile footpath to his home. From the perspective of an eagle Dickinsons Reach is a swirl of sand, water, and mud where two fingers of land pinch to create a place where the tides are constricted and the tilt of the earth can be felt. When I am there on the ground with my fingers digging deep into the grass or my canoe floating through the tide rip, I'm reminded of that swirl of land and water, and I can see myself within it. More than any other place, perhaps even more than my own farm, this place has helped me to connect to the earth.

A few years after meeting Bill I got the phone call that Helen Nearing had been killed in a single-car accident. She had hit a tree on the dirt road not far from her home and, apparently, just after going to the post office, because I would get a note from her just two days later. There was some talk that perhaps it wasn't an accident so much as something she intended. I needed to go there quickly and to reach my own conclusion about her end, to confront what had taken her life. It wasn't hard to find the maple tree where she had died on impact. I had traveled that stretch of gravel road from Forest Farm to Brooksville, Maine, many times, even on a few occasions with her, and

Sail and Anchor

I knew where the tree would be. I expected the maple to be mangled, crushed, but the tree had but a small scar from the impact of her old car, much smaller than what I would have imagined from a crash that had taken a human life. There was another woman, I had been told, who came upon the accident while the car was still smoking and who claimed to have seen Helen's spirit walk away from the scene, but I was not one to believe in ghosts. I parked my own car and slowly approached this maple and gently touched the garland of sunflowers wrapped around the scar.

The sun was low and the air was cold later that fall day when I drove away from the tree that killed Helen Nearing. I felt particularly alive, awake, and at peace when I came to the stop sign in Brooksville and looked slowly into my rearview mirror and saw her, staring forward at me. Our eyes met. Her hands were on the steering wheel of her old car, and she was driving directly behind my car. She didn't move or wave, almost as if to let the reality of her presence sink in. She had time. I was neither stunned nor scared. I remember being locked into Helen Nearing's gaze through my rearview mirror and the feeling of warmth rising in my chest and my eyes beginning to crinkle into a smile. I felt a smile in her eyes, too, and when I couldn't stand it any longer I swung around to stare at her directly. And when I did, Helen's high forehead and warm eyes went out of focus and another set of eyes were locked with mine. There were deep lines on that face, too, and a smile, and big-knuckled hands on a steering wheel of an equally old car. It was Bill Coperthwaite. We jumped out of our cars, went toward each other and hugged like bears. He was strong and warm. I had to take a few breaths to hold back the heaves that were rising in my chest; I didn't want him to know what that moment felt like. "I knew I'd find you somewhere around here," he said.

And now, some twenty years later, I was going to help bury him.

Chapter Three

LIKE A LANDSCAPE

—Helen—

I would describe myself
like a landscape I've studied
at length, in detail;
like a word I'm coming to understand
like a pitcher I pour from at mealtime
like my mother's face;
like a ship that carried me
when the waters raged.

— R. M. Rilke

There are many ways that I feared Bill dying, but a car accident was never one of them. I imagined him falling off the sloping, shingled roof of his four-storied yurt where he might have gone to check the solar panel or devise something so that the woodpeckers wouldn't make a racket on the stovepipe brackets, or even higher, to fix an upper-story window, remove a wasps' nest from the eaves, or adjust the blue glass buoy that graced the top of what he called his aerie. I imagined him dying on the water, lost in fog in one of his twenty-foot wooden canoes, tired enough to sit down at last and rest his paddle, drifting in the waves. I could see how easily he might slip while climbing down one dewy morning from his sixty-foot-high tree house suspended on cables between huge spruces, where he had slept as recently as his eighty-third birthday and which required stepping through space and then a perilous descent through branches.

I thought about how if he was badly hurt or ill he wouldn't have a way to call or hike out, that it could be long enough until someone found him that it would be too late. I hoped that he wouldn't suffer. Most of all, I had imagined him lying frail, like a dry leaf, on a cot in his small studio yurt close to where he wanted to be buried, friends around him, perhaps refusing food and water as his friend Scott Nearing did at age one hundred, independent and intentional and cracking wry jokes to the end. I imagined having time to say good-bye.

My grief at first was selfish. I kept thinking: not now, not yet, I'm not ready, there is so much more I need to do and say and share with you, so much I want to learn.

Early on Bill and I had connected over our mutual love of literature and poetry. He had a strong collection of stories about the Arctic, and I was editing a Norton anthology on exploration narratives of the 1800s when I met him, so he was often recommending books to me. I didn't always connect with him around his theories of how society needed to change, not because I didn't believe in them but because I could find the conversation ponderous, and my mind wandered. As an editor I found it satisfying to have a hand in helping him publish his book, *A Handmade Life*, but most of what I wanted to learn from him had to do with my hands. More recently I had started to ask him questions about design—how he designed, what he thought about when he sought to create something where beauty and utility were aligned, what appealed to him in native artifacts and handcrafts, what made something feel authentic, what was beauty and proportion. Those conversations were opening doors in my mind.

As I lay in bed the night he died, all I could think was, How will we tell Wren in the morning? At nine she had a particularly special connection with "Uncle Bill," which seemed to have something to do with her curious nature and also to do with how he had softened with age. She would unabashedly ask him things, and he would bend low to hear, he let her use his tools for carving, helped her make things out of leather, and shared his magnetic ball bearings to show her how to build weird geometric shapes for which he knew all the names. Wren saw a sweetness in Bill that the rest of us rarely saw; he responded to her innate curiosity and nurtured her desire to be involved in a way that often touched and surprised me.

One August, the time that we always gathered at Bill's with other families in his community of friends, the kids collected all kinds of deadly looking mushrooms in the woods and hung them upside down in their fort along with the colorful lobster buoys and bits of fishing net they had scavenged on Hickey Island. Wren eagerly tugged Bill out to the woods by the hand to see. I feared he would object to having all that junk hauled to his homestead and hung there, but he didn't. He encouraged her.

Wren was still at that age where his place—its round buildings and snaking paths, its named features and distant islands—was a kingdom to

be explored and against which she could measure her growing abilities. The tree house was inaccessible to the youngest children, who would stare up at it in awe for years until daring to test the climb up the giant spruce at age eight or ten. In the many journeys on the water, the back seat in the canoes had to be earned, taking the paddle first while kneeling in the middle, then in the bow.

In Bill's workshop the smallest children would play on the floor, later learning how to use the drawknife to make a sword or boat, then earning his trust to use a knife and carve a first spoon or make their own knife handle and sheath. The treasure hunt that we made an annual tradition every August got a little harder each time, the circumference of exploration a little wider, across the water or all the way out to Rosy Ness to the west or Sonni's cabin against the scarp of bedrock to the east. And Bill's giant swing, which he designed as a single rope and board that you clamped with your thighs, was swung by someone else who pulled hard on a rope attached to the swing's main rope seventy-five feet up in the canopy of a birch. At age three Wren and Willow both learned to hang on; by age ten they demanded to be flung by someone strong at great speed to stunning heights in the trees.

For Wren's first visit, at four months, she took a bath in one of Bill's broad hand-hammered copper basins that he had long ago purchased in Mexico, and after sitting up in it and squirming delightedly for a hour in the warm water she emerged, her bottom and knees black from soot. The tradition of staying dirty remained, which suited her well. Bill's homestead was where children disappeared into the woods to make forts or along the tide flats flinging stones and became their wildest selves.

Wren woke earlier than usual on November 27 and crawled into our bed. It was a date she would come to remember. I told her we had sad news to share, drew her in close, and then, without preamble, said, "Uncle Bill died yesterday."

"How?" she asked after a long silence. "He can't die. He was going to live forever."

All morning she let the news seep in and the tears seep out, expressing her sadness by painting an arctic owl in the Inuit style, with outspread wings and a fledging sitting on its sturdy feet. She knew Kenojuak was his favorite artist. Rue, our shepherd, sensed Wren's sadness and came frequently to rest her head in Wren's lap. We put her painting on the table with some of Peter's photographs of Bill.

Willow woke much later, and when Peter told her the news she came down to tell Wren how sorry she was. Willow, my stepdaughter, had been to Bill's before I met either of them. Her relationship with Bill and his land had been close when she was much younger but had waned over the years; the tidal mud and mosquitoes, tree house climbs that left your hands and hair sticky with pine pitch, and cooking over a smoky fire that she had loved as a kid were not at all appealing to her as a teen. But she also seemed to perceive that she and Wren were different, that Wren might always love it there, and most of all how deeply Wren would miss Bill.

The next day would be Thanksgiving, and our families were all coming to Knoll Farm for dinner and the weekend. My grief would accompany me to the frozen garden where I snapped off the last of the brussels sprouts from their long stalks with red hands, cleaned them in the sink, peeled the ragged outer leaves and cut a cross in each stem. My grief would mince the garlic and shape the loaves of bread. The whole day I felt as though I were swimming a long distance, farther than I knew how to swim. I felt exhausted, but I had to keep going or I would sink to the bottom.

We would find out that in Bill's car when he crashed was the form required by the state of Maine for the "final disposition of his body," giving permission for someone other than a blood relative to transport his body and bury him on his land. He had been taking it to give to Julie for safekeeping. The paper was found, torn and crumpled, amid a jumble of other belongings—his annual calendars to mail and boughs of balsam to make wreaths over Thanksgiving. Later, on Bill's desk in his Library Yurt, we would find a final list he had scratched on

a piece of scrap paper: "To pack," with "Burial Authorization" crossed off. This was in keeping with the preparedness that guided all of Bill's life.

Bill lived in a swirl of ideas, inventions, plans, and enthusiasms, always studying, always investigating new ways to design yurts, tools, and everyday objects, as well as educational systems and community life. But he was also intentional about nearly every detail of his life; nothing was extraneous,

nothing left unconsidered.
And in recent years this
included his plans for his
final days. To many of us
who were close to Bill—
those who, with me, had just
attended a symposium at
his homestead to study his
many yurt designs, or those
planning a trip with him to
Mexico to study handcrafts,
or helping him to organize
another symposium on the
design of native tools, or
helping him to design the
next version of a lightweight
trailworthy wheelbarrow
(using Kevlar and bicycle

wheels) for hauling goods into the homestead, or going over drawings
for a large yurt he would build in the spring—it seemed that Bill was in
a heyday of creativity and energy. But he was also talking about death.
He was preparing, putting everything in place to go.

When I met him, Bill was already an elder. The first time I walked
into his homestead was on the occasion of his seventieth birthday,
after a celebration for him at the Nearings' Good Life Center. I was
eager to go; I had seen Peter's photographs. I was also a little nervous,
feeling a certain self-imposed obligation to like the place, given that
my relationship with Peter was just beginning and Bill's home was a
closely held talisman in Peter's life.

I had met Bill a couple of times already, first at a slide show we
attended together with Peter in which the artist showing the slides had
put each one in upside down, would laugh at himself and calmly right
the image, then go on to the next one, which was also upside down.

Bill would look over at me and subtly shake his head, his eyes full of mirth. Then, sensing two-year-old Willow's boredom, he took out of his pocket a watch on a chain and swung it back and forth, enticing her over to play. My first impression of him in that meeting, and again at his birthday, was of a person with a fierce, quiet presence alight with a quick wit and playfulness.

So although I went to Bill's knowing I was about to pass over a threshold that held meaning for me, nothing prepared me for how his land and the homestead he had created would actually feel.

There is a palpable, different sense when you pass through land that is well loved and tended by hand. And you approach a home differently that requires a long walk, with more anticipation of what it means to arrive. I took in the bright sawdust marking the trail, the hand-hewn bridges, the woodpiles that graduated in size to small rounds that many people would consider too small to be saved, the evenly spaced maples of the woodlot. And then Bill's cache yurt—now my favorite of all his yurt designs—came into view, a round weathered-gray building, ten feet across, with a generous overhanging roof, standing eight feet in the air on a stout cedar post with an elegant ladder that is hand-carved out of one log going up to the small door. It's perfectly and simply proportioned, but also odd on its perch, enticing and mysterious, a guardian at the threshold.

As we walked into the clearing that day years ago we could see Bill through the second-story windows of his Library Yurt, sitting at his desk where the windows catch the morning light and face the path. In our visits over the years it's the place I would come to know best. Across from his desk was a couch made of old sweaters cut into strips and rolled, then put flat side up in tight rows to form a cushioned platform. In front of the couch was a simple wooden table that he had made very light so he could move it aside if there were lots of people joining him for a meal, substituting a larger round one made of stiff cardboard and covered with maps of Dickinsons Reach. To one side of the low cast-iron wood-and-cookstove was his desk, and to the other was a small table held to the out-leaning wall by brackets, where he kept his collection of handmade carving tools. His desk was elevated near the woodstove, and to write

he sat on a leather-covered stool that he had designed to keep his feet well off the floor: "That way I'm always warm."

He had his stationery organized in a little slot he'd built on the side of his desk, and on shelves within reach of his left hand were all his favorite books and rows of little wooden boxes with his files and clippings on the design ideas he was constantly working on: Basketry, Boat Design, Chairs, Education, Geometry, Horn, Japanese Tools, Knives and Axes, Scandinavian Design, Shelter, Tools, Wheelbarrows, Yurts. On his desk was often a melee of various papers and projects, clippings from articles he'd been reading, lists of projects and research to do, and jotted quotes from books. He did a lot of cutting and pasting as well as drawing. Above his desk in a little slot made of bent copper bands fastened between two ceiling boards were his fine Japanese scissors, and next to them his old drawing compass with its tiny pencil kept shaved to a perfect point. On his desk was his roll of cello tape, not in the usual plastic holder but in a sturdy wooden one he had made, to me emblematic of Bill's unique ability to see even the most ordinary of objects as a call to think about better design, a higher aesthetic, to pay attention to the way the world was made, how we use it, and why.

I had never entered a space that had so much presence, that was distilled with so much creativity and care. Bill's home and nearly everything in it was intricately handmade and born out of one man's unique imagination and genius. The detail was almost inconceivable. To step over his threshold was to be given a glimpse of a very particular soul, a soul I came to love as much as the place itself, for they were one and the same.

That seamless joining of person and place, of imagination and manifestation, ignited me; it emboldened me to have with Peter many conversations about how one should live, and it invited me to move differently through the world from then on, with more attention, more attuned to the design of my own life and to the landscape of home he and I were still then seeking to find.

Chapter Four

THIRST

—Peter—

The words we borrowed from each other at the gravesite, and repeated, to express what Bill meant to us were these: grace, intention, encouragement, beauty, and, finally, solitude.

Sarah spoke about the night before, when Bill's round, four-story yurt was filled beyond capacity with his friends from all over New England who had made their way there to help with the work of bringing him home and burying him. The letters he was reading were still open on his desk. His felt shoes were there where he left them beside his bed. His breakfast dishes, not fully put away, were there waiting for him to return. His vest hung by the stairs to his bed. His bag of teaching tools, as I called them, was ready by the door. And we were there, some twenty-five of us, but he was not. The one lightbulb from Bill's solar panel, which had always seemed sufficient for him, was just a tiny spot in a house filled with headlamps sweeping back and forth like a crime scene. Though we tried to be respectful, we had the energy of a herd of deer locked in a corral. From outside the beams of light bounced off trees, swept out into the cold night like so many bats. The first thing I noticed about Bill's being gone was that our energy, unbounded by the lack of his presence, seemed so different than his. I had to leave the Library Yurt and walk down to the quiet rhythms of the receding tide at Mill Pond.

Sarah noticed this, too, and talked the next morning above his pine box about how the big old yurt finally stopped creaking and popping with all our activity and came to a rest. And then, only then in the deep quiet, did she feel Bill. Sarah reflected on the difference between our experience that one night of a crowd of us, talking, shifting, asking

questions of each other, speculating, all our scattered energy bouncing off every curved wall, and what Bill experienced for the far majority of his eighteen thousand nights in that yurt: the slow coming on of dusk, the crackling of a fire, the turning of a single page, the silence of a shooting star racing across the dark night sky.

Bill's bold experiment in living at Dickinsons Reach lasted exactly fifty-three years. He settled there on November 25, 1960, and left, not to return alive, on November 26, 2013. And though old friends and new acquaintances were often showing up and spending nights with him, most evenings, certainly ten thousand of them, he spent completely by himself. That world of solitude defined him, gave him grace and his sense of abundance. Bill's wisdom arose from drinking deeply of the solitude for which he was so thirsty.

When I think of all the nights over twenty years that I visited Bill, my strongest feeling is the healing quality of the solitude that Bill wrapped himself in. There were occasions when I tasted it: when I walked in on the trail one spring day to find him reading alone in a patch of sun or when I came upon him at night carving a bowl under the light of his single small bulb. Every night that I stayed with him, my sleep would be filled with instructive dreaming, and I relished the slow waking that Bill encouraged long before first light with the creaking open of his woodstove doors, the crumpling of old writing paper for starter, the scratch of a match or two on steel and then the slow and steady growing of a fire amidst dry wood. There was no need for the morning banter that was my habit; the words left us to be replaced by perception. Bill didn't need to speak unless his words, somehow, could be more important than what was already around us. And rarely are our words more important than what the day is already revealing, so most mornings we let the day speak for us.

I'm a husband and a father, with a family farm in the hills of Vermont, and I'm a conservationist and writer who pays close attention to the relationship between people and place, but Dickinsons Reach is the place that renews me and reveals me to myself. For twenty years I

have gone west to present myself to the world. I went west to test ideas, to give talks, to meet with colleagues; to raise money for projects I believe will make change. And for those same years I have also gone east, on the back roads and through the small towns of northern New England along Route 2 to Bill's homestead, to find myself.

When I was falling in love with my wife, Helen, and imagining a life together, I brought her to Bill's land. Coming from the mountains of New Hampshire, would she find the flatness oppressive or beautiful? Were the mud and the mosquitoes overwhelming or a gorgeous expression of wildness? Did she feel something similar to what I felt when the fog rolls in? What might stir inside her from the smell of saltwater and cedar on a thick, damp August morning—poetry or boredom? When the tide is out, do the mudflats strike her as ugly or fertile and abundant? And most importantly, would she appreciate Bill, see through his rough exterior, go past his manly stories and his dogma to find something unique, deeply helpful, loving to a core?

And later I wondered, would our daughters, Willow and Wren, come here by choice? They have grown up with Bill, known him as an older figure, a grandfather, a curmudgeon with a sense of humor, one who built towers from all our household objects, taught them how to carve spoons, always has interesting things to play with and time for adventures, and compares to no one else in our lives. And when they are free to form their own opinions and make their own decisions, will they conclude that he is a man of enormous character and accomplishment, or will they only see his eccentricities, his unkempt hair, his loose dentures, and his worn-out clothes?

Bill has a small notepad and pencil on a string attached to his door on which he has written, "Friends, glad you were here. Leave a note." Thousands of people have walked, paddled, sailed, or skied to Bill's homestead over the fifty-odd years he has lived alone there, to see his yurts, lend a hand, learn a craft, or simply pester him with questions about why and how he lives the way he does. Many scratch their heads and bug bites and leave, not sure what to make of such an existence. But for many others seeing Bill's way of life quenched a thirst, and they would stay a few days longer, or a summer, or come back again and again, their lives changed by what they had seen.

Writing in *Cruising World* magazine, two ocean-savvy sailors wrote an entire feature story about getting lost in the fog of Little Kennebec Bay and coming upon Bill canoeing out through the tide rip: "out of a tidal hole in the trees along the shore slid an ancient, twenty-foot wooden canoe. Standing in the stern was a lanky man in his sixties. His clothes were ragged. His long, thin hair was disheveled and stuck out like seeds of a dandelion. From a precarious standing position, he took long careful strokes with what must have been a six-foot paddle, moving the slender craft easily and gracefully." These two sailors, filled with their mythical vision of Bill as hermit, nonetheless came away from their two hours with him having received the essential transmission: "I went below and crawled into my bunk. Bryan's voice followed me. 'David, how many people have you met who truly make and follow their own paths?'"

Twelve years ago, when Bill enlisted Helen and me to

help him with his manuscript of what became *A Handmade Life*, we encouraged Bill to write something about his homestead and the way he lived. That was what we were drawn to: the example of a life. But Bill wasn't interested in that. He wanted to write about what might be required to design a new society, new ways of educating our children and of treating the earth. New thinking. We felt that there are plenty of people who put out their ideas for reform, but a pitiful few whose creed is matched by their deed, who practice their ideals every day in how they live. Bill is one of those few uncompromising souls, unblinded by convention, unsocialized, living an experimental life but proving it real, decade after decade.

For me Dickinsons Reach is where I see and touch all these things that society doesn't value: intentionality, skill, work, beauty, respect for people and place, and I see how valuable they are. Nothing at Bill's can be stuffed into a bank account. It's his utter security here, at the margins of life, at the far edge of town that attracts us. Bill wasn't driven here by antisocial tendencies or by a crime record. He wasn't running away from anything by choosing to live the way he did. He was running toward something, embracing the desire to live sanely in a world of death-making things. He was pulled there by his belief in nonviolence and his sense of beauty. He was searching for nonviolence because he had grown up among violence, and he was hungry for beauty because he had already seen so much ugliness. We ourselves were drawn, not to his seclusion but to these values.

Every article, and there have been dozens, that feature Bill and call him either quaint or a hermit overlook the much bigger and more important story of what it takes to make your own life, to be an introvert, to take the time in solitude to examine oneself, and then to live by what one finds. What's missing from most of those articles is an understanding of Bill's personal politics, the hard choices he made to conform his way of living to his way of thinking, and to see what one person can do to live more fully within his convictions. By that I mean Bill was motivated mostly by ideals: fairness, beauty, democratic ideals and practices that leave no one out, personal power and community health, respect for all beings. And I learned as much from his failure to live up to his ideals as I did by his successes because the failures enabled me to see him as more whole.

Years ago Bill and I were together when a census form showed up in the bundle of mail that I brought in from town. We sat together in that ever-inspiring, four-storied, and handmade home trying to answer the questions on the form. Number of phones? Number of televisions? Bill looked at me with each question and made a crack like, "What phone? Will you call them on my phone, Peter, and tell them to stop sending these damn forms?" How many cars? How many bathrooms?

How many bedrooms? Dishwasher or not? Heat with gas or electric? Garage or driveway? Bill had some fun with the form, but when it was filled out, I resigned myself to the picture that this definition of being an American painted of Bill: an old man, living alone without plumbing, television, computer, phone, or driveway, out at the end of a footpath in the distant pucker-brush of Maine.

It was a picture of poverty, but what I experienced was a man of great wealth. True wealth. What I saw was abundance. A person who had influenced thousands, left a big mark, was his own creation. And I saw sadness, too. There were things he wanted and had not done, such as truly embracing others living their lives on his land. His life was all about education, the life of a community, creating a better society, and yet he could not accommodate other people's visions and could only take people close-up in short doses. Bill achieved that really big goal of having community form and stay at Dickinsons Reach only very late in life as he was confronting old age and preparing to die.

Bill is one of those unusual Americans who shun public visibility as avarice and yet is a worthwhile public figure. While many who visited Bill did not agree with his ideas or would not be willing or able to live like he did, nearly all left challenged and inspired by what they encountered. He was authentic to the core at a time when so much feels fake, false, and undurable. I am inspired by how Bill and a few others I have only read about like Henry David Thoreau of Walden Pond or Anna and Harlan Hubbard of the Ohio River have led lives in protest against mainstream society. The same is true for Wendell Berry, a writer who has shaped—for the good—thousands of lives, including my own. Like them, Bill does not attend protests, he lives one. And when I get all caught up, as I sometimes do, in analyzing and naming society's big problems, and in creating efforts to address those problems, then getting on planes to raise money to address those problems, Bill would bring me back to fundamentals and humility with a statement like, "Peter, that's all well and good, but there's nothing you could ever say or write that's as important as how you live your days." From Bill I have learned how the manner in which my life radiates and touches people has more potential for change than anything else I could say or do.

To build something beautiful and meaningful with one's own hands is to defeat those fears of inadequacy and fakeness, so my family set out to make a home with Bill, alongside him. My own motivations changed quite a lot over two decades. At first, I was flattered by Bill's invitation to live there. But with time and experience I saw that Bill had extended those invitations to many different people, every year, going back decades, and I knew there were good reasons why no one had ever accepted. I kept some distance, though I never stopped feeling the pull of Dickinsons Reach. Proctors Point, as our land was called back then, was across the tide rip, a half mile from Bill's homestead, and felt less his domain, and I was drawn to the power of the tide rip and to the long history of human habitation. On every visit to Dickinsons Reach, I made my way by canoe across the pond to Proctors Point to walk it, feel it, and imagine living there. We cleared trails, then watched them grow over.

After a decade of hard work at Knoll Farm and largely unfulfilled dreams at Dickinsons Reach, I wanted to add our heartbeats and creativity to this land that had a growing meaning for my family. I wanted to create a place on Proctors Point that was more comfortable than a tent for Willow that might lure her back to Dickinsons Reach. I wanted to start planting fruit trees; I wanted to build a structure with my wife and my kids. I saw myself growing old there.

Bill's heart attack in the spring of 2010 shifted my focus dramatically from a future home for ourselves to an immediate place for a caretaker to live, and then, finally, our building of a yurt with Bill in the fall of 2011 became as much a celebration of his life as it was a home-building project for us. Building the yurt there at Proctors Point was an obvious, visible way that my family and I could try to honor him in his last years through our own sweat and equity.

We began this effort of home building and satisfying our thirst for meaning in the most practical and durable of ways: by digging a well.

"First thing to do is find the old well and dig it out. That's what I did." That's what Bill told me to do because that's what Bill had done himself sometime in the mid-1960s, after he had successfully assembled the lands he called Dickinsons Reach. Bill started to roam about and use the old mill site at the tide rip directly across the tidal pond from his own small A-frame cabin. At that moment Bill was thirty-five years old and at the start of an important relationship that would chiefly occupy his imagination and strength for the next fifty years. He would build yurts, and tree houses, and stone showers, and a boathouse, and a summer kitchen, but all that would come years later. In the beginning of his relationship to his place, he left only faint foot trails along the coast and his small A-frame down at the shore. Across the tidal pond, after clearing the historic mill site of its alders, he found a well that had been dug by settlers two hundred years before. "I was one of the few young guys interested in their stories," Bill told me. "Chris Proctor was ninety-five years old when I knocked on his door in town and showed him the old maps. He got down on his knees on the floor so he could study them carefully, and then the old man shared a distant memory of holding his dad's hand on a walk at the tide rip and being shown a well where an ox had fallen in. The family couldn't get the ox out so they buried it right there and filled the well with stones."

Two hundred years ago that double mill was so productive that schooners came all the way up to Moose Snare Cove to transport the lumber points south. And when all the giant spruce was cut, the mill

grew quiet and eventually burned. By the time of the Civil War the most important crop was hay for the Union cavalry, and the hundred-acre mill pond was diked at the tide rip so that salt hay could be grown on the tidal flats. That Herculean effort to keep the ocean away worked for about ten years, but then a succession of hard spring thaws pushed up the dam and scattered the enormous wood beams and braces. Today I can see how the land approaching the rip was leveled and pushed into the dike, and at the lowest tides one can see the huge broken beams wrapped in seaweed.

There was no other source of fresh water on this small point of land surrounded by salt. And when the ox fell in the well just after the Civil War, homesteading there would have stopped immediately. That ended a fifty-year pulse of human energy that began in 1810 when four families each put up two hundred fifty dollars to construct a lumber mill that benefited from both flows of tide and could cut large volumes of spruce. One thousand dollars was a fortune in 1810, especially in this remote and sparsely populated stretch of coast.

This was a valuable place, and a meaningful place no matter what gives you meaning. The Passamaquoddys had felt it first, choosing to bury their dead just across Moose Snare Cove, where the land rises. For thousands of years the pulse of human life was felt in these reaches, ebbing and flowing, humans arriving, building things, nature taking them away.

Bill was in his mid-twenties when he began his search for a piece of land to start a school and a homestead. He had found a perfect island for sale off Grand Manan in Canada, sent a check ahead to buy it, and arrived with all his tools to settle and get to work, but the owner had changed his mind and handed Bill back his check.

With that dream thwarted, Bill set off searching the Maine coastline for tide rips, rare physical features where the tidal waters are squeezed into narrows by the opposing shores to create something like a flowing river, except that the river changes depth and direction twice a day. Most humans find these places beautiful to observe, and extremely valuable to own because of the constricted energy that can be harnessed to mill lumber or produce electricity. As generations of wise people before him understood, tide rips offered a source of physical and spiritual energy for one's life's work. Bill found the lands of Dickinsons Reach having been cut over for lumber, repossessed by the town for taxes owed, and cheap enough at $3.50 an acre that Bill could buy several hundred.

Bill knew the value of what he saw even though at that moment in 1960 it looked beat up. For as far as his eye could see, the landscape was tree stumps and slash piles, having been cut over hard, then abandoned, not even worth paying the taxes on. And it was 1960 in Washington County, Maine, which was the poorest county in one of the poorest states of our United States.

It has taken time and friendships to fully appreciate the significant true wealth of the people here. They make time for their families, work hard, have a strong sense of community with less crime than other parts of Maine, and they live amidst great beauty, though are quick to say, "You can't eat the scenery." The poverty is visible, too: the rusted-out boats up on their irons, the abandoned homes, and the young man I first waved to in 1995 in his wheelchair at the end of the dirt road waving to cars. He's grown twenty years older in that chair on that corner. In 1960, when Bill first moved to Machiasport, the average adult in Washington County earned less than three thousand dollars per year, the lowest income of any county in Maine. Today 20 percent of local residents live below the poverty line. A once vital inland and offshore fishery is all but gone; lobstering prices today are lower than a decade ago.

In a word, Bill is resourceful. There are many things he chooses not to do, but I can't imagine something he couldn't do. Having mastered the hand arts of carpentry and mechanics while in his teens, he approached the buying of land with the same fascination and skill. He would do it himself, better and cheaper. He found an ancient lawyer in town who offered this young man a quick law course in how land is transferred and recorded; then Bill went into the town vaults and began reading deed after deed. He identified some five hundred acres in three separate parcels that would afford him all the attributes for a homestead, school, and community that he longed to create. The largest parcel, cut hard of trees by the previous owner, belonged to the town. The second, some one hundred acres to the west, belonged to Captain Proctor. The third, and most important, was the tiny two-acre mill site at the very head of the tide rip.

He studied the oldest official maps and the history of the mill site at the tide rips and discovered that it was once owned separately back in 1810—and therefore still was separate—from the adjacent land he was about to buy that was owned by Captain Proctor. Becoming savvy in real estate, Bill set out to secure the rights to the mill site before purchasing the rest of the land. The descendants of the Pettegrows and the Thaxters—families whose ancestors were originally partners in the deed—didn't even know they owned the old mill site but were impressed by this young man's energy and determination. "If I own it

I'll give it to you," is what each of them told Bill just before he got them to sign quitclaim deeds. That November Bill moved forward to buy Dickinsons Reach.

The last piece of land in Bill's vision was the hundred acres immediately adjacent to the tide rip and mill site belonging to Captain Proctor, who was also smitten enough by Bill to give him a "first refusal" or the right to buy his land if he ever decided to sell in the future. Seven years passed, and several competing offers were made for that same piece of land, including one from the industrialist-turned-conservationist, Thomas Cabot, but the captain remained quietly loyal to Bill, and one day he left a message for Bill at the post office: "It's time. I'll sell you my land."

It is here, on this dynamic and storied spot close to the tide rip, that Bill would help us to build a home. Thirty-five years after Captain Proctor moved out of his summer cabin at the point, Bill and I first started talking about my homesteading there one day. And we agreed that a good place for me to start a relationship with this place was the old well.

Bill offered vague directions one late fall day. "The well's somewhere there to the south not far from the pond itself." I wandered for about half an hour through alders as thick as my arm and was thrilled to find something that might be a well. I shouted out three times in excitement, "Bill, I've found it," only to hear my voice disappear amidst the seagulls. It was nothing spectacular anyway: There was no sign of a well casing or a cover, just a muddy depression with dirty milk at the surface. I was elated.

But Helen and I were just starting our lives 350 miles to the west in Vermont at Knoll Farm, and it would be three more years before we went looking for the well again. This time it was much harder to find. It was June, leaves were out, and the bank where I thought the well had been was a cage of wire brush and alders. Helen and I finally fought our way to that rim of milky water and spent hours cutting a perimeter around the well so it wouldn't be lost again.

Another two years passed, and I returned this time with the spoken conviction that I would empty the well, clean and restore it, and drink deeply from its depths. It was August 2008, and as we did every year at the end of summer, a good number of friends had gathered at Dickinsons Reach. Bill smiled wryly at my dream but grabbed rope, pulleys, three shovels, and several five-gallon plastic jugs from his boathouse, and four of us set off across the tidal pond to Proctors Point. Scott, Steve, Dorn, and I eagerly attacked the first job, which was removing all the surface water with the five-gallon jugs. Our enthusiasm swept

us through the first hour and the second, but by the third hour we were covered in mud, mosquitoes biting every part of our body, the sun blistering us, and the wooden walls of the well just beginning to appear.

"How deep is this well?"

Bill answered quietly, "It's got to be at least fifteen feet down to the bedrock."

It was a jungle scene: 85 degrees, slippery clay everywhere, clouds of mosquitoes in our eyes and ears, sweat dripping from our faces and backs.

"This is a lot bigger job than I expected," I likely said testily. In truth, I thought the job of cleaning out that well was impossible. It was too much work. I couldn't do it.

But it wasn't my work to do alone, and that was the first lesson. Five of us worked nonstop for another two days, and Bill was there alongside us the entire time, encouraging, passing buckets. We removed by hand twelve tons of rock, half-rotten tree limbs, and finally hundreds of buckets of dense blue clay. Of course, I thought about how that clay got in this well, slowly seeping in over 180 years through the narrow gaps in the well-made wood casing. This may have been a tough job, but it was also a job that would need to be done again. Imagine this if you can: me standing in a four-foot-square hole in the ground digging up blue clay and hoisting it to the surface as I slowly sank a commensurate amount deeper into the well. My friends and family aboveground got more and more distant with each backbreaking lug of mud to the surface. This was lots of work, and I thought happily about the prospects of a great-granddaughter doing exactly the same thing in, say, 2080.

By the end of day three we were down to bedrock and from there, looking up, could marvel at the oak posts and boards that were set in place around 1862. We began scrubbing clean these wooden walls and reflecting even more on the lives of the people who had made this well. How did they dig this in the first place? And how did they line it so perfectly in oak panels and posts? Where were those oaks growing? There are none here now. What were their names? What were they thirsty for?

I've been drinking from that well for five years now, just a beginning. Thirst of the body is so simply and completely satisfied by a large

glass of cold water. The thirst for meaning, community, and love is not so easily quenched.

Today by our well it is cold and foggy, and the air is wet on my face as I take my favorite walk down the path to the rip to marvel at the way the high tide fills this pond to the brim. It is slack high, and except for the fog that blows through, everything is uncharacteristically motionless. For just a second the earth is not spinning; the ocean is neither spilling in nor spilling out. Then an osprey arches overhead, I look up, the world begins to turn again, and I walk home, past the well, and am grateful to be in this relationship.

I have always felt both held and challenged by this spot, and my greatest inheritance is the relationship that Bill has given me to this place. Its beauty holds me: the eagle taking flight above, the quail that

rises up from the trail, the porcupine asleep in the outhouse bucket, and all the ways that water shows up here as a flowing mass, as white ice on black stone, as fog on an August morning, as pounding rain on the roof.

I've crossed this ninety-acre Mill Pond in all the months of the year. In June winds have blown so fiercely that my canoe and I were pushed hard to the southern shore, and I've inched along, paddling against whitecaps breaking over my bow. On a January day when it's so quiet and still, I can hear the ice pop and shift. In the winter when the direction of the tide and the wind correspond, icebergs three feet high move at six knots through the tide rip and collide with each other, sheets of ice passing over and under each other in something that sounds like large furniture scraping on a wood floor or the crackling of a big bonfire. I've crossed this tidal pond on a late February afternoon when clear open water closed in with ice so fast that I was caught in the middle of the pond icebound—Shackletoned—and had to get out of the canoe and drag it before it stuck. And on August nights with no moon, when the whole pond was a deep misty purple, we picked our way across slowly from one lobster buoy to the next.

Is it the beauty and the solitude that kept Bill there for five decades? Is this the only place where he could surround himself completely with the beauty that he found so lacking in the human world? Is this how he escaped the ugliness and thoughtlessness of modern society: the family that didn't share his values; the generations of men coming home drunk from a day of roofing or working in the boatyard; everywhere people acting like sheep not using their talents, medicating themselves with recreation, alcohol, or drugs to make life more bearable? As a young man Bill knew he had abilities, and he could recognize other possibilities for himself that he found more resonant, more whole, more filled with beauty. In coming here to this place, wild and remote, he was choosing one over the other, no matter how difficult it would be to stay.

Much here quenched Bill's thirst. I can walk through the woods and miss the long in-breath and out-breath that marks the change from summer to fall, say, or the long rest of the trees that is winter, but Bill must have felt these things in his body. And he had enough lived perspective to imagine perfectly well the in-breath and out-breath of human history, of Native Americans netting salmon at the tide rip and burying their dead, of settlers building mills that slowly decay back into the ground, of himself clearing acres of alders that grow back and are cleared again a hundred years later by the granddaughter I have not yet met. It's always been the tide rip itself that has helped me feel this place as Bill did nearly every day.

The inhale and exhale of the earth through tides is hard to miss. All one needs to do is to sit right there at the tide rip, where the mill was built in 1810, and watch the water flow. If you could sit there for a good, long time—say, six hours—you would benefit much to see the water flowing in, carrying ducks, lobsters, mackerel, ice caps, young cod, or the occasional seal, porpoise, or log, then faster and faster, then becoming standing waves, and then release. Its energy ebbs with the abundance of flowing salty water filling every nook and cranny of place and comes to stillness for just long enough to observe. Maybe one notices the seaweed slowly shifting direction, then the whole ancient flow begins quietly, almost unbelievably, to reverse, flowing out from imperceptible to fast water to three-foot standing waves, then a crashing, thrashing power that always stirs me and draws me. Then stillness again.

And if you can sit there for six hours in the deep winter, you will be rewarded the most. In with the salt water flow icebergs and sheets of ice that just moments ago formed on the surface, out of the reach of the sun, and pack themselves into the mill pond with the ferociousness of cars crashing and windows breaking. And when it is packed in tight, jagged like a mountain range, it pauses and freezes hard like a curtain drawn across the pond, and silence. Slowly, now out of sight, the ocean water will recede, flowing out, allowing the weight of the ice to compact upon itself. No canoe could ever pass over this, only a homesteader walking on two feet, carefully, and alone, picking her way across the ice field. There are many deep winter days when the temperature stays below 10 degrees that the ice never leaves the pond, only popping and shifting with the rising and falling tide.

Bill found this energy some fifty years ago and decided to live among it, not visit for a week here and there, but to live within it for five decades. He sank into this place, developing a grace that arose from here. Many of us who knew him for more than a decade saw this shift from a tough, judgmental man, wanting community but not wanting people, to someone able to create community and to give it all his possessions, even as some parts of himself remained hidden and conflicted.

Was Bill drawn here by that beauty and that energy, or was part of him running away from town? Why the air rifles and guns that we found after he died? They were never used or even spoken of in all the years I knew him, but they were hidden there nonetheless. A few months after his death, a small group of us met at his homestead for a week of sorting and planning. We had buried Bill, but we had not yet come together to understand how we would live without him. It was midwinter, cold, and yet we found warmth together. While going through Bill's possessions and putting aside gifts for others, Julie remembered a strange, brief conversation with Bill just before he died

when he told her about all his secret hiding spots and said to her twice not to forget to look under the wood shavings. Why was he telling her this? But more importantly now, what wood shavings was he speaking about? There were wood shavings everywhere. Late one afternoon, when the winter light was already low, Julie realized that Bill might have been talking about the wood shavings in his outhouse. Of course, it would have been wise

to hide something in a separate building safe from fire, and after all, who would think to look in the wood shavings of an outhouse? Peter and Julie ran there and closely examined all around the compartment that holds the shavings and eventually found a false bottom. What can explain the ten thousand dollars (more than a year's worth of income for Bill) in hundred-dollar bills neatly bound and wrapped in plastic bags and carefully marked in blue handwriting "February, 2012, $10,000" and hidden there for Julie one day to find?

In a letter written to his closest friends forty years before he hid that money, Bill ended the letter with two starkly different images. "The sun," he wrote, "has just broken through the clouds and glistens through my window off the ripples in the brook as it curls past the cedar grove—I hope this is a good omen." And scratched below his name he appended this last ominous thought: "In view of all this, the old theme of survival comes up again for me. I'd like to have a session with you laying out our needs in case of social breakdown of the government. Tuck this away in your mind until we meet." Bill would often talk about "when the crash comes," then shake his head and acknowledge that so far he had got the timing wrong. Amidst the beauty of this place and the grace that it afforded Bill, he was also distrustful. Our failed society one day, he was sure, would collapse; it was only a matter of when. Was that brilliant and prophetic, or was it paranoid and survivalist?

There's darkness here, too, I can feel it, and it's not just the weather or the remoteness. It's the darkness of being alone with yourself and not always liking the company. It's the darkness of doubt and regret. It's Bill's struggle, made visible, to carve a ladle capable of serving up a drink of community. It's the long stretches of gray days, the monochromatic stick season, and long winter nights that begin at 4:30. No one will know if you die here along the trail or fall from your boat. That's real, too. Bill needed that darkness for his soul along with the beauty. The darkness makes the beauty whole.

Chapter Five

DAWN

—Helen—

Not knowing when the dawn will come
I open every door;
Or has it feathers like a bird
Or billows like a shore?

— Emily Dickinson

Proctors Point is a rocky index finger of land that points south and ends at the edge of the tide rip. If the land across the rip were a thumb, the two would be almost touching, pinching the sea into a narrow gap that surges into a circular pond encircled by those fingers. As we began to build our yurt with Bill in the fall of 2011, we came to call the land Herons Rip, a reference to the solitary long-legged bird who stalked the water's edge, and a nod to solitude itself.

In the breaking light I can just see my breath curling out to join all the other vapors of this misty, dewy, gray landscape around me. I have slipped out of the tent and walked the few feet through the low mountain laurel and blueberry to the shore to let it sink in that I've arrived. I squat on a rough mound of rock that slopes down to the sea in front of me, my knees drawn up in the chill, facing west, the way I came in the day before to join Peter and a small crew who have begun to prepare the site for the building workshop.

The sky is pearly and ready to open, the inside of a mussel shell. The tide is very low in the cove to the north of the point, low enough

for a couple of lobster
pots to be beached on the
gray-black mud. A kingfisher
announces itself in a sudden
staccato from the fir trees
across the tide rip, makes
two swoops over the dark
water, then back to a low
perch above the splashing
waves, eager for breakfast.
When the water in the
narrow channel is low like
this, you can make out
the shadowy forms of kelp
waving their huge fleshy fronds across the mouth of the rip, which here
is about forty feet across. Somewhere down there too deep to see are
the wooden remains of a dam, encrusted with barnacles and mussels
but preserved by the salt water for two hundred–some years. It's dark
and mysterious, you can pull up large mackerel from the depths, and
sometimes eagles, seals, and even harbor porpoises come to hunt here.

We treat the rip with respect when it's low and running hard, but
at higher water and a dropping tide we can jump off the rocks at the
pond side and ride the waves through. I used to be scared of the waves
and all the seaweed tangled on the rocks, the icy penetrating bite of the
salt water that made all my scratches sting, and how hard I had to
swim to get back to shore as I was carried down. But then around the
age of four Wren wanted to join the ritual, so I had to pretend that
none of that mattered, put a life jacket on her and go for it, swimming
extra hard to tow both of us back toward the rocks.

Altogether I've pretended my way into a deep authentic love of
this place over the years. Although Bill's way of life fascinated me from
the first, his land didn't immediately draw me in. In the first few visits
I pretended to love it just because I could see how much it meant to

Dawn

Peter, how much he wanted me to care, even though the landscape
of scrubby trees and wide mudflats strewn with seaweed that sucked
at one's boots and stank of decaying organisms and brine wasn't
immediately appealing to me. I preferred the "bold coast" of Maine,
where you can hear the surf crash and rock hop along the shore, trying
not to get blasted by a wave, looking out to endless ocean, intoxicated
by all that ozone and air. Where you can hear a bell or foghorn when
the fog rolled in and find starfish in the rocks when the tide was out.
Where you can look to the far horizon and see the blue-gray sea merge
into the blue sky. Here in the inner tidal zone, without surf, without
sand, without rocky tide pools or wide horizons, it is deep and quiet

and slow. This place has a subtler kind of beauty; it took more patience and imagination to fall in love.

I remember on one early visit standing next to Peter in the dusk, on Bill's side of the pond, looking out over a flat landscape of tidal mud and scrubby spruce, birch, and pine toward a sky the faintest shade of gold. Our canoe was pulled up on shore, and Peter was photographing the boat against the mounds of seaweed-covered rocks and distant water that still held the last of the light like a half-lidded eye. Whenever we are at Bill's he always has his camera in his hand. I stood there with him, feeling the cool, dew-laden night air flooding down toward us like a veil of invisible rain, darkness falling fast, and wondered what Peter was chasing with such rapture. He must have taken fifty frames of that canoe. But later, seeing the slides come back, I was stunned. I saw the subtle light of sky and water reflected on the blue-green curve of the boat's hull, the bladder wrack almost violet instead of a rank brown, the utter peace and serenity of the pond, and its sensual curve of land meeting water. That's what he saw through his lens that I did not, at least not then.

I came to love this place. First because I was in love with Peter, but shortly thereafter because of Bill, because of what he made here. For many people Bill took patience, too. He was often impatient, set in his ways, capable of a comment that cut deep. If he didn't know you well and you said or did something that didn't make sense to him, or if you seemed awkward in his world that was made by practical and skillful means, he would at best just ignore you. Or, at worst, dismiss your question as if you were an idiot and you were wasting his time. Most significant with Bill, if you didn't ask to learn, he saw no point in teaching. With children he could be wonderful—patient, inspiring, playful—or he could be snappish, depending on the setting and whether he thought children should be contained and silent at that moment, as when gathering in the guest yurt in the evening to sing the songs he loved and had carried the lyrics to in his head over a lifetime. Not having any children of his own did not prevent him from having an opinion on how they should be raised. He believed children learned best by being in a community of adults who were creative, excited, engaged designers of their own world and ideas. Children would pick this up naturally and flourish; modern child rearing catered too much and modeled too little, he thought.

In general, opinions came cheap, and nurturing conversation cost a lot more with Bill, though that changed over the years. By the time he had lost his hearing he was actually a good listener, and even in the time I knew him he seemed to nod and to question more and express his opinion less, giving the rest of us more room to share with him, to be ourselves. It was always his stated wish to "become gentler and kinder in all things," and I saw him do that during my friendship with him in the last decade of his life.

Just behind where I crouch on the mist-soaked rocks, Peter, Wren, and I have pitched our tent on a wooden platform that was long ago the floor of Captain Proctor's cabin. The remains of the cabin, including an old stove, bedsprings, and parts of furniture, are heaped in the thick birch and fir woods behind. Sometimes Wren finds treasures there, such as the ornate metal handle of a bureau or a little bed wheel or a fragment of old blue glass. But mostly it is the realm of porcupines. At night sometimes we hear them rustling and gnawing near the tent in their slow deliberate way, unconcerned with humans. One imagines that they would have some fear of our kind, having lived for generations with Bill, who thinks porcupine one of the world's delicacies, but maybe this branch of the family feels safe over here on the point, and they move as slowly as ever when they see us.

This has been our camping spot for the past five years or so, for as long as Wren has been old enough, at around two, to handle the ten-minute paddle in the dark across Mill Pond from Bill's house and the bushwhack across the point to crawl into a tent. The platform itself is starting to rot now—people keep putting their foot through it in places—and the insect world is busy dismantling and returning

to earth what the captain built long ago. Someday this delicate area near the shore will be a wild garden of bedrock, moss, reindeer lichen, mountain laurel, and blueberry once more. I never get tired of looking at the way these plants grow together: the soft gray of the laurel against the glossy dark of the blueberry leaf and underfoot the velvety lush moss contrasting with the brittle silver stems and bright red heads of the British soldier lichen.

One year I came to the platform to make camp and found the body of a bald eagle lying nearby on the moss. It was not a fresh kill; the flesh had partially shrunk from the bones and the feathers left ragged by the rain. I left it where I found it, undisturbed except for a note that

I folded and pinched inside its beak as one of the clues for the annual treasure hunt that year. A far-ranging treasure hunt that gave our collective children more experience and independence with Bill's place was part of our tradition. (My clue leading to the eagle read: "Now I lie where I once could soar. To find me there you'll need an oar," enticing the kids across the water on their own.)

The next summer, remarkably, the eagle was still there, and what had been feathers and flesh was a perfect skeleton of clean white bones. We carried the bones slightly uphill and inland, to a high piece of exposed bedrock. Peter and I laid them out with Wren and Willow and said some words of gratitude, dedicating them on the site that we had chosen for our new living space, for the yurt that we were then beginning to design with Bill. That was in 2010, and the yurt seemed to me an improbable dream. All around the bedrock for as far as you could see was a thicket of alders, wire brush, birch, and fir, home to the happiest mosquito population I'd ever encountered. I'm not sure what Bill's so-called "wire brush" is called in the taxonomic world of plants, and the closest I've come in a plant book is a type of spirea, but there's probably no better name: imagine a vigorous brushy plant, about four feet tall, with wiry stems that spring up underfoot and resist being cut by their toughness and sheer multitude. Bill has a special hook for pulling it up by the roots. Imagine lots of wire brush in the understory and above it twenty-foot-high scrubby alders that have a willowlike tendency to sprout back from their stumps within days of being cut down, and you have a sense of our building site. What was once a field surrounding the old mill, used for pasture by the family who lived on the point until their ox fell in the well, was now so thick that we could not walk a straight line for more than a couple of yards.

The eagle bones lay on the one opening above our little piece of bedrock like a talisman and prayer: of open skies and air, freedom of movement, and of determination.

I have to credit Peter with a lot of the determination. I was not entirely convinced about building a home on the point at first. I love camping, despite the mosquitoes, and I liked the freedom of visiting Bill and enjoying the homestead he already had without the responsibility of caring for a place we had made. We already cared for a berry farm and a large flock of sheep, along with gardens and buildings, and at that time we had the additional huge responsibility of nurturing a nonprofit education center, its staff and faculty, and all the people who came through our programs. I came to Maine in large part to get away from all that. When we arrived at Dickinsons Reach I wanted to feel unburdened from what felt like a life full of complexity and responsibility. Here we were making life *more* complex, I worried, with more to maintain, and in the very place where we came to embrace and partake in a simpler way of life with the man who embodied that philosophy. Besides, all my life I have been averse to new buildings, preferring to appreciate land in its less settled state. In short, I loved going to Bill's and didn't see the need for anything different. If anything, I longed to go further toward a life like Bill's: pared down, elemental, our needs few but our lives rich in solitude and time.

One August evening, when Peter and I were at Dickinsons Reach a couple of years before, we found someone in the group to watch the girls—both young then—and broke away to go for a paddle on the pond. I told Peter my feelings of ambivalence, told him if it were me I wouldn't build anything more than a new tent platform. It felt like a kind of betrayal to say that; I knew by then how much Peter wanted this, and I didn't want to be the one to stand in the way of his dream. I remember the trepidation I felt, with the man I loved, at testing out saying that I had a different vision. It was a commitment and a strength of our marriage, I believe, that we tried to help each other fulfill dreams, but so often, because mine were more often vague and slower to form, I faced the choice of saying no to possibilities or taking the role of joining Peter's vision for things. I most often chose the latter, and this had given me many gifts and opportunities I would not have otherwise had. But I was trying to learn, too, how to speak up for my truth in a way that could give space to my own vision while not fearing that it would diminish his, to allow that there might be enough light in the forest of possibilities for divergent dreams to flourish together.

Peter spoke of some of his own reasons: about how a caretaker would need a home if Bill ever needed help as he aged, how we might want our own place when Bill was gone, how much he believed the girls would like to have a place of our own even now, how creating something here would be an expression of the love he felt for this place. I heard all this, but I didn't share the strength of his feeling then. Peter saw so much that I wasn't thinking about, had had conversations with Bill and in his own head that I didn't even know about and that were far from straightforward for him to explain. What he expressed that night were only the easy explanations.

When I first met Peter, he carried a smooth black stone around his neck in a leather pouch, a stone that was about the size and shape of a human heart. I knew that stone was from Dickinsons Reach and that he kept it with him as a kind of anchor. He had given it to me to hold and wear, once, when he wanted me to feel close to him.

In our twelve years of marriage, Peter has always seemed happiest when he is manifesting something inherently challenging. I don't shy away from challenge, but I am averse to complexity, especially when it involves lots of planning and money. And people. At heart I'm more the hermit, and anything that involves organizing a lot of people usually gives me pause. Though our differences can bring us into conflict and hurt at times, they aren't a bad complement. I enjoy being design partner to his vision, love hard work, love the present-moment challenge of figuring things out and punting if I have to, more than Peter, who would prefer not to change a plan once he has one. When it comes to any building project we have ever done—and we've done many at our farm and the retreat center—I often feel a tightness and dread at the first suggestion of the idea, while he is filled with the excitement of planning energy; then when it comes to the actual project he tends to be tense and unhappy, striving to manage the outcome he envisions, while I always do better with the present, regardless of what it delivers.

As one friend who knows us well commented, Peter is the visionary and Helen is the re-visionary. Given that I met Peter because he
needed an editor for a project he was doing at the Trust for Public
Land, the insight seemed to fit, and sometimes it helps me to remember that there is a role for the one who doesn't hold the vision. I can
hold the red pencil, or the hammer; perhaps—in my marriage at
least—that has been my more natural role.

In the end, what satisfied my heart most in going forward with our
yurt on Proctors Point was my excitement to do it as a workshop with
Bill, to learn from him how to build one of his designs by hand. The
other part that excited me was the remoteness of the site. This to me

would be the equivalent of a long-distance backpacking trip; you had to pack in everything you needed, you had to live outdoors, you were on an extended journey without detour to the comforts of home. To do this while homeschooling Wren, in the most beautiful season of the New England year, was ultimately an adventure I didn't want to pass up.

Once I decided to embrace the adventure, I was innocent and optimistic about how it would all go. What I didn't fully understand until later was that I was entering into a project that was the birth of a dream and conversation that had been ongoing between Peter and Bill for longer than I had known either of them, and that its maiden voyage was to be laden with the freight and expectations of many years in the making.

Peter comes out of the tent to sit with me on the rocks above the tide rip. We watch the water in silence for a while. Then he stretches out his legs with a slight groan, turns his back to lean against me and drops his head in a gesture I know means he could use a massage across the shoulders. At our retreat center at home in the summer it is our practice for everyone to be in silence from waking until after breakfast, and though we aren't formally doing that here, it is a ritual we both particularly love and seem to fall into naturally even when not at home.

As I work my thumbs in under his collar and along the sides of his spine, I look down at his boots and pants caked stiff with tidal mud. He has been working hard to prep the site for a week already, along with a small site crew—Josh, Malena, Dan, Emily, and Lindley—we had hired, knowing they would be critical to us to be prepared for the actual building of the yurt. I had come up after them with Wren and Clara, who would be Wren's homeschool teacher while we were building. Willow, who was just starting eighth grade and didn't want to miss school, had decided to stay with her mother in Vermont.

During long days Peter and the others had cleared the yurt site of all that alder and wire brush; cut trails through the brush from the two main landing spots, one on the pond side of the point and one on the ocean side; made another clearing midway and set up a dining tent and camp kitchen under tarps, complete with rudimentary counters for storing and prepping food; tried, in vain, to get the well water to pump; set up a solar shower bag on a wooden tripod near the shore; and started hauling building materials.

Since there is no road or even footpath connecting our rugged point of land to anywhere else, it turns out to be an enormous backbreaking task to gather all the materials needed to build a twenty-four-foot-diameter, two-story wooden yurt. In addition to all the lumber, nails, insulation, roof shingles, windows, and tools, we need all the food, cooking and serving utensils, tables and tents to house and feed the site crew for three weeks, plus the fifteen volunteers who will join us for Bill's building workshop for another two weeks after that. We also have to haul in a woodstove from our farmhouse, a solar panel, large canvas equipment tent and dining tent, propane cooking stove, a nine-foot cherry log that will be the center post of the building, and a thousand other things I'm forgetting.

When Peter and I packed the Toyota pickup back at the farm, hitched his wooden dory behind, and loaded that to the gunwales, too, I started to understand a little about what we were in for. And yet even then it hadn't sunk in. Beside everything we have to haul in from town, we also need to find and transport huge flat foundation stones on beaches up and down the reach, just a few tons of them. Some of the building materials milled just outside Machias will come in by barge; others we will row in on our dory or lash across two canoes paddled together. For hauling the several tons of stone from nearby shores, we have our beat-up seventeen-foot Old Town canoe that had brought us here so many times and was about to be tested to its true strength.

Peter and I get up and stretch, and I head off to find Wren. A path leads from our tent platform through some gnarled firs to the kitchen clearing. A long wavy row of firewood is all that is left of the alder tangle it had recently been. Peter left one tree in the clearing, a straggly young birch. Its slight form is bent under the weight of an enormous Amish-style steel bell, the bell we replaced but for years hung at Knoll Farm to call everyone at our retreat center to meals. I smile when I see it, for I hadn't known that Peter hauled it here, and it is such a strange yet familiar sight. But it is an ironic smile: I am reminded how I come to Bill's—to this place unsullied by road, or electricity, or phone service, or e-mail, or outside noise—to fulfill my need for privacy and quiet, but here we are, building another community, bell and all.

My desire for privacy and solitude on the one hand and the pull to be engaged and of service to something larger than myself on the other was a big struggle in my life. Our work with deeply engaged environmental and social change leaders from around the country at the residential retreat center we had started was work that both thrilled and challenged me. Often I wondered if I was cut out for the social demands of it: meeting so many people for short intense bursts and being required to process and deeply examine all the emotions that come up in a retreat setting, something I enjoy one-on-one but do so less willingly when prompted in a group. More and more I noticed that I sought balance in farming, which allowed me plenty of opportunity to be alone, and yet

through growing the food and sharing that food and the experience of organic farming with so many who came from all over the country, I was able to satisfy my desire to share our land, to be generous, and also to stay in touch with a larger purpose than just feeding my family and my solitary nature.

I duck around the bell and past the canvas dining tent to find Wren under the adjoining kitchen tarp with Clara and Josh. Wren is standing on a stump, stirring a small amount of hot cocoa in a giant pot over the propane stove, Clara next to her starting another burner for tea. They are both wearing wool hat, fleece jacket, long john bottoms and rubber boots, our general uniform. Josh, powerfully built, in his thirties, is wearing handmade leather shorts and a hoodie sewn together from pieces of thrift-store cashmere sweaters. He offers to make me a hoodie, when I admire it. He tans his own leather and designs clothes in the cold months and spends his summers as a trail builder and carpenter. I can tell he and Clara already have a good connection.

Clara grew up in Costa Rica and the White Mountains of New Hampshire and is the kind of person who seems equally at home

anywhere. I had met her just once on a day that past August when she had visited Knoll Farm with her mother to pick blueberries at our pick-your-own orchard. Somehow I had this sense about her, that she would be a great companion for Wren and would appreciate Bill's place, and I knew she had just graduated from college and had no immediate plans, so I spontaneously invited her along. Every other time we had come to Maine, since Wren was a baby, I had spent most of my time with Wren and Willow, alerting them to various hazards, making food, and organizing games, such as treasure hunts, building forts, or simple carving projects in the workshop. I enjoyed this, but I also yearned for more time to work alongside Bill and other friends who brought skills in building, woodcraft, and homesteading. It was a true revelation to have time now to work and to learn, largely uninterrupted.

Slowly the others emerge from the tents that they had pitched along the shore through the trees east of ours. Everyone is moving stiffly, and no one is saying much, cupping hands around coffee and letting the steam billow up, wool hats pulled down low against mosquitoes that are whining in our ears. Emily is the daughter of friends of ours in our valley and taking a semester off from her architecture graduate program in Amsterdam. Lindley and Malena have both recently been student interns at the Yestermorrow Design/Build School near our farm and have a good deal of carpentry experience. Dan is a friend of Emily's from art school and the only one I've never met. He spends breakfast drawing crazy-looking cartoons on a scrap of wood to entertain Wren.

All day we carry lumber up from the so-called beach (really a mud flat) on the pond side to the yurt site. This is no small task. Each piece of spruce and hemlock and pine has to be hauled or handed up the steep fifteen-foot-high embankment, then carried along the trail about four hundred yards to the building site. It has all been cut by Bill's friend and timber framer Tim Beal at his lumberyard, then hauled here behind a lobster boat by Danny Manchester at high tide. Each piece is stickered (meaning stacked in layers with perpendicular strips of wood between each layer to keep the air circulating) on the barge, dismantled, and stickered again at the site. Each one of us devises ways of carrying our awkward, heavy loads. Malena has a strip of plastic shrink-wrap that was around some material that she slings over her

forehead and hooks under a bale of shingles against her back. Emily and Danny use a gurney made of alder poles and a burlap sack, using the straps of empty backpacks as extra support to shift some of the weight from the arms to the shoulders. When the arms fail, there's always the back or shoulders, and when they get rubbed too sore by the rough lumber, one is back to the hands and arms. Peter figures that the most we can do without injury is four hours of hauling a day, which amounts to about twenty round trips, or eight miles for each of us. Today we did close to six hours, with a two-hour lunch and swim break.

I never realized how much volume of wood it takes to make a small building until I saw it all in one place stacked on the ground; it seems an inconceivable amount. Some of the pieces are clearly beams, massively heavy from being still green and full of sap, and others are shiplapped boards for covering the walls. But much of a yurt is its circular roof, so we also have piles of pine cut into long irregular triangles. At times Bill has ripped each of his roof boards on the diagonal on-site, and having heard him tell stories about this, I know how lucky we are to have so much of the roof cut ahead of time. We have so many bales of shingles that we stack them to make furniture under the huge canvas tool awning set up at one edge of the clearing. Two stacks with boards across make a crude workbench and another stack makes a drafting table for Bill.

Peter seems happy, like a benevolent general, driving himself and everyone else hard but still on a high from the demands of the task. I hear a few grumblings in the ranks—the crew is really tired—so I just stay positive. I know Wren, Clara, and I bring some fresh energy, but I also sense a little that we are one more thing for Peter to have to worry about, so I try to figure out what needs to be done ahead of time without being asked. We need to have the site and trails completely cleared, all the building materials in place, and the foundation laid as well as functional outhouses, tent sites, and dining and kitchen area finished by the time everyone arrives for Bill's yurt-building workshop in less than two weeks. The workshop itself is only thirteen days, and in that time we have to construct the floor, walls, insulation, roof, windows, shingling. We are nervous; even though Bill has always said that to make a yurt weathertight takes no more than ten days of labor, we can't risk being complacent; everyone will disperse after the workshop, and shortly after that we will also need to return to the farm.

That night we drop into bed exhausted, the sweet smell of pine and the stink of biotic tidal mud clinging to us. When I pull off my watch with my teeth to set the alarm for 6:00 a.m. and stash it above my pillow, I can taste the salt on my wrist from my sweat. Or was that from washing in the cold sea? I am asleep in about two seconds.

The next day we haul and sort stones. Big stones. Foundation stones. The bigger and flatter the better, unless they are bigger than a few of us together can carry. Josh, Dan, and Emily head out in the canoe as the tide drops to comb the shorelines of Moose Snare Cove just to the north, and Johnson Point to the west, for square-edged flat stones of sufficient size to hold up the footing of a house. These they haul upslope through the mud to the high point of the tide line so that they can go back and pick them up at high tide and not have to struggle with a weighted canoe in the mudflats. At high tide each stone, mud-smeared and barnacle-coated, is precariously lifted and let down with a gentle thud onto the sloping bottom of the boat. When

the boat looks in danger of sinking or listing too far to one side, they head back to the point, where the rest of us help unload each rock onto the gurney and carry them one by one up a narrow wooded ravine on the west side to the clearing. We knew we'd never get them up the trail from the normal "beach" landing on the pond, given their number and weight. The pile of stones looks huge by

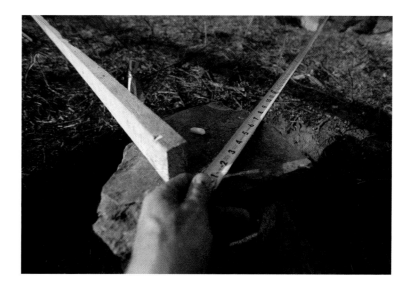

afternoon, but we know many of them won't work for our task. We estimate we need seventy-five 50- to 100-pound stones for the foundation, and probably three times that many to allow for the combinations that will eventually work.

We need to build eleven footings out of dry stone on top of the mother bedrock that will sit under the house. We put one at the center of the circle, one in each cardinal direction, one at each diagonal, and finally a couple of extras under the long beams that will stretch the length of the circle, making a cross under the house. Before setting the rock pillars we dig down to expose the bedrock. Placing the footings directly on that massive slab of Arcadian granite saves us from having to dig a lot of holes down below frost line. It was Bill's idea; one of the few pieces of hard labor Bill admits to hating is digging holes. Still, we have to dig to bedrock, which is exposed aboveground near where we are going to place the door to the west (where we laid the eagle bones two years before), then slopes downward toward the east, getting progressively deeper in the soil. In some places we dig for at least four feet before hitting solid rock. Once we have the holes in exactly the right place in the circle—itself a feat of measuring and re-measuring from our center stake—we have to build dry rock pillars that are both level and unshakable. Wren is our tester; we have her stand on each pillar to see if it wobbles. Most of the time it wobbles, a lot, and we have to take all the stone slabs that aren't lying perfectly soundly out of the hole and build it again. And again, and again.

For most of the day I am in one hole, Emily in another, and Dan in another. Josh is ferociously attacking with a pickax a massive alder root-ball that stands in the way of progress in yet another hole, beads of sweat flinging off his forehead. At one point, stopping to take a break and shoot a little video, I try my hand at getting some commentary. "How's it going?" I ask Emily. She grunts and doesn't look up. "Dan?" I ask, next hole over. "Now I know why rock is a four-letter word," he says, sounding too tired to laugh at his joke.

The next day Peter and I agree it is okay for me to peel off from the urgent work at hand for a mission I've been relishing. I creep out of the tent at 5:30 a.m., trying not to rustle my sleeping bag too much and wake Wren beside me. It is an hour before high tide, the right time to paddle into Duck Cove if one wants to avoid dragging a boat across acres of slippery boot-sucking sea mud. I pack a small bag with water, headlamp, wallet, and rain shell and launch the kayak into the water off the point. Peter fastens the compass with a bungee cord onto my bow, as the fog is thick, so thick that, amazingly, we can't even see the trees on the other side of the rip. We can hear the current fine, though, so I climb into the kayak's cockpit and push gingerly toward it.

I paddle by feel across the finger of ocean from our land to Johnson Point, then trace the outline of the shore down to where I have to start the ocean crossing to Duck Cove, a much longer stretch of water with more current and wind, and the potential for getting lost and missing the cove altogether. I have been disoriented in fog before—most memorably as a fourteen-year-old girl on my final Outward Bound expedition along this same coast when we circled in our pull boat in dense fog for two days before realizing that we had seen the same shoals before—and I knew how easily it could happen. Similarly to being in a whiteout blizzard in the mountains, being in fog can confuse and disorient the most experienced navigator. To "orient" means, literally, to get your bearings by turning to the east, but in fog or snow every direction seems entirely the same.

I drift for a moment, pointing my bow so that I have a compass bearing of due west, then make sure to paddle with my eyes fixed to the needle. "I am my own compass," I think, a note to myself that I used to carry in my wallet to better trust my intuition but which also serves as a reminder that without one's full attention to the moment even a compass (or in my metaphor, one's intuition) is useless. One has to set a bearing and follow it. To be intuitive takes time, takes attention. I was aware of painful times I had overridden my intuition and let myself surrender to the fog when, looking back, I could see that I had had a bearing all along, just not the faith in myself or the courage I needed to follow it.

Right now there isn't much else to look at besides the compass two feet in front of me. I can see the lobster buoys only when I am about to touch them, all the colors muted by the fog, the world a solid gray. The cold salt water drips off my paddle and down the sleeves of my rain shell until I am thoroughly chilled and my wrists sting from the salt. Better paddle quickly.

I am warm by the time I can just make out the pale gray shapes of pointed firs, like a line of slightly more solid clouds in a swirling mist. Then I can hear the gentle lapping of waves on the pebble beach, and I'm there, just north of Duck Cove at a place I recognize. I paddle into the little protected cove with its public floating dock often loaded down with lobster pots and pull the kayak up the rocks, hiding it in a thicket of *Rosa rugosa*. Then I find our red Toyota pickup, which is parked just up the road from the boat landing. I drive out of Duck Cove, make a left onto Route 1, and go downcoast toward Jonesboro, just southwest of Machias. I have located a farm there that milks goats, and I know that any farm with milking goats always has a few spare billy goat kids they are looking to get rid of. Peter and I have this idea that we should have a few goats with us to help us clear the land of brush. We could have brought our own sheep, but goats are much better brush eaters, and besides, the truck pulling out of the farm's driveway was chock-full. This seemed easier.

Most of the islands in Maine were at one time cleared by sheep and goats, which then pastured there summer after summer, safe from wolves and coyotes and eliminating the need for fences. I love that history. As a shepherd I liked the idea of hauling animals out by boat to a piece of land and leaving them there to go semiwild on a diet of beach peas, laurel, raspberry, and sweet vernal grass. Now, it seemed, my fantasy was about to come true. Well, almost true. It turned out our goats preferred bagels to sweet vernal grass, and at the rate they ate wire brush we could have used three dozen goats, but it was a worthy experiment.

Don and Kim have an impressive flock of Alpine goats and are making some delicious fresh chèvre blended with rosemary and other herbs that they are selling at local markets. They also have a rambling house with a new litter of cloud-soft kittens playing on the steps and two small children who run out to greet me. They lead me to the young billy goats, who are separated from their mothers now that it's almost breeding season, in a hoop-house structure behind the garden. After a lot of chatting about the relative merits of goats and sheep, and after nearly adopting one of the kittens for a camp pet for Wren, then thinking better of it, I settle on two small white male goats with shiny hair and scraggly adolescent beards. Much less skittish than our lambs at home, they remind me of puppies—curious, naughty, and totally adorable.

Our plan had been to have a goat roast at the end of the yurt-building workshop, but already I am revising that plan in my head as I load them into the back of the Toyota pickup. I decide maybe I'll "rent a goat" instead, and right away Don and Kim kindly agree to take them back if necessary. On the way to Duck Cove I even name them: Jack for the one with upright horns and a bright face because he reminds me of a Jack-in-the-box character, and Tommie for the smaller hornless one, Jack's sidekick.

Peter had arranged for Danny Manchester to pick me up with the new recruits in his lobster boat. I had never met Danny and wasn't sure how he might look upon this harebrained project, but Peter had said Danny had been happy to help our prep crew all week, barging lumber and building materials to the land when it got to be too much to do by canoe. When I pull in to Duck Cove with the billy goats, some of Kim's fresh herbed chèvre, a few giant cabbages and squash from the jungle of the farm's fall garden, and a few pounds of chocolate from the general store, Danny is there waiting. His boat, a powerful-looking and well-worn lobster hauler with an open cockpit, has *The Floating Farmer* painted on the side in large block letters. I'm set, I think, and wave from the gravel road as I pull down to the boat-loading ramp.

Danny is a big handsome man with black hair and an easy smile, and with the kind of strength and quiet grace that comes from hauling lobster pots on a rolling sea year after year. I admire his boat and ask lots of questions; he tells me that he started lobstering here with his own license when he was just fifteen. He chuckles at the goats but

carries them aboard his small skiff almost lovingly and ties them up near the outboard motor with a piece of baling twine that I had in the truck. I am imagining doing this with a panicky sheep and am not sure how it will go, but I follow his lead.

"If they jump overboard, how well do they swim?" I ask.

"They'll probably just stand there," Danny said, and indeed they do.

Danny hooks up his big lobster hauler to the skiff, I throw the kayak on board, and we set off, dragging the little loaded boat behind. The goats stay standing, swaying, looking around at the churning water with wonder but no apparent alarm, all the way to the tide rip and through it to the other side. No self-respecting sheep would have caused so little fuss.

As Danny and I pull in through the rip with the goats, I see Bill paddling one of his twenty-foot wooden canoes back across the pond toward home. He always paddles standing up—it is one of his quirks, though I'm sure he has explained to me the good reason for it—and there he is in his familiar faded button-down shirt and wool pants and battered canvas hat, artfully guiding the boat past our wake. I feel sorry to miss his visit as I haven't seen him yet since we arrived. Usually it is the very first thing I do: find Bill, get one of his enveloping hugs that squashes my head into the top of his broad chest and the woodsmoke smell of him. This flat-out pace of ours is not normal. He doesn't wave—not that it would have been easy to do while standing in a tippy canoe—and I have the sense that our bulk and engine noise are obnoxious to him. I myself have never come in by engine before, and I feel uncomfortable. In our need to use Danny's motorboat to help us, are we being disrespectful of all that Bill had built here and believed?

To build his own sixty-foot-diameter, four-story yurt, little by little over the years, Bill brought every piece of wood in by canoe or on his back. I am always astonished by this fact. We could have taken on that challenge, forgoing Danny's help. We could have loaded the goats in the canoe, too. (As I write this I can hear Bill making one of his favorite plays on words: "We paddled in with a goat . . . well, actually it turned out to be easier with a paddle.")

The past winter, Peter, Julie, Bill, and I had come to the site to set up a wooden tripod topped by a long pole and red bandanna to test whether our yurt roof could be seen from any other part of Dickinsons Reach (it couldn't), and the conversation turned to how we would get materials there. Bill did the calculation for us on the back of a board: over forty trips with four paddlers and two canoes lashed together just to get the lumber to the point. But since the tides are not that cooperative (to say nothing of the weather) and paddling in and out of the rip and in and out of Duck Cove is only possible when the tide is at the right height and flowing in your direction of travel, there was no way around it: We needed a bigger boat, unless we had more like sixty days to do nothing but bring in materials. We didn't. So we are grateful to Danny. We offer to pay him to help us, though many times he refuses to accept it or takes some payment but shows up with heaps of vegetables and lobsters for our dinner.

This thought reminded me of a story Bill once told about buying an entire lumberyard's supply of 3×3s. No one wanted the odd-size lumber, so the owner offered Bill a deal. The more pieces Bill committed to buying the cheaper the price of each piece became, until Bill—laughing at himself for his folly—found himself buying an enormous truckload of the stuff (he still had gobs of 3×3s in his lumber shed decades later). He had it all delivered to Duck Cove, loaded as much as he could on his canoe catamaran and had some friends help him paddle it in. He said they were about halfway across

Johnson Point when they realized they were all pulling as hard as they possibly could and moving backward in the current. So they gave up and retreated. Bill found a lobsterman who had a barge and agreed to help them, even though it was a Sunday. Bill said they all rode on the loaded barge, which nearly went under at one point from the weight, a giant plume of water arcing over the top. When they got to Bill's beach, soaked and exhilarated, Bill asked the man what he owed him. "It being a Sunday and all, how about twenty dollars," the lobsterman said apologetically. Bill handed him forty and saw a huge shy grin spread over his face. When telling the story Bill said, "It was the only time I ever saw him smile. It was the best money I ever spent."

Still, even with this memory, as we motor in I feel graceless, and I can't help wishing we were building only if we can really take our time and attune our attention as Bill has. It's not always easy to be around someone you admire so much, whose way of life you aspire to but so obviously haven't reached. This building of the yurt was underlining what I already knew but wasn't comfortable with: how different we were in the life choices we'd made.

In Bill's world time is the most valuable currency. Time, not money, is what you want to earn; time is what will allow you to do what you want. And contrary to what modern life would like us to believe, it seems to me that money—though it could—does not create time. In fact, it seems to do the opposite. It is often the case that the people who have the capacity to earn the most and save the most money, those who have the most material wealth, are the ones who talk about having the least time. In our drive to achieve some conventional measure of success, to stay afloat with modern demands on our bank accounts, to feel self-satisfied with our social status, time leaks out of our lives, our children's lives, our creative lives, out of our sense of consciousness altogether. In fact, in chasing material gain one can become fearful of time, as if it were an opponent to conquer. We speak of it in so many ways as if it too were something material or something animate—time can be killed, squandered, wasted—we can take time or need time and yet rarely do we have "just enough." Our obsession with managing time becomes a never-ending conversation about "finding balance," which seems to be largely illusory and a setup for meaning high achievement without a nervous breakdown. "Balance" rarely means slowing down in any real way, at least the way I hear people use the word. In fact, having time on one's hands tends to mean boredom, or a lack of success, ambition, connection, or potency in our culture these days—like something you'd want to wash off.

By most of the world, people who live like Bill, far from Main Street and without modern conveniences, are spoken of mostly in the pejorative: eccentrics, dropouts, curmudgeons, throwbacks, or, at the very least, quaint. Too few see the brilliance of what Bill demonstrated:

that time is far more important than money in creating a meaningful life, and that money is not in fact a prerequisite to having time. In fact, money, and the materialism it is tied to, along with the conspiring cultural notions of what is required to be successful in others' eyes, only makes it harder to allow oneself to live a spacious and self-created life.

Bill, who did not come from money, did not make his choices padded by the security of a trust fund or savings account, found a way to live on very little a year, under ten thousand dollars. Having escaped the world's notions of success, he had time for self-fulfillment, to pursue what he felt was most important to learn and do. He read Erich Fromm and *The Humanure Handbook* and worlds of books in between. He designed everything from ethereal wooden yurts to the wheelbarrows that would withstand a rocky trail. He cut and split an enormous amount of wood by hand, thereby keeping himself warm, his back strong, and his woods full of light and eliminating the need for fossil fuels.

But as I came to know him, I learned that his motivation was not just about time, not just a personal preference for manual labor, or a retreat from the world. His choice to be free of the cultural pressures and norms most of us live with did not share a great deal with other homesteaders I knew, who were in two loosely connected categories— the überfrugal who had found a way to live self-sufficiently to escape the working world and "suck out the marrow of life" doing what they most wanted, or staunch environmentalists who didn't believe in using up more resources than they absolutely had to. Bill's notion was less environmentally motivated—though he did care about that—and deeply rooted in his belief in nonviolence and social equality. He wanted to step away from a social and economic machine that he saw as undeniably exploitative; to participate as a consumer, and especially to strive for affluence, was to be part of this engine of exploiting others. And he saw learning to make by hand what was necessary to live your own life, and sharing that example with others, as the antidote to this. He believed that people, from a very young age, needed to feel competent and useful, needed to understand how they could contribute to their own elemental needs such as shelter and nutrition, and by doing so would have a greater sense of self-esteem and altruism. And he often worried that the ways in which growth and prosperity removed people from working with their hands and feeling competent and connected to the sustenance of their lives contributed

toward a growing apathy and disinterest in making a better world.

So many of these values I agree with and long to carry out more fully in our lives. To build this building Bill's way—with hand tools— felt like more than just an outback adventure full of hard labor. He was passing something on, something more than skills. And we were privileged to be shaped by what he was giving us. Bill believed in hand tools because they were democratic, anyone can learn how to use them and obtain them, in many cases even make them (Bill made many of his own tools). If you build a house with hand tools, you have to make a connection with each step, each cut of each board, each nail. You are less likely to make waste, make mistakes, let yourself be distracted. It is like walking through a landscape instead of seeing it through the window of a speeding car. You are more likely to take in, and remember, what you are seeing. Just as if you have to load and unload your canoe with all your supplies and carry them on your back, you will not likely take more than you need. If you have a large boat you will fill it and only notice later that you now have to spend twice as much time maintaining all that you brought on the passage with you.

Another point, to state the obvious, is that to use power tools you need power. Which usually means you need a road, and a power grid, or at least a gas-powered generator or solar technology. For these you need some capital and the ability to maintain that power source with money or time. There it is: A hammer builds you a shelter, then that same hammer takes no time to maintain when it is hanging on the wall; a power source isn't so simple. You have to go out and earn some money to get the power, then keep earning money to keep paying for it, and if it goes down, most likely you have little control over fixing it and yet have become dependent on it to work. What's more, power tools, Bill argued, are designed only to make it easy to mass-produce something. That didn't interest Bill: To make strides in efficiency of production to sell something was again part of the same exploitative economy he wanted to get away from. He spent lots of time designing hand tools that improved one's efficiency or made a job simpler so that more people would want to build their own shelter or carve their own bowl. That kind of efficiency interested him.

Bill wasn't categorically against technology, not a Luddite, and in fact was fascinated by technology whenever it demonstrated what

he felt was good design. He loved his tiny solar panel on the roof that powered one light bulb and a radio. People would bring him things, let him try them out, and sometimes—like that solar panel—he would adopt them. Mostly he wouldn't—much to others' frustration—like the rocket stoves both Peter Lamb and Dorn brought for the outdoor kitchen that burned much hotter and cooked much faster, with less smoke, but he never used it, preferring to cook everything on his open fire pit. Besides that solar panel and a few modern building materials that he readily embraced, like Kevlar for his handmade wheelbarrows, I actually can't think of a single thing in his homestead that would count as modern (meaning twentieth or twenty-first century) technology. No phone. No sink. No refrigerator. No appliances. No computer. He loved inventions, but he felt that most new technology, especially technology that created convenience, took more away than it gave. It narrowed people's opportunity to use their biggest asset—the capacity of their imagination. And he was so much about nurturing creativity in people. "The thing I think about most," Bill told me, "is trying to encourage people to think and do for themselves, not just be fed information. It feels like that is more and more rare, and I see a lot of technology being part of that, so I distrust it."

When Bill was setting up our yurt-building workshop and making the supply list, he suggested to Peter that he rent a generator to charge a couple of power drills, much to our surprise. Bill appreciated the speed of a power drill with a group and how much better screws work than nails for securing ceiling boards when you had to work from underneath. So power drills were our one power tool on the site. Almost as if it were mocking us, the generator, which also became the hub for a surprising number of cell phones that rang and chirped around it, was the one thing that broke constantly, daily, and gave us no end of angst, causing Peter extra trips into town and awkward muscle-wrenching journeys with generator-in-wheelbarrow along Bill's long, rugged footpath.

Danny and I make shore and unload goats and groceries from his skiff, and I send an excited Wren to dip the animals some fresh water at the well. Peter comes down to say that Bill was over to see how Lindley and Malena were progressing on the very small yurt that will be the outhouse for the site. Like Bill's own "yurt johns," this will be a conical structure with a tipped-back roof and skylight, giving people just enough room inside to stand or sit, do their business into a bucket set in a wooden bench, sprinkle in some sawdust, close the lid, and leave through the arched door. A square outhouse surely would have been easier to build, but Bill's yurt johns are gorgeous. He had built one for us at Knoll Farm, next to our Mountain Yurt, itself a thirty-foot wooden-frame yurt covered by a canvas, which we had constructed from a kit made by Pacific Yurts. Bill never approved of our canvas yurt, even though the company Pacific Yurts bowed publicly to Bill as the inspiration for their designs. So he openly ignored that we had it there, but all the same he made us a tiny exquisite outhouse next to it.

And we are here, on Bill's homestead, so we build round buildings. This is both a matter of respect and of something akin to submission: We love his designs, but in our bowing to them we also convert. Bill had that effect on people, though I'm not sure he realized it. He spoke so much about the importance of collaboration, and yet ultimately he had an opinionated streak as wide as his four miles of coastline. As a case in point, the discussions about building at the tide rip many years prior began with Bill saying, "I'll be really curious to see what you build over there," and Peter said something to me about a very small New England saltbox or cape in keeping with the place's earlier settlement history. But before any plan took form, long before I even knew we were building anything for sure, Bill was sketching out the design for a thirty-two-foot yurt on a sheet of lined yellow paper on a flight to Mexico with Peter and making his pitch.

We quickly saw that a yurt was the only right thing to build, to properly honor Bill and his landscape populated by round dwellings. So by 2010 we talked it through in detail, gave Bill our ideas and desires, watched him sketch it all out, met a few times that winter.

Now, here on the land, Bill's lumber order already milled and plans drawn, we are soon to find out that he has taken most of the specific ideas that Peter and I added to his design of our yurt and conveniently forgotten (or abandoned) them, so that only the pure elements of his own design remain.

Chapter Six

FINDING AN ELDER

—Peter—

For a week after his death, I walked down to our mailbox, certain to receive a letter in his distinctive, always blue, handwriting. The top left-hand corner of every envelope, saying volumes about relationships, would have his simple return address "Bill 04655." I had seen my last letter to Bill opened in the middle of a small pile of others exactly where his hands had left them on his desk the day he died. It was a strange thing to see it there, a portrait of myself calling out to Bill but him being gone, only his vapors and last acts visible in the way things were left that morning. Surely he had read my letter and written back.

All spring, summer, and fall before he died, we were unable to have the conversation I was thirsty for. I needed Bill's help, maybe more than ever before, and I didn't know how to ask for it, and he didn't know what to offer. The way things were, with Bill using only the mail and picking that up but once or twice a week, and my seeing him only five or six times a year, an important conversation could easily take, well, forever to unfold. A few times he showed an interest in knowing about the transition I hinted at. What's important to you right now, he asked? I fumbled the answer, not being honest and direct, instead likely offering up some platitude to hide the truth: I no longer knew what was most important to me; I was in between stories. For the twenty years that Bill had known me I would have answered that question with a clear eye and a quick response, leaning in, with ideas that would likely draw others in. More than a few times I've been talking to colleagues in a public place, say, a restaurant, and had strangers walk over to ask more about what we did with our lives. For years I had been on fire with beliefs and dreams and actions, but now I was humbled, unclear, doubting, sensing something underneath the surface that I could not yet see. This conversation needed intention and time; I needed to ask Bill for help. I needed Bill to see that I was adrift in need of a sail and an anchor.

Over the last several years our conversations had become routine, pleasant and supportive without much new being revealed. Bill would tend to talk with me about conservation initiatives in the bay, about friends in common, and about trips he was dreaming about, and always about the pros and cons of new tools he had created. In short, he would talk with me about what interested him. It had been years since he had talked with me about my work, and I could never really tell if that was because he didn't understand it, he didn't approve of it, or if in these last years it was harder for him to connect with ideas outside his world. I was not a new friend, and I had a clear sense of where Bill stood on most things, and my expectations were in line with that. In the first decade of our friendship our lives overlapped constantly, and more recently we had become two circles standing comfortably beside one another, shoulders rubbing, but eyes gazing in slightly different directions. We informed each other's thinking, we kept in close touch, but Bill didn't engage as much as I might like in my world. And my sense was that showing up for each other, standing there beside

each other, even if there wasn't as much overlap as either of us might like, was a commitment that we both appreciated.

In July of the year he died I wrote to him that one of the first buildings we put up at Knoll Farm ten years before had burned and how hard that was, and now I understand that my metaphor of loss was not explicit enough. I needed to say what was hardest to say: that what had been my dream and work for twelve years had burned. A large and important part of my life, my family's life, and the lives of quite a few others, was over. Bill wrote back immediately saying that the burning of that building was sad, it's true, but that it gave me the chance to design something new. Damn, I knew that, but what I didn't know was did I have the strength to do whatever might come next? Did he believe in me? Help me, Bill, to understand to trust myself. When November rolled around, Bill had finished building his last yurt just fifty feet from where he hoped to be buried. I knew I had better write, skip the metaphors, and ask him straight up, what should *I* build next?

I knew Bill's patterns, and there should be a letter today or the next arriving for me. It had just been delayed by the holidays. Bill would have arisen early that morning to answer the pile of mail that he had picked up a few days before. He'd have stuffed the addressed letters in his leather bag and slung it over his shoulder. On his way to town he would have stopped to drop the letters with Ann, the postmistress, who would have stamped them for Bill, taking the stamps out of their vault on "account" for Bill, a service that was provided to him and no one else.

When I first met Bill I was thirty, and now I'm fifty-two; I needed a guide and an example then, and today I needed something different: a counsel, a fellow traveler, I needed a peer. Just then, I needed a friend willing to dig a little deeper with me, observe me, hear me out, and tell me what he saw. That's not where Bill was able to go with me, and my work wasn't something he would comment on. I still don't know if that was out of deep respect or plain disregard. Nowhere at Dickinsons Reach is there a mirror for one to look into and see your reflection; it was never that easy. It's not that I needed to look at Bill and Dickinsons Reach in order to see myself, but that's what I wanted. I wanted his encouragement. I wanted him to tell me what to do.

The letter never came. The most important questions in life we are left to answer on our own.

It was Bill and just a handful of others who had inspired this lifework in me, and I had spent more than a decade manifesting what I had learned from them, kindling it, gently and not so gently nurturing the ideas, inviting people to be part of it, raising money to enable it to flourish in the form of Center for Whole Communities, and it had grown quickly into something authentic and substantial with dedicated staff and board, eventually more than a thousand

alumni, and an integral mission of change, but my well had gone dry, the energy exhausted. Long before meeting Bill, I recognized how an experience of nature had healed me, helped me to grow and be strong. But it was my friendship with Bill that offered me the encouragement to believe that I could be so bold to offer that experience to others. And that's what Helen and I set out to do at Knoll Farm. We had no training, no advanced degrees, no directive from anyone; and truth be told, we had little experience, little infrastructure, none of the basics to make a program work. But that didn't stop us from believing that an experience of nature could transform others, help to remind conservation of its vision and values, and to bring together the different worlds that I saw at Bill's and elsewhere: the wholeness of people and the wholeness of nature. Helen and I set out to create a place at Knoll Farm where people from all walks of life could come together to have conversations that mattered and that transformed the way we think and behave about the life of community and the life of the earth.

In my work as photographer and conservationist, I saw a lot of broken and divided things: fear of each other, organizations working to stop things and in opposition to one another, failed efforts to protect nature that excluded people, and ineffective efforts to help people that didn't recognize the role of nature to healing. Helen and I believed we could offer just a taste of something different in weeklong experiences on our hillside farm. The originating vision of Center for Whole Communities was to reduce some of the tension between saving nature and meeting human need by creating a safe and inspiring place at our farm on which to bring leaders from those two worlds together in dialogue, to create relationships, and to begin to see how their work shared a common destiny and was dependent on each other's success.

If we could live it ourselves, and invite others to feel it for a period of time in their own bones while in the programs at our farm, then we might create some change. And in order to set this table for all, we'd somehow make it tuition-free. We did all of that, for more than a decade, with lots and lots of help from others, for the benefit of

something like fifteen hundred citizen leaders around this country. It was hard work, real work, because as we faced the brokenness we had to live within the wounds. The result of becoming more aware of the ecological and social divides is, as Aldo Leopold says, "to live alone in a world of wounds." We didn't seek to be alone, and the bringing together of a great many people to join this work made it more bearable and shared.

After twelve years of working and manifesting nonstop, however, I was no longer offering up what had drawn others toward us. And the good people that gathered around us for those years mostly stopped coming and writing. What had been an energy-rich, authentic, successful, collaborative offering to the world was coming to a close. The resources and the energy were flowing in other directions now because I, as one of its originators, could no longer carry its fire. I needed space to grow again and to find what was even more radical and on fire inside myself. I knew that was what I most needed, and I also knew that this could be viewed as giving up and letting others down. Could Bill help me again to discover and trust what was inside myself?

And there was smaller stuff that worried me: the workshops that we had annually invited Bill to teach would end and there would be one less reason for him to visit. And the kind of help that I once joked about was exactly what I needed right then. For example, Bill came to our wedding at Knoll Farm many years ago and spent all that weekend, except for the ceremony itself, up in the woods building us a yurt composting toilet similar to the one he had at Dickinsons Reach. Many friends joined him up in the forest by the Mountain Yurt working quietly amid the song of the hermit thrush. We needed a toilet there because it would soon be where retreats gathered. Bill being up there working while we were getting married was such a practical, loving, direct way for him to say to us: "I believe in you, and I believe in what you can do here. You will need a toilet, so I will build one for you." I needed that kind of help again. What did this moment ask of me? What can I do with my talents that might take me and my family closer to wholeness? Now that I've had fifty years of becoming a person, did I like what I saw?

I'd had experience asking myself important questions long before knowing Bill, but meeting him there at the Nearings when I was just thirty gave me my first living example of some answers to consider close up. When Bill invited me to join him for Thanksgiving twenty years ago, I didn't hesitate, though I had no idea where I was going. I set off on a long journey that would begin with me following a trail in the woods and coming upon an entirely new place.

> Turn right at the salmon factory. Follow the dirt road
> for half a mile. Park when you can't drive any further
> and then begin walking. Don't take any side trails (not
> yet). I'll be waiting for you.

And he was. On that Thanksgiving Day I made it to the end of the trail, where I found myself staring through a young stand of maples at the most unusual and impressive structure I had ever seen. It was large, sixty feet in diameter at the ground, round, of dark aged wood, elegantly sloped walls, bands of tightly spaced square windows under each brim of roof. With its four shingled rooflines each perfectly sized to sit atop the one below, this structure spoke of wholeness, elegance, and simplicity. It was not a house, but a ship. And somehow I knew it would take me on an important journey, so I eagerly climbed aboard for that first Thanksgiving dinner.

Several days later, I went home with a borrowed edition of Erich Fromm's *To Have or To Be?* The six-hour drive back to Cambridge was time well spent processing all that I had seen and heard. It was all so new. Everything in his home Bill had made with his own hands or helped someone else to make. He lived on a small amount of money to be free to do exactly what he wanted with his life. His library was extensive, most of the books unfamiliar to me and all of them

intriguing. Tools everywhere, in their right place, to do the work of life. Hardly anything there could be purchased, only made. The land outside was reflected inside, and the man inside shaped that wild with all his creativity and strength. It was a place filled with story and purpose and intention, and I was intoxicated by it all and greedy for some of that for myself. He offered no lectures and no advice, and yet I left feeling that I had learned something important. What he gave me were invitations, things to consider, examples to ponder, questions to pose to myself, and, most important of all, an open invitation to return. Would I accept?

Many years later, a younger friend, Jen Marlow, met Bill at about the same point in her life that I was when I first met him. Jen was in law school and already birthing an ambitious and heartfelt response to climate change that had her mobilizing others from all over the Americas. She wrote:

Bill's way of teaching is like a light streaming in softly through the window. A beckoning, an inspiring call: Not, you should live like this. But, you can live like this. For an old salt, he is gentle with ideas. He may have an opinion, but he was still interested in hearing yours, even if you're fifty years younger and don't always know what to say when he asks: What do you want to see? How do you want to spend your time here? I knew what he really meant. How could I be more empowered to direct my experience here? How carefully could I seek to see? What was I ready to learn?

I returned to Dickinsons Reach that first March after my Thanksgiving visit. It was gorgeous early spring weather. Bill and I launched one of his twenty-foot wooden canoes and paddled out for the first time through the tide rip, down into Little Kennebec Bay, and out to Hickey Island. I paddled in the bow, working hard to deliver clear, steady

strokes, and Bill stood in the stern with his long, six-foot paddle, striking an iconic pose on the water known to hundreds of lobstermen and sailors. But that day he and I were alone on the bay, and I felt for the first time something I have often felt since when my canoe is pointed due south toward the open ocean; it is more than beauty, more than the alertness of being in an open boat in the open ocean, more than relaxation or joy, something akin to deep relationship. That day I took my camera and tenuously began taking pictures of Bill in that place.

And I've never stopped observing, never stopped taking pictures, and never stopped piecing together new understanding about what Bill's bold experiment in living means. I understood, first, that these four miles of coastline and estuary gently shaped Bill, and Bill gently shaped them in a marriage that lasted till he died. They lived together, they cohabitated, they shared a bed. No, more than that they shared each other's songs. That's not quite it, either. Bill's consistent quality of care and attention to this wild landscape made them inseparable. Like the relationship between hunter and hunted, Bill and that place shared the same soul. This is why it was impossible for Bill to speak of it. Some years ago Bill and I did a series of recorded interviews, two hours every morning for six days, to explore a book project about his relationship to Dickinsons Reach. I hoped to write about Bill's "sense of place." The stories flowed easily about how he came there, what it took to assemble the land, how he did each thing there, but the why he would not touch. Despite all the different ways I asked, he wouldn't go there, and

I grew frustrated that he could not express what it all meant to him. He would not share with me the "sense" of it because it wasn't as abstract as a sense; it was real and it was private. This wasn't the reticence of an old Yankee to talk about himself; it just wasn't right to talk about the qualities of your lover.

Bill was undomesticated before he arrived at Dickinsons Reach, but I believe being there kept him wild and, when he needed it, such as after long trips into America and other cultures, re-wilded him. In observing Bill's relationship to Dickinsons Reach, I too have remembered, felt again, the times of my own re-wilding: a young child with a green parka lined in fur tracking raccoons in snow, a six-year-old camping along a gentle grass streambed, a young man walking alone on a high trail in the Mexican sierra, a young adult hiking at eighteen thousand feet in a cloud bank in Nepal, or an older man walking the Rio Grande through the night until morning. Being with Bill there at his place helped me to remember the smell of burning juniper, sweet grass, ponderosa, or the sound of water on rock, and all the times that I have rediscovered that mysterious place inside myself that has always sought out nature to find the soft place for the animal in me to rest. Being there alongside him reminded me how much I appreciate people who cling to the earth and how much I have sought a life that clings to this earth.

He built nests for the osprey, he gathered his water from hand-dug springs, and he made footpaths through her woods, where after years of pulling fir saplings by hand he created a spruce forest. The *Rosa rugosa* on the point, he planted that. The cedars that gently wrap around his outdoor shower by the ocean, he shaped them for forty years. That unusual split round stone the size of a picnic table, there at Rosy Ness, that sits just magically atop the water at high tide, Bill figured out how to fracture it and place it there. The small pea stone where you haul up your canoe, five hundred bucket loads were gathered miles away on a distant shore and brought here over two decades. Those giant half-ton granite sea slabs that form the wall of his ocean shower, and which have stayed in place through thirty-five thousand ups and downs of salty tides, he winched them and smashed his bony knuckles getting them into place. He transplanted the smallest of flowers and the heaviest of stone to make his place complete. He hammered and split granite to create a landing for his canoes, and he built a beautiful, unique home by hand from wood and sun. And perhaps most lovely of all for its aesthetics

and intentionality, he gardened several acres of maple saplings as a six-ty-year-old man into the perfectly sized woodlot for a ninety-year-old man. And he did it all without the violence of petroleum, without the wrongs of a society to which he took exception, with the beauty and strength of his own mind and his own hands, and—importantly—with the hands and backs of his many friends who have touched this place with him. And this also is true: the wildness of this place inside of him made him gentler and helped him in his lifelong journey from his head to his heart to become kinder to the spirit of all things.

I desperately needed Bill's story, like oxygen, to help me breathe. I had grown up in a material culture of striving, close to the generation of Russian immigrants who had changed our name and identity to be more American, more affluent, more visibly prosperous and who had worked long and hard to give me objects and placement in a privileged culture, in which I was finding less and less meaning. In the practical sense that I did not have the last name that my grandfather had, I was a child of a broken lineage and needed someone who could initiate me into the process of understanding who I was. My father's reinvention of himself was complete down to his selection of the last name "Forbes," which he must have chosen so his children would pass into a world that he had been denied access to. Bill was as committed to reinvention as was my father, but their aspirations were almost completely opposite. I had benefited enormously—the good schools, the lack of debt, the material possessions—from my father's reinvention of himself, but my soul was hungrier for what Bill's life of beauty, nature, and nonviolence offered.

I felt guilt about turning away from my parents, shame about what my dad had turned away from in the first place, and yet I was just as hungry as they were to reinvent myself. I appreciated all that my mother and father had given me, especially those long walks in the woods and the excellent schooling, and yet I was also trying hard to escape a culture where status and privilege seemed more powerful than direct experience and wisdom. I was searching for things that felt real and meaningful. I was looking for ways to be in service and had begun my journey with a naive and embarrassing affair with politics, then refound the threads of my life in my midtwenties as a photographer, then a conservationist. I had explored life in cities and in rural places, in South America and in Nepal, and I was hungry for examples of how to live in my native New England.

So Bill and his life were a tonic, an antidote that I drank of deeply and frequently. After that first Thanksgiving visit Bill and I crossed miles of open water to explore a stretch of beach that might yield rope, or whalebone, or a revealing conversation about abundance and fairness. We traveled to California, Canada, and Mexico looking for friends, for unique tools, and for ways of being. My relationship with Bill is not unique; there are many others who could write a story about how he has influenced their lives. Indeed, some of them have become my closest friends: young men, mostly, for whom Bill presented a starkly different example from what their parents offered. Through this gentle way of experiencing a place together, Bill became a teacher of the things I would come to value the most. From him I have come to understand intention and the craftsmanship of a life. How do I stay alongside what is most meaningful to me when there are so many pressures to do otherwise? What do I love, and how do I stay with what I love? How do I shift my life when others want me to stay the same? How does one build a life around one's talents and joys rather than around a source of money? Schools, family, and books had given me knowledge, but I didn't yet know how to apply it to make a life. I was not yet discerning, still easily influenced by what others wanted and expected. Still absorbing and being swayed by every bit of information about what I should like, how I should dress, what I should wake up thinking about.

The early letters from Bill, like this one from 1998, spoke directly to my biggest questions about life.

> Part of democracy, Peter, is to live a self-chosen life, so long as it does not impede others from doing so. Some have led lives of direct, vigorous civic engagement in the general use of the term. Society, in general, would not consider my life one of civic engagement but I would disagree by saying that there is also the Thoreauvian concept of how to be a good citizen. The ideal is democracy, and that our lives can express our criticism.

Earlier still, in 1995, Bill wrote the same handwritten Christmas letter to several of us:

> A Question: Why is it that other cultures, for example, Inuit and Indians, had such beauty about them in their

daily lives—and we have not? Is it important? I suspect that it is extremely important for ourselves, for our children, and for our friends that we seek to surround ourselves with beauty. Suspicions: I suspect that how a culture defines beauty greatly affects its success as a culture. I wish I could persuade our world to see life itself as a work of art. Music and paintings are fine, but of far less importance than how we live. It is important that we find ways to use our hands and bodies as well as our heads and talents, if we are to grow to our fullest and if we are to create a positive environment for those who touch us.

Other letters followed:

Work and Play. I have a friend who in twenty years has not realized that I am no longer interested in play or sport as our society at large sees them, but in work, in finding ways to work that are so enjoyable that the concept of sport becomes meaningless. Our daily lives lack adventure and excitement. I'm not referring here to the excitement of winning a race or scaling rock face, but the excitement that lies in discovering a new way to phrase an idea, the mental adventure of seeking to live in harmony with the planet. The joy of finding a new way, a simpler way, to make a chair.

September 6, 1995: It is glorious to be in the tops of some of these old trees. Sitting atop the grand white pine by the tiderips, I saw a bald eagle close up. It must have flown within 30 feet of me. It was certainly one of the highlights of the summer. Another highlight was the morning's design of a shaving horse. It's really

wonderful to work on something hardly anyone cares
about . . . a [way to] make it more efficient. I've been
riding on a cloud all day!

March 1996: My resident ermine is in transition to
becoming resident weasel. Today she was ivory colored.
She makes the day allowing me two audiences of about
ten minutes each. I think she had a brood—a clutch—
boggle under the shop floor.

July 1998: We have been honored by a lone loon. I think
it is old and blind. It has taken up residence on the Mill
Pond. Twice this week it has been resting on our beach.
Yesterday, I came within 10 feet of it with no reaction. I
moved my arms up and down (in a white shirt) and it did
not notice. In the evening, a young eagle attacked it and
the gulls mobbed the eagle. I think it does not have more
days. Come as soon as you can—stay as long as you can.
It will be good to have some days to explore and talk.

A decade of friendship passed in which I helped this man to protect
the land he loved. I used my position as the Trust for Public Land's
regional director to draw attention to Bill's story and to his land, and
TPL acquired an important inholding at the homestead, kept it largely
wild through conservation agreements, then enlisted the active participation of the State of Maine and Maine Coast Heritage Trust, whose
efforts, in a matter of five years, resulted in more than a thousand acres
on and around Dickinsons Reach being cared for as conserved lands. I
brought new allies to Bill's way of life, and through conserving the land
and getting some money into Bill's pocket for those rights, we helped
Bill's vision for that way of life to be possible long into the future.
And he helped me tremendously by honoring me as the illustrator
of his book *A Handmade Life,* and even more so by giving me open

and loving access to that way of life, which was transforming me and evolving my own thinking about the purpose of land conservation.

The more Bill helped me to stretch away from what is secure and comfortable, the more I have grown, and the better work of service I believe I have done. Because of my relationship with this man, everything was shifting for me, and I believe, things were shifting for him as well.

I fell deeply in love with Helen Whybrow, who had been part of the editorial team for Helen Nearing's last book, *Loving and Leaving the Good Life*. The kind way that Bill swept Helen up into his life and the enthusiastic way that she took to him and his place became a validation of our growing love and partnership. It was Helen and Bill's friendship, I think, that brought Bill more frequently eight hours west to our home, where he became a presence in our daughters' lives, Willow's and then Wren's. And Wren and Bill would develop the closest and shortest relationship of anyone in our family. Though they only had nine years of friendship, they enjoyed and trusted each other a great deal. One of the last times Bill was in our home, I came downstairs early in the morning to find him seated bare chested in a chair by the woodstove, then-eight-year-old Wren trimming his long, errant white hair. So she had already entered terrain to which I would never be granted access.

The death of my parents when I was still in my thirties gave me an unexpected modest inheritance that raised questions for me about what I had learned from the Nearings and then from Bill. When I confronted myself, I wasn't content about stuffing that money into a savings account to save for myself or any future children I might have. I was convinced then, as I am today, that my kids' future is more dependent on the health of the community than on the size of my bank account. He didn't tell me what to do with that money, that wasn't his way, but I wouldn't have known alternatives for an inheritance without having known him. I carefully and quietly gave the inheritance away, helping modestly to strengthen the fabric of our community, and helping to make possible the new work I saw possible at Knoll Farm.

There were other steps I took into a new life. Bill and I had connected through my work in conservation, and observing Bill's life close up offered me my first very personal story of why a renewed belief in human stewardship of land was so important. You couldn't miss the obvious visible story of Bill, living there the way he did, while all around him the coast was being developed into golf courses, eight-thousand-square-foot summer cottages, private beaches, while local people lost access and ways of life. What a stark difference Bill's values were to those values. If a hundred years from now, there still survive osprey and fisher cat, salmon and black bear, and wild stretches of coast, it will be because of that kind of conservation.

But his life offered a firm challenge, also, to the conservation I was used to. At a time when the highest ideals of conservation, offered up by relatively privileged white folks like me, were concepts of wilderness that didn't include people, I was learning things from Bill about the opposite: that land and nature are not whole without people and that people are not whole without the skill and craft of living well in place. At the same moment that "Leave No Trace" was the ethic and the slogan for how people like me should enjoy land and nature, I had this seventy-year-old friend who was leaving a huge trace, proud of it, and I saw wildness in him and humanness in the nature, and it all seemed healthy and durable to me. It was confusing; Bill was mixing it all up. His life was asking me to consider my own human potential, and our collective evolutionary potential, as a goal of conservation, too.

And his example was helping me begin to express a new philosophy of conservation where it may be possible, as Terry Tempest Williams had so eloquently written, "to translate the soul of the land into the soul of our culture." That's exactly what I saw Bill doing in himself and everyone who visited him, and Bill's life became my standard for what conservation and relationship to place could mean. And seeing the possibility in how Bill lived, and also having that reaffirmed, over and over, in how others were living in distinctly different places such as South Central Los Angeles or Central Harlem or the dry ranchlands of

New Mexico helped me to recognize some difficult things about my own profession. Conservation had its own ideology about what was possible and not possible, about who was with us and who was against us, and it included some self-loathing: We humans, we can only screw things up.

The learning I experienced with Bill was reinforced from new relationships I sought out with urban gardeners in Harlem, New York, and ranchers in Colorado, and traditional taro growers in Hawaii, which dramatically shaped a new story for conservation that I began to speak of louder and louder. Bill had helped me see the meaning of land as bigger than wealth or beauty or biodiversity, and he helped me consider a new promise of conservation as being about creating relationships between people and nature. That career gave me the reason and an audience to talk about what I was learning from Bill about integrated lives that care about place and care about how people treat each other. He gave me the strength and the evidence to confront my own profession that I respected, and then he helped me move beyond that profession. By observing Bill's life I realized how a life lived in conservation may be even better for the earth than what I was doing: working in offices, facing a computer, sitting at a table negotiating real estate, raising money from others. Bill's resolute focus on personal responsibility—who you are is more important than what you do—cracked open the shell I was in and asked that I confront how I was living.

I wanted something more than that career in conservation; I yearned for a life in conservation. I wanted to leave a trace, to touch this earth, not just talk about it or read about it or legally protect it. I wanted one day to be eighty years old and to know that I cared well for a place that could sustain and influence my family and my larger community. At the very moment when I might have made a career last forever, I exchanged it for a life on a small farm. And I feared that my choice, which arose from what Bill taught me, would leave him without his helpful inside player on land issues. I was his friend, no doubt, but I also had a role when it came to fulfilling his dream of protecting that big

stretch of coast that had nurtured him. And I was right: As I launched my own life, I wasn't as helpful, and our relationship grew apart.

A magazine article I wrote a year after Helen and I moved to Knoll Farm captured where my heart was, which was still with Bill and that early experience of Dickinsons Reach:

> We came to this hillside in search of a more satisfying bond with the world around us: one about community, not isolation. We came here out of the growing recognition of what might nourish our family most. We came here to engage and to serve differently, and we sense that knowing this place well leads us to where, in our best selves, we really want to go. We want to trust and be trusted. We want to be firmly rooted here, independent and self-willed, with a sense of security that is as deep as the list of people we can call when things go wrong.
>
> We all have relationships and some aren't good ones. We enter into them with the aspiration of being at our very best, but the truth is that we aren't always perfect. Often I fail. My relationship to this hillside is transforming me. It is teaching me how to pay closer

*attention, to go beyond what I see on the surface, to be
more patient. I see that all we need is already at hand.
I am slowly cultivating myself by attending to the
particulars of the soil, the flow of water, the diversity of
life, and the burden this land and we can carry. This
land is filled with both seeds and ashes, and my struggle to understand both has made for a more mature
love. Our relationship to this farm is about health and
wellbeing: the lands, our neighbors', and ours.*

I didn't move to Dickinsons Reach, but to the hills of Vermont.
Moving to Knoll Farm, exchanging a career for a life, finding my
vision, manifesting it, rolling with all the changes it required of me
and of those I loved should have earned an A+ in Bill's School of How
to Make Your Own Unique Life, but it didn't feel that way to me. I was
pouring all my life energy into something new that was, in fact, pulling
me further away from Bill.

Jan 28, 2003: Thank you for writing the letter you gave
me at Knoll Farm. I appreciated the pain and effort it
took to write it. First off, I want to thank you for the
amount of time and effort you've put in over the years to
help me, the yurt foundation, and the effort to protect
Dickinsons Reach. Our friendship is one of the most
beautiful parts of my life and I thank you for that gift.

I understand your need to focus on the big piece
of work you've undertaken at Knoll Farm—and I'd like
to help you with that in any way that I can. Of course,
I'm disappointed at not having you as a neighbor in the
foreseeable future. I also have this nagging feeling that
in some way I have failed you. To the extent that this is
true, I'd be very grateful if you could spell it out for me
so that I can grow in a better way.

I didn't launch Center for Whole Communities and bring our lives to Knoll Farm because of Bill, but I did have some dream that he might become more integral to it. I imagined he would visit us for months each year, not days, and that his presence would be more of a foundation. And I have to confront the reality that I may not have been present had this happened. It wasn't long before I was getting on airplanes to spread our word and to raise money more than I was home living the dream on the land. This new life kept me busy, perhaps even busier than the previous career in conservation. All those times Bill was up in a tree watching eagles, I was headed off in an airplane somewhere.

He may have agreed with the purpose of what we were doing but not the form. And he likely saw things in how I was living my life that disappointed him. But there should have been parts too that really excited him. Bill's lifework was about helping people, especially less privileged people like himself, to create better, more fulfilled lives. The yurts were just a way, a tool, to get there. He started his lifework in his early twenties in rural Mexico, then worked in Philadelphia, rural North Carolina, Georgia, West Virginia, Venezuela, Alaska, Japan, Siberia, and Scandinavia. He cared so deeply about human development; why did he not engage more with what we were doing?

One answer, I think, is how hard it was for Bill to talk about many of the things that he experienced so deeply. He didn't know how to talk about social justice even though he still remembered carrying a young dead Mexican boy on his shoulders, killed in a bar fight because of the influence that privileged white people from a different culture can have. Though Bill's students arrived from the United States in the back of an open pickup with almost no possessions, they still had more than the villagers did, and that difference between having more and having less created conflict that led indirectly to this boy's death. The further something is from our hands and hearts and our backs, the less accessible it is. But that young boy was on Bill's heart and back, and he still couldn't speak of it. Surely Bill felt too that one can't talk about being a whole leader; you have to try to walk in different shoes first as a whole person. At the one retreat at Knoll Farm I could convince Bill to attend and be part of, one about the exchange of learning between generations and the roles of mentors and apprentices, Bill summed up his views with, "I would rather struggle with how to be a whole person and let all this talk of leadership fall where it may."

Up on his turf, at Dickinsons Reach, the conversation would sometimes turn to finding one's original work versus attending to the original work of others. In theory both of these are essential, and in practice Bill could offer encouragement to others in their pursuit of original work, but he was primarily interested in his own. He had an ambivalent relationship with what it meant to be a teacher. "Don't call me a teacher," he would say. "I want to be a learner alongside you." While it is true that he didn't aspire to be seen in the hierarchical position of teacher, it's the role he most often put himself into, and the role in which he was most potent. It's also true that Bill saw—even reluctantly—the many hundreds of people who walked the trail into his homestead as potential students.

I like to believe that as a result of the decade of collaborative work at Knoll Farm the boundaries are more permeable now between those who care about a river and those who care about people having a home. The work was deeply important to me, occupying every ounce of my heart and soul for those ten years, but it wasn't something that I could talk about with Bill. I never understood why. I don't think Bill knew how to help me with my original work, which was in tangible ways so far from his own, and like that nonexistent mirror up there, if I needed to see something in myself, I had to look to see how Bill was reacting to me. His distance was his answer. There's a limit to what we can learn from our mentors.

Because he taught me how to be discerning, I have discerned what parts of his life I can adopt and what parts I cannot. I learned from Bill how I want to live: I want to inspire, not make demands. I want to forgo privilege and memberships and be more faithful to my own spirituality, my wildness, to my art, and to my love. I want to always struggle with balancing being grounded in a place and aspiring to make change elsewhere. I want to accept my own limitations but at the same time have the courage to always try to do what is enough; to not get fearful and stuck like a deer caught in the headlights of an oncoming car.

I once asked Bill what is, for him, the most appropriate form of protest: to participate in an action like Occupy, visible and political, or to carve a spoon, practical and personal? Bill looked at me in disbelief at my, well, stupidity, then turned and asked Sonni, sitting beside us, if she had read my "spoon manifesto," implying that I already knew my own answer and his, and why was I questioning myself? How could I waffle like that? So I have learned that I am not as resolute or uncompromising as Bill and therefore, perhaps, not as effective an example for others. I actually do think both ways, I walk the edges between worlds, I make compromises, and I'm more tolerant than Bill of the things I cannot accomplish, but the greatest gift from Bill is that I know, even when I can't always live it, what it means to be radical, radical being the willingness to do *enough*.

Chapter Seven

KNOW YOUR OWN BONE

—Helen—

"Do what you love. Know your own bone. Gnaw it.
Bury it. Unearth it and gnaw it still."

— HENRY DAVID THOREAU

"If your dream came true, would you want it then?"

— GREG BROWN

On the first night of the yurt-building workshop, fifteen new people have joined our family and our prep crew. We are all packed on wooden benches around the two honeycomb-shaped tables that Bill built for our dining space—honeycomb because they work as round tables when single but can also be fit together in a line. Bill is always thinking about the function of design and prefers not to build shapes with right angles. The dining room itself is inside the large canvas tent set in the clearing with the black iron Knoll Farm bell and attached to a smaller makeshift tent where we can do all the cooking on a four-burner Coleman stove.

Peter rigged up the dining tent using long maple saplings that he cut at Knoll Farm and hauled here, knowing that there would be little in the way of straight wood to harvest on this land. The floor is dirt, which is perfect because Jack and Tommie, our resident goats, have

already developed the habit of sleeping under the tables and no doubt having a morning piss there as well, and the door consists of large flaps that tie back at one end. People's backpacks and extra sweaters hang from the maple saplings across the doorway, and all around the edges are small piles of books and magazines, art supplies, and carving projects. On the tables are oil lamps, a collection of found objects—beach stones, whelk and periwinkle shells, a porcupine skull—and stacks of oval wooden plates, the slabs only half-carved with crude edges.

Bill, who arrived over the pond earlier in the day with his bedroll, moving in for the week of the workshop, brought these plates so that each of us can make one for ourselves to eat on before week's end. He included a kid-size one for Wren. It is a gift so emblematic of Bill—practical, half-made so that you can have the satisfaction of finishing it, made of birch he harvested on his land, costs nothing, with an intrinsic beauty without being ornamental.

Taylor and Catherine, two friends Peter and I hired to cook for the group, stand at the door end of the table, where the big canvas flaps are tied back in an upside-down V, serving and passing around bowls of steaming lobster stew from a harvest Danny generously dropped off when doing his rounds of his traps in the cove. One of Bill's oldest friends, JoAnna, spent the afternoon pulling the tiny bits of meat out of the lobster tentacles; as I saw her there, sleeves rolled up, doing the messy job that no one else would have wanted or bothered to do, I was struck by how lucky we are to have her here with us.

Over my many summers of spending time at Bill's homestead, JoAnna, a person of almost ageless vigor and enthusiasm and agility, has become one of the people I most admire and look forward to spending time with. She has been a loyal friend, brought her three children here to Dickinsons Reach every summer for years, and participated in countless yurt-building workshops with Bill since she met him more than five decades before. I'm guessing that she was one of the first names on Bill's list of fifteen friends to invite.

All day people arrive on foot, then by boat from Bill's side. Most are from New England, but one couple flew in from Seattle, and JoAnna drove from Baltimore. Margaret is the most local and simply paddled across from Johnson Point in her kayak; George sailed his small wooden sailboat for several days up the coast until he turned his nose into Dickinsons Reach and all the way through the tide rip. Some of these people Peter and I know well, and others we are meeting for the first time.

I pause for a moment and look up at everyone:

friends of Bill's, as well as our prep crew whom we've grown so fond of, all together for this one night. Tomorrow the people who have helped us get this far will head out, and the workshop with this new crew of builders will begin. I take in the warm breath of the soup mingling with the cold breath of the sea air, the flames flickering and the shadows shifting on the tent walls, the soft sound of spoons on wooden bowls and the murmur of the tide rip behind the sound of voices around the table, trying to let it sink in what we are about to do together, taking in this calm before I feel again the sense of rushing against time. Wren comes over to find a warm lap, her head fuzzy with braids that I haven't redone since we left Vermont two weeks ago brushing just under my chin. She senses that Bill is about to tell a story. He has always had this way of entering the calm, containing a group's energy, drawing people in to listen.

Bill starts telling his story of meeting, in the 1970s, Peter Andrews, a British professor in the School of Architecture at Cambridge University and the world's expert on native yurts. Bill was traveling by train in England, on his way to Bath to visit a friend. In his train compartment was a formally dressed man reading Rappaport's *Native Architecture*, a book Bill admired, so he struck up a conversation and was promptly invited over to the man's house for tea. The two men were contemporaries, and both studied yurt design but did not know of each other; it is hard to imagine two more different personalities or career paths converging on the same idea. Andrews, a British academic out of another age, fluent in over a dozen languages, including Turkish, Persian, Ottoman, and Mongolian, and having spent over a decade documenting his subject in Asia; Bill, inspired to experiment and build yurts after seeing a photograph in a magazine and on a quest to build a simple, inexpensive shelter as a way of teaching design and autonomy. Andrew's dissertation was eventually to become, in two volumes and 1,059 pages, *The Felt Tent in Middle Asia: The Nomadic Tradition and Its Interaction with Princely Tentage*. Bill later acquired both volumes, oversize hardcovers full of the most intricate hand drawings and notes—an "exhausting study," he jokingly called it—and always kept it in a place of honor above his desk. Bill clearly admired Andrews, though he also loved to tell stories about how Dr. Andrews was the kind of brilliant academic who couldn't hold a hammer or follow a map. From that first meeting they stayed in touch and twice traveled together through Europe. Peter and his wife, Mügül, even visited Bill at his homestead in Maine (getting lost on the way in, as Bill tells it) and "enjoyed a porcupine."

As the inventor of the wooden yurt, Bill led nearly three hundred yurt-building workshops, all over the United States and as far away as Rome, India, and China. It was in 1962 that he read an article in *National Geographic* and recognized the genius in the mobile design of the indigenous yurts of Mongolia, thus beginning a lifelong study of translating that design into wooden dwellings that would endure the climate of his home ground and be simple enough for people to build themselves.

From the beginning Bill saw his wooden yurt design not only as a beautiful and functional home for his own climate but as a way of

sharing his ideas about cultural blending and what he called demo-cratic design. Democratic design is the idea that things can be both functional and beautiful and that that their construction can be acces-sible to everyone; something with a democratic design does not exclude participation, does not require being mass-produced in a factory or crafted by only those who have the exclusive knowledge or tools.

As an extension of this belief in the democratic design process, all of Bill's workshops have been with volunteers—their currency is sweat, and what they earn is knowledge. Early on, until he realized that even he, as a homesteader, needed a meager income, Bill himself was also a volunteer. He resisted being called an expert, a designer, or even a teacher, holding instead the ideal that we are all learners and teachers. It is testament to his knowledge and charisma that he put out the call to fifteen people about our yurt raising and they all came, not just to check it out, but to stay and camp for two weeks, rain or shine.

I feel humbled by this, and nervous, wanting everyone to feel rewarded yet having no idea how it will all go. I know it makes Peter nervous, too, not just worrying about how well the experience will go for everyone but also that as soon as we switch over to having vol-unteer labor under Bill's direction, at Bill's pace, Peter will no longer have control over how much gets done, or really even know the plan. His three weeks of executing the vision he sees is pretty much over. He'll have to trust Bill's agenda, where giving people the experience of building is more important than how much gets accomplished.

Although modern yurt design is what he was most well known for, Bill didn't feel that this was his central idea: Experiential education and designing a better way to live was. But yurt design itself was a lifelong fascination. "Fifty years after I built my first wooden yurt, designs are still coming to me," he says. "I never get tired of this form." And then, in a roundabout way, he starts telling us "my life in yurts."

When Bill first became interested in architecture, in the 1960s, Buckminster Fuller's geodesic domes were at the cutting edge of the quest for shelter that was more energy efficient, more sustainable, and more affordable for a greater number of people, so they sparked Bill's interest. I grew up on a small farm in New Hampshire next door to Donella and Dennis Meadows, whose 1972 book, *The Limits to Growth*, described their systems model of how the earth's resources would be exhausted at our current rate of consumption sooner than anyone imagined. My hands-on rural childhood was full of talk about self-sufficiency and conservation and whether technology could save us. As I listened to Bill I suddenly had a memory from the late 1970s, when a friend of Dennis's constructed a geodesic dome back in the woods. I didn't understand my parents' and neighbors' fascination with the weird-looking house, but I loved climbing the spiral staircase and touching the endless triangle panels on the inside walls. Bill said that he played a little with the dome shape in his own designs but never liked it aesthetically. He preferred the roof delineated from the walls. Nor did he agree that it was essentially democratic. Bucky Fuller's basic dome could supposedly be made from a kit, but it also required some high-tech materials that the average person couldn't easily obtain, and ultimately its concept relied on mass production, something Bill didn't believe in. But he was fascinated with the economy of surface-to-area ratio that circular structures offered, and drawn to the lightness and free open space of their interiors.

Bill was teaching at The Meeting School in Rindge, New Hampshire, in 1962 and decided to do a math seminar with high school seniors on the geometry of circular roof structures. That was when he stumbled upon the *National Geographic* article on Mongolia, with photos of yurts, showing their light basketlike structure of lattice walls held together with woven fabric tension bands and tied to roof rafters that were held in place by a circular compression ring at the center peak.

There are many design variations on the yurt among nomadic peoples in Asia, but in general Bill interpreted the design with two consistent differences: He eliminated the central roof ring (which was traditionally made by soaking and bending layers of wood into a circle through which holes were burned at intervals with a hot iron to allow the roof rafters to peg in), and he leaned the walls out at an angle. This accomplished a few things. The roof was given its structural integrity by the way the roof rafters or boards met in the middle, making their own compression ring and simplifying a step. And the sloped walls, leaning out against a single tension cable at the eaves, gave structural rigidity to the walls, eliminating the need for crosswise supports or multiple tension bands and providing more spaciousness. Aesthetically, the walls leaning outward also give Bill's yurts a profile closer to the ground; inside, one stands not next to a wall but upright under the roof, so the walls can be as low as four feet.

"Why did you lean the walls out, and how much?" someone asked from the darkness, the dinner dishes long ago cleared away and the oil lamps making shimmering pools of light in the center of each table and shadows dance on the tent walls.

"I saw some photos of little Swedish hay barns that had walls like that, and it was very appealing to me," Bill answered. "And how much? I found the angle by leaning back in a chair until it felt comfortable and going with that. That way people can sit on the floor or a simple bench and have a comfortable backrest." He wouldn't give degrees for the angle he liked; he said things like degrees put people off. "We learn in school that math is scary or competitive, and then we stop being curious about numbers and learning on our own as adults," Bill said. Because of this angle, Bill is often written about and credited as the inventor of the "tapered wall yurt."

After experimenting with his math students at The Meeting School, Bill built his first proper yurt with students in California at the John Woolman School in 1963. They arranged the roof saplings in a latticework; the way their ends met and put diagonal pressure on each other in a circle at the top meant that they could not collapse inward. Bill's first yurts, what he called pole yurts, were made this way, with saplings serving as the structure for the lattice of the walls and roof and fabric covering. One summer a group of us built a pole yurt at Dickinsons Reach, and it may be the only one that still exists. It replaced an earlier pole yurt that had been covered by birch bark as an experiment for a natural wall and roof covering, but it eventually rotted in the rain, and Bill pulled it down.

Bill described yurts as the skeleton and the skin. In traditional yurts this meant the wooden lattice walls and roof rafters covered with wool felt. In his first designs he also used a wooden lattice, covered by cloth or boards. Next, he wanted to build a yurt that eliminated the need for the skeleton, where the angle of the boards created its own structural strength and became both skeleton and skin. He did a number of small yurts this way, leaning the boards at an angle and overlapping them in a lapstrake design, rather like a dory is built. It was strong but not practical—too much work, Bill decided. In the next phase he started making the yurt strong not with an overlapping structure but by making a perfect rigid cone, "like an old sap bucket." The first of these he built in College, Alaska. It was winter and cold, but luckily the design proved easy to erect, and Bill and two others put up the walls and roof in seven hours. It didn't have a floor, so Bill covered the frozen ground with hay bales and slept on them. He was happy with this advance in the design but felt it was still too complicated. It required cutting each board at an angle lengthwise, with the proportion he wanted at the top of the walls and at the bottom, then making each pair of boards into a tongue and groove. Same for the roof. The math required to figure this out was not easy, and in the end Bill decided that this design was not democratic either.

The small yurt Bill built at Harvard in 1971 was a big step forward in his design thinking. He didn't nail the wall boards at an angle, nor did he cut them tapered. Instead he overlapped two layers of straight-sided boards and leaned them out to the angle he wanted. The Harvard yurt had a twelve-foot, eight-inch base and was approximately sixteen feet at the eaves, given the angle of the walls. Once this went up, Bill made the roof as another "skin" at an angle to the walls. The roof boards connected to make a central ring at a skylight, then lay across the span to sit on the tops of the walls at the other end. He nailed the roof boards at right angles so they stood up to make small triangles at the skylight end and large triangular windows where they met the roof. This gave Bill the ability to make a simpler, stronger roof with less wood and was his first discovery of a lampshade roof, a shell construction that was strong without any interior rafters, beams, or supports. This gave the building a wonderfully spacious light feel as well.

The Harvard yurt also represented a leap in Bill's thinking about how you can apply design to how people learn and interact, that not only the building process but the space itself was essentially democratic: "Perhaps the Yurt's most satisfying quality," he wrote, "is the effect it has had on the majority of people who have visited it. They are moved to talk not only about the beauty of the enclosed spaces but also about the space as an environment for group interaction. Visitors trying to formulate the difference between this space and others they have known, often become conscious of spatial quality for the first time. At a time when visual pollution is so great, it is of extreme importance to develop sensitivity to environmental quality. The spatial quality of the Yurt is conducive to discussion. As a seminar room, the structure has the advantage of easily bringing people into a face-to-face relationship. It is unnecessary to arrange chairs in a circle . . . no need to ask people not to sit behind one another. The curved bench echoes the wall, is set at a comfortable angle to lean back, and places people within pleasant conversation distance. It promotes group process since there is no one place more prominent than the others."

Bill built the Harvard yurt with fellow students right there on the university campus—in a single weekend, he claims—and lived in it for a year while he was a graduate student. It was right in the middle of everything, a small, ground-hugging wooden yurt with a curved door surrounded by massive historic brick buildings. He didn't have any heat in the winter other than a two-burner hot plate for cooking, which he claimed also kept him warm (I didn't believe him, but then again Bill never seemed to me to suffer from the cold). One year he broke out for a little more power: a friend came to visit him for Thanksgiving, bringing a duck he had shot, and they figured they could cook it by suspending it and spinning it between two propane space heaters borrowed from a classroom. I didn't believe that story either, but then again, knowing Bill, it could have happened.

Bill was thirty-eight when he studied for his PhD at the Harvard Graduate School of Education. If you believe it the way he always told it, he got through the program by writing a dissertation but not taking classes for credit, giving lectures in his yurt on sustainable design, educational philosophy, and indigenous crafts and auditing other classes that interested him. And when he did audit other classes, he would sit on the floor and sew moccasins, a current fascination and perhaps an irresistible way he could demonstrate his originality and counterculture radicalism in the halls of Haaa-vard University.

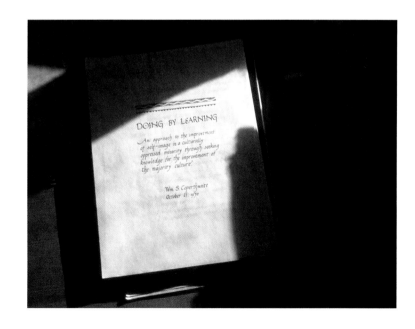

Bill's Harvard yurt eventually got picked up by a massive crane and moved to the Radcliffe campus to

**The 15 Books I Would Save
If the World Was Burning Up**

BY BILL COPERTHWAITE

Ends and Means by Aldous Huxley
The Anatomy of Human Destructiveness by Erich Fromm
The Way of Life by Lao-Tzu
Not by Bread Alone by Mohandas Gandhi
Reconstruction by Way of the Soil by Guy Wrench
On Becoming a Person by Carl Rogers
Sir Gibbie by George MacDonald
Looking Backward by Edward Bellamy
Walden by Henry David Thoreau
Pagoo by Holling C. Holling
Small Is Beautiful by E. F. Schumacher
Living the Good Life by Helen and Scott Nearing
Shantyboat by Harlan Hubbard
Wind, Sand and Stars by Antoine de Saint-Exupéry
The Road to Mecca by Muhammad Asad

make room for a six hundred million dollar library. "My yurt cost less to build than Thoreau's cabin," Bill said when he told that story. His Harvard design became his first yurt-building plan, exquisitely hand-drawn and lettered by a young friend, Tor Faegre, on a single sheet of 23 × 35-inch paper, original price $3.50 plus postage. He and Tor went on to make other plans, and they are works of art as well as incredible guides to Bill's mind at work. They are sprinkled with quotes ("make yurts, not war") and opinions ("plant flowers on your roof," "a power tool . . . separates rather than joins people together," "don't be led astray by newness and glitter"), encouragement to readers to share their experiences of yurt-building and "utopian quotes on simple living," and with the caveat: "This plan is not meant to be a complete set of instructions but a guide to the most difficult parts for those who want the adventure of building their own Yurt. If you perchance get hung up, have a swim and try again with a clearer head." Harvard was Bill's first yurt-plan customer, ordering a thousand copies for Harvard Graduate School of Education alumni. Such was 1972.

Bill called that time at Harvard "his experiment in getting an education." As well educated as he was, he never portrayed himself that way and never talked about having a doctorate. Years later, when he was invited to teach at the University of Massachusetts for a year and once again led the students through the building of a yurt on campus, then used it as his classroom, one of his awestruck students, impressed with all that this unconventional and anti-establishment guy knew, asked, "Bill, you ever think of going to college?" Bill roared with pleasure when he told that story.

"Back to Buckminster Fuller," someone said from the darkness around the dining room table, calling me back from my own memories of all Bill's stories over the years. "Did you ever meet him?"

"Sure," Bill said. "I invited him to come to the Harvard yurt once and talk to a class. I had picked him up at the airport and driven him to deliver one of his eight-hour lectures that he was known for, and the next day he came out to the yurt. He was very polite, but I could tell that he had no idea what we were trying to accomplish there. And I felt like few people could really understand his thinking. Personally, I'm not interested in buildings that you can't build. Our craft world is full of specialists. I'm interested in design that anyone can build and people can gather around. I might get less credit as a designer because of that, but doing something democratic, based on cultural blending, is more interesting to me. We all stand on the shoulders of thousands of others."

Bill stands up from our table, stretches, clearly done with the day. He says goodnight, asking us all if we'd be willing to gather early the next morning. He pulls out his tiny LED light, around which he had sewn a leather case with a seam so that it won't be cold in his hand or roll off a table, and turns up the trail toward the yurt site and his cot stashed a hundred yards or so beyond in the scrub forest of spruce-fir. It isn't a particularly attractive spot, sort of cobwebbed and dark with plenty of spiky blowdowns on the forest floor. He is the only one not sleeping in the meadow, and the only one without tent or sleeping bag. He has a small tarp rigged up over his cot and a blanket. He says he likes the quiet, which is true, but it reminds me how he is essentially a loner, despite his love of company and interest in community building.

He is an introvert who likes company, but on his own terms. Back there in the realm of porcupines and mosquitoes he seems most at home.

The first day of the yurt raising we all meet at 7:30 at the dining tent. The air is clear, and the sun breaking over the low trees sparkles on the frosted grass. We pull the tables outside onto our "lawn" of roots and stumps to sit in the sun. Bill has some drawings of our design that he spreads out—hardly what you would call a blueprint, because he doesn't believe in blueprints, and in fact, much of the design of our yurt will end up being done on the back of a shingle or in the middle of the night when Bill's friend—"the fellow who never sleeps and lives just above my right ear"—understands midstream that he needs to make a slight change. The wisp of knowledge that exists outside Bill's brain this first morning is hand-drawn in blue ink and gives us the overall dimensions—twenty-four feet at the base and twenty-eight at the eaves—and the design, a concentric yurt where a smaller upper story is hung, like a stacked basket, inside the larger bottom story. Our upper story is going to be eleven feet in diameter, with triangular windows, and the roof will be slightly convex, curving up to a skylight at the center.

This concentric multistory design is one Bill has built many times, starting with his own Library Yurt in 1976, which he built with students from Earlham College. The advance with his Library Yurt was its nestled multitiered structure, where each story was suspended inside the one below. The roof boards of the lower level could rest one end on the half wall of the level above. Above the half wall were windows, then a roof, so the windows of the upper level shone out above the roof of the level below, but the floor was actually halfway between. In his own yurt Bill started with two stories, then decided a few years later to build a light aerie on top and a fourth, very large story at the bottom of the structure. With simple jacks, working by himself, he raised the whole house, put beams under it, and built a wider circle—sixty-four feet in diameter at that point—around it, attaching the roof of the new bottom story just under the windows of his original house. When someone in our group, clearly thinking of Bill's huge circular house and trying to visualize this feat, asks, "But how did you *really* do that?" Bill says in a typically wry response, "very slowly, because I didn't want to break any of my mugs upstairs."

When Peter and I started designing our yurt in earnest with Bill before his trip to Italy where he suffered a heart attack, we stood at the window of the Library Yurt and paged through binders of photographs of the many yurts that he had built over the years, each one distinctly different as he tried out new ideas and forms. Bill's most dramatic designs, like the one at the Woodland Institute in West Virginia, have curvilinear roof shapes that swoop down between each contact with the wall, resembling the patterns one sees in a pinecone or flower, symmetrical but organic. To look at all his designs together really gives one a sense of how Bill played with form and geometry— part architect, part origami master.

In that meeting we told him what we liked and planned a kind of composite, taking elements of design from several that we were drawn to. We liked the triangular windows in the aerie of the small yurt he had built for Helen Nearing at Forest Farm in the 1980s. The year before Bill had experimented with a concentric yurt in Oregon where the second story was held up by a single post, and we wanted to reproduce that for its feeling of spaciousness and for the elegance of having a live-edge tree trunk at the center.

Perhaps the most important part of our concentric yurt design was borrowed from Bill's own Library Yurt: the idea of a small addition that bumped out from the main circle on the ground level and provided some privacy. Bill had built two of these in his workshop, one as a place to put his shaving horse and a workbench and another as a sleeping space; both had glass on all three sides as well as the roof, letting tremendous sunlight and warmth into the space. On many a sunny winter afternoon, very cold outside and almost as cold inside Bill's workshop, the sun would feel warm enough to induce a catnap in that sleeping nook. We imagined one fairly large addition like this, divided in half so that each of the girls would have a private bedroom of their own. We imagined a built-in bed for each of them against the outside wall with cupboards underneath for storing their clothes, curtains across the doorway, windows all around, and a sliding window between the two beds so that they could open it and have their heads together if they wanted to. They are six years apart, and close, but also need their own space from each other and from us.

I have always found that children react strongly to their built environment and that small private spaces are often what they gravitate to most. For the very young, private spaces invite the imagination—a burrow or hideout—and for older children such spaces become a place to establish one's identity away from the rest of the family. Bill agreed with us and was fully engaged with planning this part of the design.

But there are no such sleeping sheds in the drawing that we all gather round that first morning of the workshop. I take it on faith, for now, that they are coming later, but I'm also worried. Maybe at the last minute Bill felt it was all too much, though I wonder why he hasn't said anything to either of us as we've laid out the plan.

After we look at some sketches, Bill suggests that we divide into teams. Someone needs to lay out the foundation beams, others can start cutting wall posts, still others can build a rack for all our tools under the tarp at the work site, and there is still more material to haul. He puts me on the foundation with Scott, an old friend of mine, an artist and musician and one of the most patient people I know. When Scott isn't playing percussion in his wife Rani's band, he works at a children's museum designing and creating 3-D interactive installations of pirate ships and dragon catchers and undersea worlds. He can do just about anything with his hands. Good person to be with, I think, since I am good with my hands but know next to nothing about building.

Scott and I spend much of the morning righting the stone foundation pillars that, once bearing the weight of our 12×12 beams, start to look much less level. But by about midmorning we have something that looks solid and level, and we start cutting the beams to length. Jen, a friend who first met us and met Bill at a "mentors and apprentices" retreat at Knoll Farm and who is a brilliant young lawyer in Seattle with a flash-bright smile, comes over to help us. She got married to Dane not too long before, and he came with her, but now he is down with the flu in their tent. No one has seen him yet. A software designer and cartographer who works long hours at his office in Seattle, he might have collapsed from exhaustion and a sense of total disorientation about where he has found himself. Jen and I have equally little experience with carpentry, and we find out that it's not all that easy to cut a perfectly square line with a small hand saw through a twelve-inch-square green spruce beam; Jen, who is probably also worrying about Dane, is close to tears. I, too, am frustrated, knowing enough to know that this beam should not be green, and what's more, noticing that we are one beam short.

Scott heads over to talk to Peter, who has already realized this. Bill says he thinks there might be an old beam of the right dimensions under Sonni's cabin, which requires paddling at high tide across Mill Pond and down a tidal creek to access the trail to her place. Peter Lamb, a close friend of Bill's who I soon learn is one of the most level-headed and skilled people at the workshop, and Peter head off to find it. When they do, and haul it back, it's a beam the right size but punctured by beetle holes and clearly the worse for wear. Peter is nervous about its integrity and wants to ask Bill about it but expects the usual put-down from Bill for not knowing the answer himself, so he reaches out to Peter Lamb instead who says that it seems sound.

Bill, who I can only guess is embarrassed by this oversight of not having ordered enough material for the sills, tells me and Scott to "put it in the back of the yurt and the client won't notice the difference." I know what just happened, a barb in the form of a joke, and when I

glance up at Peter I see that it sunk deep. I've seen this side of Bill before, his dismissal of someone's intelligence and care, and I am left trying to understand where it's coming from now. I also want to ask Bill what we will use for the base of the bedrooms since we are already short on beams, but—cowardly or wisely—I decide to pick a different time.

By the end of the day Scott, Jen, and I have laid out the two massive crossbeams along with others that are cut to a point and notched into each of the four corners at the center. Still more beams link them at the perimeter to make an octagon. We spend a lot of time with a tape measure, a level, and a long piece of scrap lumber that we nail to the center of the circle as a diameter jig and swing around in all directions, trying to get all eight sections even and on the same plane. We measure and adjust in one direction, only to find it's slightly out in the next. We shift a beam ever so slightly to align it with the others, then find that we have destabilized the pillar of rock beneath it. Finally, incredibly, it seems as close to perfect as we can muster. I stand up on the tripod where each day Peter is taking a time-lapse photo of our progress, and I can see the footprint of the yurt laid out on the ground below my boots. Here it finally makes a mark, a circle of our intention. I turn in each direction to orient myself from this center point: tide rip to the south, bare bedrock to the west, fir woods to the north, scraggly larch trees to the east, spreading their misty green limbs against the sky like cormorants drying their wings before making ready to fly.

The weather has turned gorgeous as we work, the late afternoon glowing with the amber light of late September. Scott, Jen, and I head down to the tide rip, where Taylor has already jumped in for his second swim down, dark sleek head bobbing like a seal. I find Wren and Clara on the rocks, reading Laura Ingalls Wilder. They have returned from Bill's guest yurt across the water where they go to do their school lessons, when there isn't too much mud to get there. I ask Wren how she likes the kind of school that is open only when the tide is right, already knowing the answer. This fall of adventure as home school is her ultimate heaven.

Over the next two days most of us work on putting the deck—or floor— together. As Bill reminds us, yurts are not really round, but you can make them look that way by the number of sides you build. Our structure will have thirty-two sides, so we build the floor with thirty-two "corners," on which will stand the wall posts. We build the floor frame in four identical sections. Each time we build a quarter frame, nail plywood over it, and trim all the edges, a group of us lifts it up, carries it to the side of the clearing, and flips it over, using the giant burn pile of alder brush to break its free fall. Then we carry it back and place it in the opposite corner from where we built it. This way, very efficiently, we have our frame with plywood nailed on the bottom so that we can insulate the space between the floor joists, then nail the tongue-in-groove flooring over that.

Peter paddles back from a trip to Duck Cove and town with Isaac, the nineteen-year-old son of Michael and Elizabeth who is no stranger to hard work, having been brought up on a small homestead in Vermont. But he's a teenager, too, and wasn't at all keen on coming along to something that his parents felt strongly about, away from his friends. But I can tell he is starting to arrive and engage; I watch Peter picking him for the hard paddles and any kind of adventure he thinks Isaac will awaken to. It's starting to work; I will end up really appreciating having Isaac there, who is a strong and steady worker. And having Michael, a filmmaker who like Peter in any spare moment has a camera in hand, and Elizabeth, an artist whose public art installations focus on woven natural materials, is a joy, as they are not only skilled but consistently full of positive energy.

Today Peter and Isaac have brought back more materials from the hardware store, including several boxes of caulk and a caulk gun to seal the joints in the deck before the insulation goes in. Bill thinks caulk is unnecessary and tells Peter so. Caulk is a level of finishing detail, and probably expense, that Bill doesn't believe in, that he doesn't think matters. "Let it rot and replace it later" sums up most of his attitude on the subject of weatherproofing. I can tell Peter is frustrated at having to make runs into town every day, thinking ahead of all the things that Bill has forgotten or not deemed important on the materials list, then not being sure he has gotten the right thing, or being doubted for what he does get.

Peter isn't a builder, isn't fluent in the language of carpenters and lumber orders, and yet he was having to figure all this out on the fly, with disdain rather than support from Bill. And rather than fulfilling a

dream of helping construct
this yurt step by step with the
rest of us on this land, he is
mostly in town waiting in a
line in front of a cash register.
He comes back, having spent
more money than he wanted,
and doesn't really know
what is going on at the site,
doesn't have a role. And at
this point it looks like we are
making slow progress, with

a lot of people standing around, which only inflames Peter's anxiety
and sense of powerlessness, especially being someone who is all about
action. His style—so organized and driven—and Bill's are very different;
I can see that immediately. Bill spends a lot of time at his makeshift
desk under the tarp, pencil in hand, figuring out the math and angles
of the structure as we go. People keep interrupting him to ask for
another task, and right now he seems overwhelmed and tired of all the
questions and people, having trouble hearing, waving his hands at them
to go away. At one point Peter hands me the caulk gun and tells me to
seal up all the joints in the plywood and the deck beams, and I can only
guess that he is tired of being the one catching Bill's disapproving looks.
So I climb around on each quarter deck where it teeters against the
brush pile, working as quickly as I can before the next one falls in line.

Before we stuff the fiber insulation into the deck spaces, Peter
Lamb suggests we all draw outlines of our hands on the frame, to
symbolize the community holding the house above the earth. The
hands that created our handmade house with us are Bill, JoAnna,
Clara, Taylor, Catherine, Isaac, Michael, Elizabeth, Margaret, Peter,
George, Jen, Dane, Mike, and Scott.

That night Taylor makes pizza on the fire, dozens of pizzas balanced precariously on rocks and scraps of lumber arranged around the

flames to brown. We pull up stumps and makeshift benches and eat in a big circle as the brightness of the flames and the early darkness draws us in. Bill doesn't stay long to tell his usual stories; at some point I notice that he has slipped away. Isaac brings out his guitar, and Scott accompanies him by playing percussion on empty caulk tubes that he has cut to different lengths and screwed to a board. The repetitive plunking percussion with the melodious tune on the strings is mesmerizing, especially in my sleepy state. Taylor feeds small squares of scrap lumber into the fire, making houses of cards and seeing how long they will last in the flames. Next to me Wren is snuggled up with Clara.

Peter is writing in his journal by the oil lamp in the dining tent, alone. I can see his silhouette, head bent intently, from the fire where I sit with the others. I keep thinking he will join us for the music, or at least come and say goodnight to me and Wren. But he doesn't. He slips away into the dark.

I find him in the tent, getting into his sleeping bag. Is everything okay? I ask, knowing that of course it's not, but not really knowing how else to begin. Peter says how frustrated he is by the lack of planning and organization, his worry that we will not be able to build the yurt before we run out of the people and the time we all thought it would require, and Bill's quick dismissal of his concerns. "I'm not even sure we will be able to get the main structure up and weatherproof," he says, "let alone build the addition for the girls' rooms, which right now we don't even have lumber for." He went on to describe how important those were to him, something codesigned with Bill and something he could offer Wren and Willow, a place of their own in the hopes of deepening their sense of belonging to this place.

Sitting there, awash in Peter's emotions, I feel a helpless sadness. I, too, had a different version of how this would go, and probably Bill has yet a third. Peter imagined that the yurt would be weathertight by the end of the workshop and he could spend that time that we will have on the land enjoying what we had accomplished, with Bill. He was looking toward the fulfillment of something long imagined. And I had my own dream, which held little in the way of a goal for the final form and was all about having a shared experience of work with people I love. I realize I longed for something with Peter like homesteader Harlan Hubbard described of his days building his shanty boat with his wife Anna in a book Bill had shared with us called *Shantyboat*: "days of near ecstasy. . . . In this wild place we come to ourselves again." Now my version seems foolishly romantic, the reality much more full of anxiety and tension, and I, too, am flooded by a mix of emotions too tangled to name.

That night Peter and I couldn't really talk about what was going on. Peter couldn't find the words to tell me what it felt like to be the one pushing forward the building of a yurt that symbolized a decade of yearning for partnership and neighborliness and respect with a man who meant so much to him, to feel like he was fulfilling a dream that Bill shared and had urged him to fulfill, only to have it fall far short of that, to be treated like a client more than a friend, and an inept client at that. It was too painful then to explain how

he felt he was just seen by Bill as the person who could get something done, not someone who could be a creative partner or a craftsman, that Bill had never given him that chance. Why was Bill so dismissive of Peter and his ideas and desires for this project? Why did he decide to ignore the very pieces that Peter had told him he cared most about and not take the time to explain? Given his attachment to Wren, how could he not want to design a space for her to have as her own?

That night I started to understand the extent to which we were testing Bill by building this yurt. For so many years—for decades—Bill had yearned for community here. And before that he had yearned for family, for children of his own. How many times my heart had ached listening on dark fall evenings to his wistful readings of his "Willy stories" about the boy named after him who lived at Dickinsons Reach with his father, mother, and sister and had adventures such as finding a whale in the tide rip and figuring out a way to domesticate her and have a taste of whale milk. His longing for a role as father felt so palpable in those pages.

Bill's offer of a piece of land for us to build on was genuine; it was a gift that showed his love of us, and yet it was also a plea. *Come and build something; I need to fulfill a need for something larger here than just my own home; I want to walk my talk about creating community.* So we came. We actually said yes, we will invest our time, money, and most of all our hearts and hands there with you. Peter was the first to answer that call after all those decades. Now I had to guess that Bill, at eighty-one, might be having second thoughts, even grave doubts about having others make a home on this wild point of land he had enjoyed alone for so long, and it was making him tense and closed. What should have been the fulfillment of a long-held desire was beginning to look more like the clash of a long-held ideal with the reality of his inner nature. What would it feel like, I wondered, to hold a map in your hand for sixty years of somewhere you longed to go, then finally get there and realize that the trail felt all wrong? For all his lovingness, for all the ways he was beloved, I think for Bill the trail of intimacy was the hardest, most untraveled walk of all. We were seeing him stumble.

Chapter Eight

FINDING NONVIOLENCE

— Peter —

The work yard of the Nunzo brothers in Santa Clara del Cobre, Mexico, had changed very little in the fifty-odd years since Bill had been there. He and I found the place in 2007 just as he had back in 1955, by walking the dusty streets and listening for the rhythmic pounding of iron on copper. Just a ten-minute walk from the main square, the work yard was buried inside a compound of connected *tiendas* and family homes, down a long alley that opened up into a large work yard surrounded by four thick adobe walls, in each corner of which were fire pits, forges, and polished steel anvils. Soot darkened the adobe walls around the forges. Hung or leaning against the long walls were hundreds of handmade tools for pounding out copper vases. The ground in the work areas was packed earth, and chickens were everywhere under feet. Every view of this place felt warm with the labor of seasoned work and experienced craftsmanship.

It was exciting to be there, and both Bill and I had many questions, though the craftsmen paid no attention to us, not unfriendly but absorbed in their work. Bill remembered the brothers as young creative scavengers like himself, buying for almost nothing one-ton balls of recycled copper up at the border and bringing them here to their home, where they melted them and pounded them into vases for everyday use. Bill was eager to reconnect with his old friends and maybe find something handmade and useful for his homestead.

But the Nunzo brothers had all moved to the United States long ago, and I understood the gaze that this young relative gave us that day: We couldn't afford what they made. He spoke to us in perfect English, wearing a crisp polo shirt, about how every piece they made was headed to a museum or to a wealthy home in Los Angeles or Houston. Bill said nothing, hiding his disappointment from me, but voted with his feet and was gone from that alley before I had even politely finished my conversation.

Bill was intent to move on quickly to his next memory of his years in Mexico doing alternative military service, then graduate work in the 1950s. And he had a mission: He had returned to Mexico to find something. That week in 2007 I was in Michoacán for no other reason than because Bill had invited me to travel with him. A one-sentence letter had arrived a month earlier: "I hope your girls will let you sneak down to Mexico with me next month. I'm looking for a batea (a farm bowl)."

The short letter was folded around a mint-condition 1948 Humble Oil road map of Mexico. I should have known that the inclusion of the map was his suggestion that I plan the trip. But neither of us planned the trip, so when we arrived in Mexico City at 11:00 p.m. at night, we didn't have a place to stay, a car, or an idea for where to go next. I realized that we had spent the entire flight from Boston to Mexico

City talking about a concentric yurt that Bill had hoped we would one day build on his land at the tide rip. He had designed the yurt in the seat next to me and come up with a basic lumber order and the rough estimate that the project would cost us no more than thirteen thousand dollars to build.

I was confused: For years Bill had repeatedly told all of us that he was excited to watch what each family would create on their land. Helen and I had taken him at his word, and for our side of the tide rip we had been dreaming about a simple saltbox one-room cabin like what might have been there in 1810, or about the cob structures that we had already been experimenting with at Knoll Farm. There was lots of clay available at Dickinsons Reach, and we were excited about what it would be like to build something there of that earth. We loved the natural feel and building process of cob combined with post and beam. But none of that seemed to interest Bill, and he handed me his sketch of a concentric yurt and a lumber order. The two-story yurt was beautiful and exciting to me but not something we could ever build on our own. Bill and I were about to spend a week together roaming Mexico, and the building of anything on Proctors Point in Maine seemed remote and many years away, so I didn't press my need to have my own thoughts taken more seriously by him. Still, Bill was asking me for a commitment on when we would start construction of "my" yurt when the steel tube in which we had been hurtling through the sky landed gently in Mexico City, a place of twenty million people. That was the first miracle.

There was a lot that felt overwhelming at 11:00 p.m. in a new city: the enormity of the airport, the smog and 95-degree temperature, and the realization that Bill's idea of where to stay was a 1954 address in his head for a hostel once operated by the American Friends Service Committee. The second miracle was that it was still there, still a hostel, and that someone could be roused from their sleep to raise the steel curtain over the entrance when we leaned on the buzzer at 1:15 a.m.

The next morning we bought fruit from street vendors, found a car to rent cheaply for a week, and started off on the six-hour nerve-racking drive south through the city's sprawling traffic to the southern state of Michoacán, the village of Santa Clara, and to Bill's fond memory of the Nunzo brothers. They would surely help us get started on our adventure. They did, but not in the way Bill had hoped, and less than eight hours later (six of which were spent sleeping in a much-too-expensive hotel) we said hasty good-byes to Santa Clara and headed off.

We made our way to the city of Tacambaro, where Bill remembered from his youth a fabled market town where he had spent days marveling at the handmade creations coming in from the hills and being sold in the open air market. I was drawn right away to the ancient and sleepy feel of the town, we found an affordable place to stay on the main square, and I discovered the roof that offered me hours of focused attention as I sank into my art of photography: clotheslines with white sheets and blue sky, terra-cotta rooflines, egrets roosting in trees, cats sleeping in clay pots, mothers pounding corn. The next morning was market day, so we were up and out at 5:00 a.m. and surprised to find the streets in town empty. When we found someone to ask directions of, they pointed us away and down onto the valley floor. Bill remembered the market in the center of town on the main square, but we accepted that things had changed and enthusiastically began a walk along a road that dropped

down into the valley, where it quickly became a highway choked with cars and trucks and motor scooters belching black smoke. Soon Bill and I couldn't even hear each other talk, so we walked in silence until we came to a newly constructed, twenty-five-foot-high cement wall with an entrance through which all those vehicles and people were pushing.

There were no fires burning, no smell of copal, no old men and women in shawls, no well-used horse-drawn wagons, no pack baskets filled with goods. No tradesmen laying out their wares, or shamans selling plant medicines and minerals, or religious people hawking their faith, or kids begging for this or that. No one's eyes even met. It was straightforward, no-nonsense capitalism in an undiluted form that would have made the most brazen consumer fear overdosing. There were more than five hundred vendors in four long rows of stalls selling the same six things, all appearing to have been made in China. What we saw was a sea of bright red, blue, and yellow of endless plastic dolls, plastic balls, plastic shoes, washing machines, T-shirts and jeans of every kind. It was a global free-trade market, not the traditional market Bill had hoped for.

Bill loved traditional markets and market people because they are maker culture, like him, people who live close to the source of their inspiration to create and who create out of necessity. People who live close to the source of their love to create can be found in many places: in dance studios, in boat shops, in libraries, alongside anagama kilns; Bill feels connected to these people everywhere he finds them and especially connected to those who use their hands to create and who believe that all they need is already at hand. They were his people, but these were not those people. I watched Bill's face closely as he took it all in, feeling my own sadness at his disappointment and worried even at what might become his repulsion. I worried that he was doing the calculation in his mind that I was doing: that his maker culture was gone from this Mexico of his memories.

And while I share many sympathies with Bill, I am not Bill. There were parts of this market that I found interesting and deeply human. It interested me how distracted we were from one another; no one returned my morning greeting. Why within these walls of commerce did we not talk and were we so fearful of one another? Where were all the children? Why had so many people come for such a narrow selection of things? What was the pull here?

Almost in defiance of that obituary of his maker culture, Bill seemed desperate that morning to find something handmade to learn from. He wouldn't be proven wrong. Himself a maker, and experienced with traditional markets all over the world, Bill is a discerning, opinionated, and exciting person with whom to walk a market. Once, years before, when Bill and I were just becoming friends, he visited me in Cambridge a few days after I had returned from a photography assignment in Nepal, and he picked up from my desk a small, rough Tibetan bowl I had traded for and calmly and directly told me it was the most beautiful and useful object in my entire apartment. So when Bill started to make a second pass of all the vendors, I suppressed my hunger for breakfast and my skepticism of the market to walk alongside him.

He settled in on a husband and wife selling mass-produced wooden spoons and mass-produced wooden tortilla presses. They weren't selling anything Bill could possibly want, but he was negotiating with them. I stood aside, feeling that I needed to be present for whatever state Bill was in. He had spotted a low, stout chair the wife was sitting on, made like a yurt of crisscrossing bamboo. He asked them if he could buy it, and the woman did reluctantly sell it for two hundred pesos, which struck me as a great deal of money. I was confused by what happened but aware enough to not ask questions. Bill and I walked out of that market making light of the transaction, headed back on our long walk up to town, and I never saw that chair again. I assume he intentionally left it behind somewhere.

At a moment later that day, I confronted my own growing panic about this trip's becoming some awkward elegy to Bill's past and a bad validation of how threatened Bill's present way of being was in the world. I knew this place, Michoacán, and his days there in his twenties working with the Quakers were influential. I didn't want him to feel that such an anchor in his life was gone. And yet I also didn't want to keep confronting places that had changed so dramatically. So I turned away from Michoacán of 2007 and began to ask him more and more about his experiences there in the 1950s, and for the first time I heard about the other forces that created Bill Coperthwaite.

In 1949, on the eve of the Korean War, it must have been a huge transitional moment in Bill's life to be eighteen, to be the first person in his family to be headed to college, to score a perfect five hundred on the Navy Reserve Test, to be offered a full scholarship to attend Annapolis Naval Academy, to have his older sisters all married to military men, and then to flatly turn Annapolis down. This may be the first strong evidence of Bill's unique response to life taking form. At eighteen Bill was guided by a force inside himself that only he recognized and that only he could honor. Five years later he and his college girlfriend, Sonni Chamberland, would read Gandhi's autobiography aloud to one another, and Bill would form an enduring commitment to crafting his own life based on answers to the questions he found most meaningful: what is true wealth, what is a healthy person and a healthy culture, how are we to be in relationship with others? Sonni and Bill did not become husband and wife but lifelong friends who remained consistent in their devotion to one another: Sonni buying a cabin within Bill's Dickinsons Reach and Bill growing to love her children as his own kids and grandchildren.

Bill received an athletic scholarship to attend Bowdoin College, the prestigious private institution in his home state, but at the end of his freshman year, when Bill decided that competitive sports was not the education he wanted, Bowdoin took away his scholarship. If you don't run competitively, you don't get our money. Rather than run, Bill got more serious about staying. He gave up his shared house to buy a car. He used the car to commute twenty minutes every day to Bath Iron Works, working for sixty cents an hour, forty hours a week, to stay in school.

Bill knew how to get by under tough circumstances from his father, a proud and charming man with skills and intelligence, whose formal education didn't go beyond sixth grade, who taught Bill how to build anything, and also taught Bill the crushing effects of both alcoholism and the Depression. At eight years old Bill walked alongside his dad selling Fuller Brushes door to door in South Portland. They loved and respected each other, but Bill's dad didn't make it to see his son graduate from college. And he would die alone in a rooming house seventy miles away from his family when Bill was twenty-six. None of this was lost on Bill; he carried it with him everywhere he walked.

When Bill slept in college, which wasn't regularly, it was in the library at night. He kept clothes stashed in friend's rooms. He showered in the gym. He was strong of body and mind, and he began to see many things differently. He made work the hard combination of full-time labor and going to college, and it was a dark time in Bill's life that shaped many of his thoughts about justice and fairness, the corrosiveness of competition, what it means to be whole, and all the forms of violence that impact our lives.

On the car ride out of Tacambaro, Bill told me about being summoned one day into the office of Bowdoin's president, Kenneth Sills. Bill had been seen by many students and professors spending his days working underneath his car. The college president was ready to give Bill an education in values. He opened the conversation swinging verbally, challenging Bill and asking him how this young man could dare to waste his college experience fixing up a car instead of going to his classes. Wasn't Bill grateful for the education Bowdoin was giving him?

Bill didn't finish the story, and we let the bright sun and dust of the Mexican countryside speak for both of us for a while. About an hour later in the trip, Bill turned to me and quietly picked up the story. "When I told Sills that I was constantly fixing the car so I could get to work welding for forty hours every week so I could pay for his damn education, he reached into his own wallet and handed me a hundred-dollar bill, which was the full amount of tuition that I owed for the semester." It was at that moment that Bill also said to me, "I was in a dark place, and then I read Tolstoy's *Resurrection*, and the sun came out. The sun's been out ever since."

I've asked Bill a few times since our trip to Mexico what was it specifically about reading *Resurrection* that brought light back into his life, and I never got an answer. Nor do I know exactly when he read it. Once I heard him say it was at Bowdoin. On another occasion he said it was when he was laid up in a Mexican hospital bed recovering from a near-death experience of a burst appendix. What's clear is that this strong, intelligent, caring young man was wrestling with big questions about how to make his own handmade life.

One of the commonest and most generally accepted delusions is that every man can be qualified in some particular way—said to be kind, wicked, stupid, energetic, apathetic, and so on. People are not like that. We may say of a man that he is more often kind than cruel, more often wise than stupid, more often energetic than apathetic or vice versa; but it could never be true to say of one man that he is kind or wise, and of another that he is wicked or stupid. Yet we are always classifying mankind in this way. And it is wrong. Human beings are like rivers; the water is one and the same in all of them but every river is narrow in some places, flows swifter in others; here it is broad, there still, or clear, or cold, or muddy or warm. It is the same with men. Every man bears within him the germs of every human quality, and now manifests one, now

*another, and frequently is quite unlike himself, while
still remaining the same man.*

LEO TOLSTOY, *RESURRECTION*

After two years of sleeping in the library, going to classes, and working forty-hour weeks at Bath Iron Works, Bill needed out. He had a college friend who lived in Austria, and that seemed as good a place as any to spend a year. But Bill needed money for that experience, so he headed first to Aroostook County, where he was born and had lots of relatives, to pick potatoes for $1.50 a barrel; thirty-five barrels would have been a great, backbreaking day. A month later he took a boat from New York to Genoa, Italy, and arrived there with thirty-nine dollars in his pocket.

Making his way hitchhiking from Italy to Innsbruck, Austria, Bill happened to pass through the small Swiss border village of Soglio, where he came upon a group of young people singing songs and swinging pickaxes. Bill would stay with them for a month: a chance

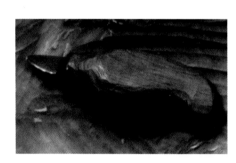

encounter that would affirm his most important choices in life and set him off in new directions.

When I first met Bill in 1993, he was telling anyone who would listen that his favorite book of all time was Pierre Cérésole's *For Peace and Truth*. Pierre Cérésole was a Swiss engineer of great privilege and wealth, born in 1879, who refused his inheritance (later giving his wealth to charity) to become a pacifist and community healer for much of Europe after the World Wars.

When Pierre was thirty, in about 1910, he left Europe for a long journey of discovery around the world. At various times in this four-year-long trip, he needed money and tried many different kinds of manual labor for the first time in his life. He worked on road construction, he built foundations for houses, he dug graves, using the pick and shovel that became important tools and symbols for the healing that he later brought to others. Pierre came to understand that the young who were trained to kill and destroy could also be forces for peace and healing. He put them and himself to work. He went first to the battlefields of Verdun to initiate civil service work. The next time Pierre assembled volunteers from different countries was to help in Switzerland, where avalanches had caused severe damage. Between 1928 and 1953, when Bill connected with them, more than five thousand volunteers from twenty-five countries joined in the reconstruction work in Europe and later in India. Pierre Cérésole's work camps became International Voluntary Service for Peace.

It was one of these work camps that Bill had the good fortune to come upon in Soglio in 1953. Leading that camp was Lise Cérésole, Pierre's wife, who was continuing on her husband's lifework after he had died, in 1945, of malnutrition and an illness acquired in a prison. That had been Pierre's eighth prison term for various crimes of the heart: refusing to pay taxes that supported war, refusing military service, speaking out against the war. Bill had found two human beings leading lives of intention grounded in principle that gave him rich examples of how to live his own life. This emphasis on the value of hand labor, on song and joy, on the healing of violence would become foundations of his life.

When his year at the University of Innsbruck was over, Bill was broke again but ever resourceful, so he parked himself in the seaport of Genoa for a month waiting to get hired on a crew of an America-bound ship. When he finally arrived in Galveston, Texas, just a few days before his last year of college began, Bill had three hundred dollars in his pocket, nearly enough to get him through the next year.

The experience of working his way through Bowdoin College and his one month in the Cérésoles' work camp in Switzerland must have been the inspiration Bill had, upon graduation, to go to Mexico and to do alternative military service—using a pickax and shovel—even though the Korean War had already ended. It was his sense of service, of appreciation of the Quakers' emphasis on nonviolence that brought Bill to Michoacán in 1954.

At this point in his life Bill seemed to have left behind any real need for his life to fit a standard form. He had already figured out how to pick potatoes and move across the world gathering experiences and return with money in his pocket. He had discovered what it means to think for himself. He had the examples of other people living fully within their own convictions. He had come to recognize himself, even though the family he dearly loved did not. In 1955 Bill wrote this letter in a strong and clear hand on thin paper to his sister Vivienne, explaining his decision to become a conscientious objector and not do military service. He was in Georgia, between trips to Mexico, and he valued the communication enough to pay the double airmail rate of six cents.

Dear Viv,

This is a hard letter to write but I will do my best. You seem to feel that I am acting rashly and without having thought this through. Believe me this is not the case. My duty in this situation has been considered and thought on almost constantly for many months. More thought has gone into this decision than any other in my life. So it hurts to have you, who understand me better than most, think I have acted irresponsibly.

Some think this is a position of cowardice. I do not think you feel I am a coward. For it is much more difficult to do what you feel is right when your family and friends do not understand and believe you are acting wrongly than it is to go as a soldier.

Most strongly you feel that I have been selfish— holding to my ideals when they cause pain to Mom and others. You may be right, but I have thought about this a great deal. This thought has bothered me more than all the others. I cannot bring myself to feel that Mom would want me to do what I believe to be wrong, dishonest or unjust. To do so would be to negate all that she has done and taught me. In due reverence to her I cannot do other than what I believe to be right and good.

At the moment I am in Georgia trying to pay off my hospital bills [for his burst appendix and three-month hospital stay]. Morris Mitchell grew some Christmas trees. I have just cut them and hauled them here and am now trying to sell them in Gainesville, Georgia. I have been here a week getting ready. I start selling them today. I've rented a vacant lot and am decorating a tree with blue lights to attract business. I expect to be here about two weeks longer.

This little poem of Emily Dickinson's is one of my favorites. I hope you like it.

> *Hope is the thing with feathers*
> *That perches in the soul.*
> *And sings the tune without the words*
> *And never stops at all,*
> *And sweetest in the gale is heard*
> *And sore must be the storm*
> *That could abash the little bird*
> *That kept so many warm . . .*
>
> E. DICKINSON

Love,
Bill

For four years, on and off, Bill would return to the villages of Michoacán to serve and to learn. Ever industrious, Bill worked for USAID and two Quaker schools, bringing himself and students into deep relationship with village life. No matter for whom he worked or the purpose of the

trip, he did the same things: be humble, travel light, see how you can help, use a pick and ax, learn by working alongside. Three summers in a row, Bill filled a pickup truck with students and drove nonstop for four days from New England down to Michoacán to do a month or two or longer of service projects.

While teaching at The Meeting School in New Hampshire in 1962, Bill built with his students a place called "the Shed" that was his first exploration of using a hand-built structure to educate and to create community. It had all the characteristics of his later-life yurt workshops: democratic, community driven, educate by doing, working together.

In the shed we eat bread of our own baking. The five of us who live here share in the cooking, sweeping, grinding the grain and in trying to get the holes patched before snow flies. The cook pumps the necessary water and the dishwasher (the cook) washed up by the light of an Aladdin lamp. The wood box always seems to be empty (as do the lamps) although it has always just been filled. We are considered odd by those who live in "comfort" in the other school houses but are tolerated good naturedly. It pleases us that they like our bread. The main room of the shed is a combination craft shop, classroom and just plain living space. The leather tote bags we sell (to fund these trips to Michoacán) are lying about in varying stages of completion so that anyone with itchy fingers can pick up one to sew one during the class discussion. Also in various stages of completion can be seen the soapstone candle holders and bone belt buckles . . .

In this picture of the life Bill was creating, there was no difference between teacher and student and no education that was drudgery and nothing important that couldn't be made by yourself. It was men and women working together, learning together, and growing together. And Bill wasn't their teacher leading a program, but the slightly older guy who knew how to make things. The school community was so transformed by their experience of Bill that upon his leaving they offered an official resolution: "Almost all of us will think of the shed. Here was a simple place of fundamentals, a place of workmanship, and a place of creativity. Here people met to talk and work. And here was another sort of meeting—the rough and the delicate, the simple and the complex, the practical and the visionary, the exciting and the restful. The shed was an individual expression, a conscientious objection, a deliberate suggestion. The bags, the beams; the logs, the light; the pump, the people—all contributed."

As beauty exists in the world of our making, so does violence. "I have some feelings I would like to share with you concerning a killing we had in our village recently," Bill wrote in a letter home to the parents of a group of these American students who had traveled with him down to Mexico to do community service. "Just after we returned

from a day of work a man was shot in a cantina fight. One of our boys
took him to the hospital where he died the next day. I wasn't very close
to this situation. But a week later a stabbing occurred which hit closer
to home. It was another cantina fight in which a young fellow of 25
was stabbed seven times, staggered homeward and was found some
hours later dead where he had dropped in the street. We carried the
body to the coroner in town some 12 miles away. I happened to be the
one to bring the body home. The scene as we carried the coffin into his
parlor was one of the most heartrending I have ever witnessed. Here
was his wrinkled, weary old mother who had nursed him as a child
and raised him for 25 years only to have him killed senselessly in a
drunken fight. The thought I would like to pass on to you is not a
moral one but a practical, vital one about alcohol in the Mexican

village . . ." Bill felt "healthy, well-educated friends from the United States" were encouraging the use of alcohol in rural villages, and he wanted nothing of that example. Here was Bill placing emphasis on what he felt was most important: the corrosive influences of a privileged American culture on Mexican village life where two people of their age had been murdered, not the relative safety and comfort of his American students. He was teaching these kids and their parents about solidarity and what it means to be an ally. It was experiential education, social justice work, and sustainable rural development all wrapped together decades before we had those words to describe it.

There are two generations of men and women, now aged around seventy and around fifty, who grew up under Bill's guidance when he was a formal teacher and later when he was living his life at Dickinsons Reach when these men and women were teenagers. Their parents valued Bill enough to give their kids over to him for large portions of the year. All of those people, men mostly, remain close to Bill, arrived to help bury him, even though they may have chosen to stay away for much of the time he was alive. Bill loved them all and had unrequited dreams of their moving back to his homestead with their families. Bill wanted that so badly with one friend that he asked me if I would help him to buy a piece of land—an important inholding—that had just come available within Bill's land. The real estate was easy to arrange, but what was painful were the conversations that arose about what might be acceptable uses of that land by Bill's younger friend. When the dialogue turned to the type of house and the use of technologies such as trucks, driveways, and chain saws that many people living in rural places reasonably use, Bill wasn't comfortable and said so. There was an important part of this younger man that wasn't being seen by Bill: the part where he took everything he had learned from Bill and applied it as best he could in his own life. And so Bill's philosophy about nonviolence—that the use of a chain saw was a violent and unacceptable way of life—led to another form of violence, which was the disrespect shown to his own friend.

It was in 1999, early in my friendship with Bill, that we were together in Northern California at a gathering hosted by a musician friend on a wild hillside directly above the Pacific Ocean. A group of twenty-five scientists, musicians, teachers, writers, and artists had come together to consider the universe story and how to tell it. We were camping, and our days were filled with conversation, preparing food together, and taking long walks. I worried that Bill, who came at my invitation, wouldn't be comfortable at an event that was more about talking than about work, but there were people there he wanted to meet. He seemed to enjoy it, and many others were enjoying learning from him how to carve a spoon, and he even chose to join a circle where we had been invited to talk about times in our lives when our values were most challenged. When it was Bill's turn to speak, he rose to his feet, and I feared, for just a moment, that he was walking away. But he was choosing to stand before us to tell us this story.

Just a few years before he and I met, Bill was at the zenith of a troubling relationship with a neighbor who Bill felt was disrespecting his own land and Bill's. They shared a trail to Bill's border, which Bill walked and carefully tended to with wood shavings and on which his neighbor rode an all-terrain buggy. The ATV caused ruts in the trail that made winter foot travel quite hard, made a racket in the woods, was a symbol of many things Bill disliked, and offered an invitation, he worried, to lots of other motors to come zooming into Bill's world. In fact, that rarely happened, but once was enough. Bill was down at the shore cooking dinner at his summer kitchen when he heard the loud whine of a dirt bike fairly close. Since the nearest road was almost two miles away, Bill knew that the dirt bike had to be on his trail. It got louder and louder. It sounded as though it was at his yurt. Bill started walking the quarter mile up to his home, and the incessant growling of the dirt bike stole away his composure. He swung into the guest yurt to grab the first big object he could, a twenty-pound peavey for moving logs. He might have been sixty years old then, and he was running up a hill with a peavey in his hand toward the growling engine. When he got within sight, what he saw made him even angrier still. The dirt bike was zooming around the perimeter of his hand-built home, revving its engine, sending grass and dirt flying. Bill ran to the front of his yurt to block the next pass of the dirt bike and raised that peavey high over his shoulder like a baseball bat. And then Bill saw that it was a young kid, maybe not even fifteen years old, looking in horror at this old hermit man about to swing at him with a bat. At this point in telling the story, Bill sank to his knees with his big shoulders shaking. "I could have killed him."

Is that what Tolstoy meant in *Resurrection* that Bill found so meaningful as a young man, that "every man bears within him the germs of every human quality," including the very things we hate the most? That boy was not much different from or younger than all the boys and girls Bill brought with him to Mexico, or not much younger than the dead boy Bill carried from the streets to the morgue, or not much different from Dan or Taz or Tigger, whom he loved and cherished with all his heart, whom he thought of as sons.

I think of all the experiences in Bill's life that must have instilled deep anger and resentment in him—how hard he had to work to stay in college or watching his father not find meaningful work and die—and I realize what enormous medicine it was for him to commit to nonviolence as a way of life. He named violence, along with the bottle, as a destructive force that he would not allow in his life. But violence was there in him, which made his decisions to step away all the more profound.

We all live lives of contradictions. Embedded in these contradictions are some of the most important promises we can make to one another: "I will live my life according to what I believe" and "I will love this place in all my actions." And Bill wrestled with what to do about those who did not share these convictions. There had to be a struggle inside Bill about how to live out his values. Like Tolstoy, Richard Gregg, Gandhi, and Nearing, Bill asked himself, how can I live according to what I most believe in; how can I believe in a moral precept and not live it? The Kentucky writer Wendell Berry asks the question this way: "If one disagrees with the nomadism and violence of our society, then one is under an obligation to take up some permanent dwelling place and cultivate the possibility of peace and harmlessness in it." Bill did feel an obligation to cultivate the possibility of peace and harmlessness, and his life was a long arch toward that lifelong pursuit, but it was never easy.

In the small village of Tzintzuntzan on our last day in Michoacán, Bill and I meet a Purépecha man, Jose Alejandra, who is himself a tool-maker, who suggests that he knows a fine blacksmith just a two-hour drive away. From that simple statement Bill concocts a dream that lifts his spirits because it affirms that handcrafts still exist in this part of the world now very obviously to me overtaken by drug trafficking. Bill's convinced Jose will take us to a forge where we can have a gauge made even better than the one I brought with me from Knoll Farm. All of this leads Bill to say, "This has been a good day." I doubt we'll ever see the toolmaker again, but I'm encouraged by Bill's enthusiasm.

We do not see Jose Alejandra again that day, and Bill and I resign ourselves to making the six-hour drive back to Mexico City and to leave. We are enjoying a large bowl of tripe on a corner of the *mercado* in Patzcuaro the next morning when Jose appears to tell us we must go with him right away to meet his friend, who is not a metal worker but, in fact, a bowl maker of the large *batea* that Bill most wanted to find. I am even more dubious than before, but Bill is elated, so we jump into the car and turn in the opposite direction from Mexico City toward the coast with Jose next to me as our guide. I drive for hours on sandy dirt roads and ask Jose about each crossroad that we come to: There are only abandoned houses, no villagers, no kids, absolutely no men. It doesn't make sense to me. Where are all the villagers? Only occasionally we see another vehicle, and it's always a new Toyota truck with blacked-out windows. I am far more interested in this current story of Michoacán than Bill is, and I'm told by Jose that the multinational corporations have bought all this land and that it has become very dangerous. Later I would learn that "multinational corporations" was a euphemism for the Knights Templar drug cartel. He reminds me every twenty minutes not to slow down. When I suggest we pull over to take a break, Jose firmly says no and urges us on with his hands.

Finally, we reach an oasis of trees, simple wood homes, a river, livestock grazing at the forest edge, and plenty of kids playing. I exhale for the first time on the trip and find my camera, long since buried at the bottom of my pack. Jose introduces us to Israel Hueta Garcia of the village of San Miguel Charahuen. Bill tells Israel that we would like to buy one of his bowls and would like, if possible, to understand how he makes them. He agrees with a big, easy smile and brings us over to a yard behind his house where he works sitting on the ground, carving the bowl between his legs.

I've never watched a craftsman work with such skill and speed. He hand-saws a twenty-four-inch round of wood from a tree felled adjacent to his yard. He splits it cleanly with a single blow from an old, rough froe. At each step Bill and I find each other's eyes and smile at each other. Bill urges me through gestures to start taking pictures. Israel takes the halves of wood and sits down with one, each of his legs straddling either side of the round of wood. He picks up

the adze and with powerful, deft strokes heaves out the wood in the center of the bowl. It takes him just twenty strokes of his adze, creating twenty sculpted curves, to remove all of the wood on the inside of the bowl. With a few more strokes the twenty-four-inch bowl with a flat bottom is completely done. His adze is so sharp, and the strokes so clear, that sandpaper is not needed. He laughs and smiles at us, stands up quickly, and puts the bowl into a barrel of sawdust to dry slowly. I look at my watch to see that just thirty minutes have passed. Israel catches my eye and says, "*Quieres un otra?*" ("You want another?")

I stood back to take in the scene. There was Bill sitting on the ground making paper toys for Israel's children. Then Israel's wife brings us mugs of hot water, heaps of sugar, and Nescafé powder. We all enjoy the coffee, even Bill, which means that he doesn't stop talking in Spanglish for the next hour. Israel asks us if we can give him a lift back to the *mercado* in Patzcuaro where he intends to sell his bowls, so we make the two-hour trip back together.

We arrive in time for dinner, and Jose takes us to a small kitchen off the *mercado* where everything is cooked over an open fire and all the tools and utensils are made by hand. Bill is animated and joyful, his Spanish flowing from his lips as it must have fifty years before. He has rediscovered his tribe. It's dark when we leave our friends, and we are a long way from Mexico City, but Bill looks at me with a big smile and says our work is done. I drive us to Mexico City, and we arrive the minute that they are lowering the old steel grate over the entrance of the American Friends Service Committee in downtown Mexico.

As we pack up in the hostel of the American Friends Service Committee, finding space for the few treasures we will bring home, I note that Bill has worn the same clothes for this entire trip: heavy white wool socks over thin gray flannel socks, blue button-down shirt, handmade red underpants. The gray flannel pants, which must have been so hot in the Mexican afternoons, cost him two dollars a pair, and Bill tells me gleefully that he bought four pairs on his last time through Cherryfield, Maine.

Chapter Nine

RAIN CLOUDS

—Helen—

give me shoes that weren't made for standing
give me tree-line, give me big sky, get me snow-bound,
give me rain clouds, give me a bed time . . . just sometimes. . . .

— GREGORY ALAN ISAKOV

When Bill had a bad dream it was often about numbers: He's trying to figure out a math problem, but it won't work, and numbers keep slipping off the page or changing form. Even when sleeping on a cot in the fir woods, Bill kept a pencil and piece of scrap paper by his bed so he could jot down equations in the night. It is often after a dream that he solves a real problem, he tells me at breakfast. By night he has been trying to stay several steps ahead of us with the yurt. Sitting in his favorite seat in the back of the dining tent so he can look out the door, he already looks tired, his broad shoulders slightly stooped, little pale pillows under his eyes.

By this fourth day the workshop has fallen into a rhythm, and everyone is feeling a little sore and tired, but excited to see real progress. It's 7:00 a.m., and people straggle into the tent with steaming mugs of coffee and bowls of oats. Some like their oats cooked, some prefer granola. Bill eats his raw, which he mixes with grated apple, yogurt, and raisins and calls "horsefeed." I notice that he has become more or less vegan and is now substituting soy milk for the yogurt. This surprises me but is good evidence of how willing he is to change. Ten

years ago he looked askance at any protein source less rugged than a steak, and now he is asking me for tofu recipes. He doesn't drink coffee or tea, nor any hot drinks. Never has, classifying them as "drugs." Nor does he drink or approve of alcohol, though over at his place he makes a concoction he calls "hooch," sitting grapefruit juice on his window ledge until it gets just the right bubbly pinkish-green scum on the top. I have never dared taste it; the smell is enough to make me gag.

Bill waits until everyone is around the tables, then lays out the day, in rough terms. This is also when we can all ask questions about how the yurt is going together, but we know not to ask too much. He doesn't hear all that well in a group, and he is anxious to get going, his mind full of numbers, his wispy white hair standing on end after a night of calculations. At lunch we also need to leave him be to take his nap in the woods, so most of us take a swim, rinse off in the solar shower, then thaw out from the experience by lying in the sun, or sometimes keep working if we know what we're doing.

Which I mostly do not. Today I am looking forward to some serious instruction in yurt math. This might be the biggest difference between building a yurt and building something square; one has to abandon simple equations in favor of geometric ones. Even though trigonometry has been around since the third century BC, and so, one would imagine, essential, I honestly think this is the first time in my life that I've had to use it. Much to my astonishment, I am loving it.

What I am not loving is the clear realization that I have to take on building the girls' bedroom addition, that Bill does not intend to design it, let alone build it, and probably doesn't even want to be asked to think about it. I know that to Peter, Bill's abandonment of this part of the design, without comment, is symbolic of all his fears that Bill does not see him as a friend with whom Bill would like to collaborate, so much as someone who will serve Bill's own agenda. And for Bill maybe this is bordering on overwhelm, given his general ambivalence about having a building here at all. There is such emotional freight around it for both of them that it seems to me virtually impossible that Bill and Peter will talk about this and work it out.

This is my building, too; I could step in. But do I really want to bring it up with Bill myself, I wonder? I know my own tendency to let things go all too easily, to lower my expectations so as not to be disappointed, to not speak up for fear of hurting someone or getting hurt myself. But something about this galvanizes my will. I really want it for Wren. She asks me about "her bed cubby," as she calls it, almost every day, having already made a

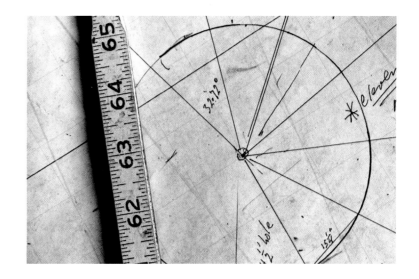

strong claim to this imaginary hideout. "When are you going to build the sleeping cubbies, Mama?" she asks, assuming I can just whip it off. One day she lies down in the dirt to test out which direction her bed should go and asks me to put boards around her to show her how big it will be. And Wren's right: The only way to help the whole situation is to start building the damn thing myself.

I decide I will ask Bill what dimension he thinks it should be so it fits proportionally, how I might attach a rectilinear room to a circular building sharing the same roofline whose walls are under five feet tall, and a few other simple details like that. I am sitting next to him at breakfast for this reason, stirring my oats around and around in my bowl. I have a sinking feeling that my questions will classify as the clueless kind in Bill's scheme of things.

Surprisingly, Bill does not give me a hard time. Nor does he explain why he blew it off, or apologize, but he thinks there may be enough lumber left over for building this extension of the yurt, he says, and I can use lighter lumber for the sills and floor joists since it will not bear much load. He suggests that the addition come out six feet from the main yurt. That's the one dimension he gives me, six feet, and a piece of graph paper to figure out the rest. "It would be good for you to take this on," is about all he says.

Peter and I had planned it on the north side of the building, where it will be cooler in summer and where the ground slopes away slightly. This is important because the addition will need to be designed with a step down from the main yurt so that we can add fifteen inches to the inside wall and a person can still stand up inside. To keep the slope of the bedroom roof in line with the main roof, the outside wall of the addition will be as low as four feet, but if we build bed platforms along this outside edge, it won't matter, so long as there's enough room to sit up in bed without bumping your head.

I draw a crude sketch with the side walls of the cubby coming out at an angle to the yurt that is in line with its own geometry; if you cut the yurt into pie slices and extended the lines beyond the circle you'd get the shape of the bedrooms like two parallelograms attached to the circle and to each other on the outer ring. Actually attaching them in the material world is another matter, since the full deck of the yurt is already completed and overhangs the joists I'll have to nail my foundation to. I immediately go and find Scott to help me plan it out, resolving to begin as soon as we have the materials we need—which, I know, will require of Peter another trip by canoe across the bay and into town.

After breakfast we all head up the hill, where there is something starting to resemble a building, or at least a flat-bottomed basket. To

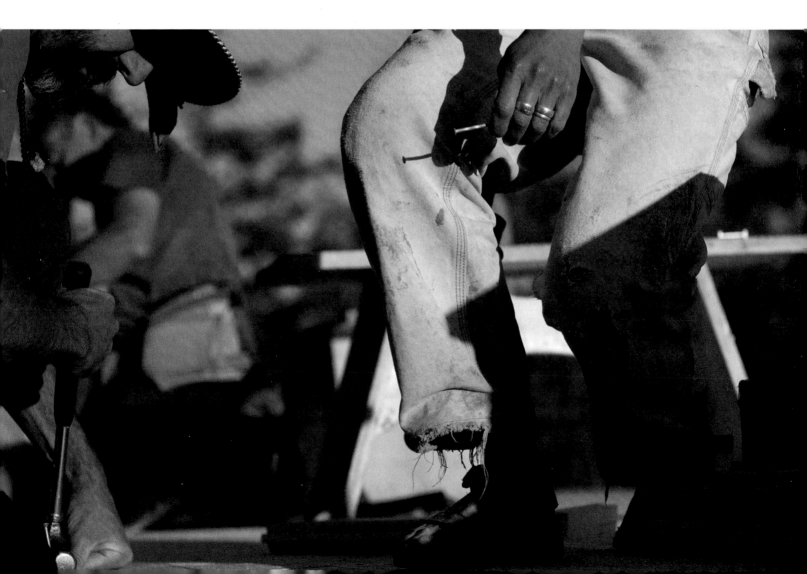

the finished main yurt floor we have attached the 4×4 wall posts—cut at the appropriate backrest angle on the bottom so that they lean outward—to our thirty-two "corners" around the edge. These posts are stiffened and tied to one another by the lintels, horizontal members spanning the space between them at the top. The whole thing still seemed a little wobbly at that stage, but Bill explained that the tension cable that wrapped around the outside of the lintels—under the eaves of the first story—would take care of that.

The tension cable may be the most important structural part of a yurt's design, holding the upper walls tight so they can support the weight of the roof. Bill has a favorite photograph of a group of friends helping him attach a cable to the eaves of a yurt in the 1970s. Seven people stand in a line, legs braced, pulling with all their might to tighten the cable around the building. Bill, young then and shirtless, his lean back muscled under the strain, pulls closest to the building, maybe so he can see when it's tight enough and can quickly secure the clamp. For years he attached his cables that way, a tug of war with a piece of inflexible steel. But over time he figured out a way that just one or two people could do it, with a claw hammer and a bunch of nails.

He'd pull the cable as taut as he could about six inches below the eaves, then hammer in nails equally spaced around the top of the wall for the cable to rest on. Then he'd move in a circle and pry the cable up over the nails with the claw. Because the walls leaned out, the cable would get tighter as it went up, and in tiny increments it didn't take a lot of muscle to get it there. But Bill loved that photo, remembering the folly of it. It represented progress in his world. Each time he built a yurt he came up with countless small innovations and efficiencies like that, and each time he found a way that something could be done more easily, moving people closer to self-sufficiency, he felt good.

Our next step, after tightening the cable for the first story, is to build the floor and interior walls of the second story—the nested basket, supported by a single post. Bill explained on our first morning around the table that what is new about our yurt is using only a single center post to hold the second story, rather than the four posts he usually uses. He is counting on the tension of the outsloping walls of the second story against the tension cable and the roof of the first story below to distribute much of the weight. He doesn't know if it will work, but if it does it will free up even more visual space inside and will be a step forward. (In fact, we find out later that the building has settled around it, and some other support will be needed.)

The center cherry post is beautiful. Bill doesn't have any cherry on his land, a wood we use often at the farm to make spoons and bowls in carving workshops. It possesses a deep red color that grows richer with age and a smooth texture under the knife. So it was a cherry tree Peter cut down for the centerpiece of the yurt; he skinned the bark and let it dry slowly, the naked wood revealing a twisted grain shaped by a windy Vermont hillside. It took Peter and others a whole day to paddle it in, suspended between two canoes; to create a miter box to hold it level and cut it to length; then to set it in the center of the yurt floor, toenail it in place, and screw a metal plate to the top to later secure the beams of the upper story.

Today we build the second-story platform, essentially an octagon of stout beams centered on the post with floorboards nailed across it and trimmed to a circle. At one side of the circle we will cut a smaller circle into the floor and make a ladder to poke up through it, to access from below what will be our sleeping loft. To each of the eight "corners" of this platform, just as on the bottom story, we screw in outward-leaning wall posts and connect them at the top with a horizontal lintel to make the second-story wall.

Next, and this is one of the most exciting parts for me because I really come to understand the concept of the lampshade roof, we screw the ceiling boards of the first story across the span from the bottom story wall to the top story wall. We work in pairs, one person crouching on the upper floor holding one end of the board and marking where it should go in the circle, the other person fitting it into place on the outer edge. We hold it up, mark the angle it needs to be cut on each end, and sometimes take a notch out of one end to fit around the window posts, then trim it and screw it in. It is so hard, craning one's neck up and holding a heavy long pine board steady, trying to measure an angle with a bevel above one's head, then remembering which side of the board should be facing down, trimming corners with a knife where it doesn't quite fit in the smaller inner circle but also having to make sure that there won't be any gaps in the larger outer circle anywhere when we are done. This way, slowly working our way around, we create the unique angle of the roof, which gives the interior an airy feeling; arcing above your head is a clean span of pine boards, overlapping in two layers as they radiate around the circle. Without any interruption or rafters or corners or angles, this lampshade roof has an elemental grace and wholeness to it. I don't want to take my eyes off it when we are done. We are all kind of stunned by it. It feels like we have just created a group mural or a sculpture, certainly not something that was following a formula. Which of course we aren't, following a formula, that is.

It is late in the afternoon, and we have already done so much. I bring Bill a cup of tea and a clementine and put it on his makeshift

desk under the tool tent. He probably won't drink the tea, but he looks really tired to me, and I am worried about his stamina. After all, he's 81, it wasn't that long ago that he had major heart surgery, and here he is working ten-hour days, guiding eighteen people with a wide variety of skills and nonskills, sleeping in the woods without a tent or sleeping bag, scampering around on scaffolding, and doing complicated math problems in his head. It's like watching someone run a grueling race. But he doesn't let up the pace. He has called me, Margaret, and Elizabeth into his "study" to take on a new assignment for the next day.

On the brown paper covering his desk Bill starts to sketch out how we will need to figure out the size of the upper-story windows, which

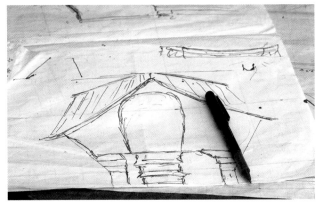

will make up the entire section of the second story that shows above the roof of the first. The windows are going to be triangular, one row at the bottom, a second row of inverted triangles above them, making a strip of light 360 degrees around the building. So beautiful! But not easy: The walls lean out, so the bottom dimension of this strip is some as-yet-to-be-determined amount less than the top dimension, meaning that the upper and lower tiers of windows have to be slightly different. It also means that the interior dimension of each window frame is slightly smaller than the exterior dimension, so we need to figure out the angle at which to cut all the material. No scale drawings on this, and everything is being built by a team of amateurs, so no doubt anything we might have had on paper would be slightly different from the reality anyway. At first, I can't even imagine how we will figure all this out.

Bill explains that if you are a yurt builder you need to know two numbers in particular: π and $\sqrt{2}$. Pi comes into play all the time when you need to calculate area, or volume, such as how much insulation we need for the roof; and the square root of 2 comes in when you are dealing with triangles. If you have a right angle triangle and the two shorter sides are equidistant (as on our windows), then the longer side is calculated using the square root of 2. Mike, hearing this mini-lecture, drifts over to the tent to join us out of curiosity. Bill gives us the number of windows around the circle and the perimeter of the circle and asks us to calculate the length of the bottom of each window, then the height of the windows if they are to be equilateral. It's like a high school geometry word problem.

"Where's the calculator?" Mike asks. Mike is someone who showed a keen interest in Bill's yurts, so Bill encouraged him to join his workshops and learn how to build them, but Mike's question makes me realize how Bill has rarely shared the actual design process with anyone. In fact, since he usually figures out a whole lot of it in his head, there is nothing transparent about his process.

"Calculator? Don't fall back on that," Bill says. "Just write it out." Mike, feeling unsure, starts to talk through the numbers out loud. "Okay, don't fill the air," Bill says, waving his hand at Mike in a moment of impatience, like combating a swarm of gnats, and gets up, having already figured it out. "Calculate it, and tell me what you get."

"People let math intimidate them," he says to me where I am figuring in the other corner of the tarp, "probably because they had a teacher who made them feel stupid so they gave up trying." I don't say anything, feeling rather like giving up myself at that moment, shingle and pencil in hand. Bill then tells me the story of going into a stationer's to buy some stiff brown paper: "The clerk brought out a giant roll of wonderful stuff, so I asked him how much it would cost for the whole thing. Well, I don't know, he says, we only sell it by the foot, and there's too much here to unroll. I took out my ruler, measured the roll, did some calculations, told him how many feet were on the roll, and made him an offer. Poor guy was too astonished to say no. Thirty-some years later I am still trying to use up that damn roll," and he laughs, pointing at his desk.

One thing you can be sure about Maine is that the weather will change, often dramatically. When I pick my head up from my shingle full of numbers, not much the wiser and feeling a sudden chill, I see that the fine wavy clouds of midday have thickened from something that looked like wisps of sheep's fleece to a solid gray wall. The breeze is picking up. "We better round up a team to cross the pond and get that big green tarp that's in the back of my boathouse," Bill says, looking up at the sky.

With considerable trouble, and well beyond dinnertime and dark-fall that night, Scott, Peter, Mike, and Michael pull an enormous dark green tarp over the construction site, and we all help to tie it out from the perimeter with an obstacle course of long sapling poles and miles of rope. We stash all the tools inside the yurt or the tool tent and pull a piece of plastic over the generator and its brood of nursing cell phones. I head down to help Taylor and Catherine tighten the lines on the kitchen tarp before bed, which is already flapping loudly and coming loose at one corner, over the totes of dry goods and tins of matches. No more lukewarm solar showers or grilled pizzas and guitar-caulk tube music by the campfire, I think to myself.

But that's not the worst part. I realize that at the end of this challenging long day I have only just laid out the most basic sills of the bedroom addition, have a good idea of how lacking I am in needed materials to continue, and now it is about to rain. Seriously rain. The rain, in fact, will pour down off the edge of the giant tarp exactly where I should be working, making a mud hole. For the first time I feel beaten and discouraged rather than energized by the challenge in front of me. I lament how much easier this would have been had we planned it from the beginning with the main building, and I begin to have grave doubts that I can pull this off. I have to remind myself to keep asking for help and not stubbornly do it alone, as can be my way.

I trudge off to the tent with Wren. I kneel and lean in, my dirty boots sticking out the door, to rummage amid the mess for our toothbrushes and a headlamp that still has a bit of strength left in it. I am bone tired. Finding new batteries right now might put me over the edge. The wind is flapping at the tent fly, and I wonder how well the stakes will hold in this rotten wood. I long to just crawl into my bag but force myself to brush my teeth in the dark, showing Wren how to spit with the wind, not into it, and how to spray the toothpaste by putting her tongue behind her teeth so it doesn't leave a nasty clod on the moss or on her foot.

Given that I spend most of my time farming, I'm used to being dirty for days on end. But here, where the most of a shower I've had in the past month is a trickle of cold silty water from a plastic bag hanging awkwardly from a tree branch at chest level, my overall feeling of encrusted griminess is getting to a critical phase. Salt water also has a way of stiffening one's hair better than the strongest hair spray. Finally, Wren and I crawl in, and I pick up our book where we left off, with Laura Ingalls still on the sun-blasted prairie. I am thankful when Wren falls asleep at once because the text is swimming off the page, and I have the vague feeling that I'm making up words.

Sure enough, the fifth day we wake up to a cold driving rain. It pours all day. The goats hunch in the brush with their heads bowed, tails to the wind. Under the monster green tarp it sounds like thunder. I know Peter is still feeling worried that we are way behind schedule,

and this weather is not helping. The wind and rain are reminders of how perilous it would be to leave a building without windows, doors, or a shingled roof as the weather turns to winter. These triangular window frames are really bogging us down, and until they are done we can't do anything more on the second story.

We also can't build the first-story roof until we insulate it, and Dane and Jen have just discovered in trying to do so that we have half the insulation we need. Besides, it's damn difficult to work under this huge tarp. It flaps constantly in the wind, which makes it impossible for Bill to hear us; it sheds pools of water violently and without warning; and it hugs the roof in places where we need to get under it to work. Bill is fond of pointing out any idleness by looking around, throwing up his hands, and saying, "Ah, two sitting, two moaning, two coming, two going, and six with cameras."

Bill tries to keep everyone going, but not only is he figuring this out as he goes, it's also clear that he doesn't like to give instructions. He'd rather have people learn by experimenting, not by being told. This, in fact, is central to his educational philosophy. He'll send you off with little information, let you stumble about and even start doing it wrong, then ask you, "Why in God's name are you doing it that way?" You have to justify yourself, and occasionally you end up finding a good solution, which he admires, and you glow in his praise, but usually you dodge the veiled insults at your incomparable stupidity and are greatly relieved when he shows you how you might get it right. Some learning happens, no doubt, learning you don't easily forget because you were the author of it, but also plenty of time wanders away in the process. Which wouldn't matter if we had all the time in the world. But we only have eight days to finish!

The building of our yurt is both democratic and autocratic, I decide. If it were any more democratic we'd never finish it (and we might not anyway) or it would look like hell, and if it were any more autocratic we would probably all quit and go fishing. Between the two—the time it takes to learn by our mistakes versus what we accomplish under orders—is a tension I am constantly aware of, as if that taut cable holding up the ground floor is wrapped around my chest.

Peter offers to take the materials list that Scott and I make and scour the local and not-so-local hardware stores for the materials we need. Hardest to find is more of the same kind of insulation we have been using, and that takes him two hours' south to Ellsworth, racing to make it back in time to paddle in the huge red bundles just before Duck Cove turns to a sea of impassable mud.

While he's gone, I take a break from being around so many people and paddle the kayak over to Bill's house on my own. I turn the kayak over on the gravel beach, walk over the bridge and up the rain-soaked meadow, where a few wizened blackberries still bow their heads over the path. Inside Bill's Library Yurt it's quiet and smells like resinous wood shavings and walnut oil and the pages of old books. In the deep quiet of the place I study Bill's construction of the additions that stick out from his round workshop walls, photographing the details so I can remember it when I am back at our site. The addition is built essentially the same way as the yurt, with an outside wall that leans out, windows at the top, and a lampshade roof making the span from the top of the windows to the roof of the main building. The side walls of the addition that cut back to the yurt will be the only vertical walls in our entire structure. I feel some measure of confidence having already done many of these steps on the yurt itself. What still feels most challenging is to see how this rectilinear shape will get attached to the circular one, and what shapes and lines for things like the windows and the siding and even the roofline will look and feel harmonious with Bill's design. Those are the things I look for over at Bill's house, though somehow it isn't all that helpful, partly because I'm not accustomed to looking at how the layers of buildings go together and don't quite know what I'm seeing.

All the same, over the next week Scott and I work it out, piece by piece, and mostly it looks amazing. I am really happy with our corner windows, the dimensions of the space, the way we manage to make it feel proportional to the round main yurt, even though it's a very different shape. Less successful, ultimately, is the roof. We figure out how to build the lampshade ceiling, insulate it, and lay across the final roof boards, making the line from the main yurt sweeping out to the far edge of the addition as harmonious and unbroken as possible. Scott climbs around on top and nails it down.

"You know," Scott calls down to me on that exciting day when we have nearly completed the hardest part of the work, "I think we should have a nice overlap of the roof boards on the sides of our addition, to soften the corners where it joins the yurt."

"Good idea," I say, not really liking the stark look of the straight side of the addition where it meets the outward-leaning wall of the yurt. Bill hears us talking, and having not commented at all on our work in any measure since the beginning, comes over to tell us no, that we have to cut the roof off flush with the walls. "Someone up there shingling is going to step on that overhang and have an accident," he says emphatically. Scott and I protest, arguing that the whole yurt roof has a substantial overhang and Bill doesn't seem worried about someone stepping on that. He's not listening, so we talk between ourselves about making brackets to stiffen the overhang and make an accident less likely. We aren't at all happy. Not only do we think it will look bad, Bill's demand at this point feels so arbitrary, almost antagonistic, given how little interest he seems to have given to what we are working on. He's a person we hold in high esteem for his sense of the aesthetic, and this decision seems to be against the grain—rude and contrarian, in fact. But ultimately we give in, we cut it off, make the roof flush, even though it looks amputated. Ultimately, even though it is our design, Bill gets the final word. So the end is anticlimactic, even maddening. But honestly, even that can't diminish how proud I feel for what I took on and was able to accomplish with Scott's help in such a short time.

Rain pools on our sleeping platform, dribbles under the tarp and soaks up through the floor of our old tent. Everything inside is damp—our sleeping bags, our clothes, our books with covers curling up, the inside of our rubber boots, our bodies. The trails through the brush turn to mud, which cakes on our boots and tracks indelibly across the bright new yurt floor. In the dining tent the benches are beginning to sink and list. Only the rocky hillside where we are building is firm underfoot. And only Wren seems to revel in it, pulling on her caked jeans every day from their damp corner in the tent, splashing through the puddles to make more mud, and even dealing with all the mosquitoes that have come back in droves by making a morgue display of all the ones she kills on the dining room table.

In fact, the one good side effect of the bad weather is that it brings Wren off the water and up to the site. I get to spend time with her for the first time in days. She is a spark of bright cheerfulness and energy, running around the building with a long stick, pushing it up underneath the heavy pools of water that are trapped on the tarp and releasing them in a sudden flood, jumping in and out of her bedroom door with delight. One day she comes up from the shore and tells me that she and Clara capsized in the tide rip in the kayak. She had been riding in Clara's lap in the cockpit and a wave flipped them; she went tumbling out and popped up some distance from Clara and the boat. Clara yelled to Michael, who was on shore and able to jump in the canoe and paddle out for Wren. Wren told me all this matter-of-factly, but from then on she didn't want to cross the pond with Clara for school or get in the kayak for any reason.

At the work site I try to find things for Wren to do that are useful and might require a little math. I devise a game in which she has to find different geometric shapes in the building—hexagon, parallelogram, rhombus, circle—and draw them. I think about Bill's idea that all people, but especially children, need to feel competent and useful, need to feel that they have something to contribute "if they are to develop a sense of belonging." Wren seems to belong here about as

much as the kingfishers and the wire brush and the rain. I had worried
about her being here so long without another kid for company; worried
about her feeling homesick or not liking the cold, the relentless bugs,
the lack of any place to go indoors, get comfortable, and have a snack
she recognized or a chair to curl up in. But there's not a peep. Every
day she seems to find endless ways to occupy herself, to connect with
everyone around her, to form her own personal and deep experience
of this place. I already have the sense that when I look back on this
experience, what will matter most to me, beyond all the laughter with
friends, the incredible beauty of the yurt, learning carpentry from Bill,

will be the adventure of living entirely outdoors with Wren and the way she has found this profound sense of belonging in the natural world.

On the next to last day of the workshop, I work under the big tarp cutting windowsills. I have Wren measure out the rough dimension, thirty-seven inches, mark them, and hand-saw them. Then I hold her boards up to the window opening and mark the inner dimension, the outer dimension, and the angle in between and cut those, then hope to God it fits. Because the building is round, and the walls lean out, meaning that the diameter changes in two directions, I'm dealing with two compound angles, front to back and top to bottom. And each window opening is slightly different because there was no way that thirty-two wall posts could be set by hand exactly evenly around the circle. When I have cut my second board in a row a fraction too short, Bill comes over and shows me a trick to the marking, which I still cannot explain, but it works. He comes back again to make sure I've got the hang of it and that they are all fitting snug. "That's looking good," he says, and I stand up a little taller, even as I marvel at how it is that this man can make me so mad one minute and the next minute so grateful for his praise.

Nearby, JoAnna holds the boards for Wren to saw and helps her along in her enthusiastic but rigorous way. Like Bill, she doesn't give praise easily; only encouragement, believing that the praise should come from within or a child will grow up looking to the outside to feel good about herself. I've had many conversations with JoAnna about child-rearing, about how her Chinese parents raised her with the "three Ds—discipline, duty and deference," and how she translated that rigor for her own children in American culture with an American husband. Now, in her seventies, a slight woman whose energy radiates in every quick decisive movement, she is an educator and mentor in the prison system. She has built more yurts with Bill than the rest of us put together. And in many ways I think she might also understand Bill better than all the rest of us. JoAnna moves through life shaping every experience as an opportunity for learning, for herself and for everyone present. It is the lens through which she sees the world. Bill, for all his reputation as a yurt designer, builder, homesteader, is the same. More than anything else, what he cares about is learning and helping others to learn.

In the 1950s, at the Putney Graduate School of Teacher Education, Bill met Morris Mitchell, whom he once described to me as his "intellectual father." Bill felt that Mitchell was the first person to confirm his idea that real education came not from schooling but from firsthand experience with the mistakes, triumphs, disappointments, and joys of everyday life and work. During Mitchell's early years as an educator in Georgia, he started several elementary schools, leading the teachers and students through the first year of the curriculum entirely designed around building their own schoolhouse. Mitchell's theories of education were strongly connected to his Quaker faith and passion for world peace, which he believed to be possible only if young people developed a social conscience and self-worth that allowed them to work for a better world. Bill came to share Mitchell's desire to redeem education from personal ambition and career advancement and to find its calling to address worldly social and ecological problems—hunger, racism, poverty, environmental degradation, and war.

For many years after buying Mill Pond, Bill was a student, then a teacher at a succession of high schools and colleges. Even before he himself settled at Dickinsons Reach, Bill dreamed of starting a school there, a school that would "be close to the land and animals, and give a direct intimate relationship with the source of life."

"Among other things," he wrote, "I want to find the secrets to building into a school program such elements as—Responsibility (personal and social . . .), Integrity—to search for the truth, and Courage, to stand for what we find; Manual and Intellectual Ability and Self-Confidence in these abilities; Awareness and sensitivity to man's and nature's needs . . . Leaving the world in a better place than we found it."

It appears, looking back, that Bill's school nearly happened. He had many connections and brought many groups of students to Mill Pond over the years who would learn and work with him in residence. He wrote about it extensively. He experimented with his ideas about experiential learning in every school he taught in and workshop he led. He hosted many Outward Bound groups. Why did it stop? Why did he turn only to leading yurt workshops elsewhere as his vehicle for teaching, and abandon the idea of a school? He ultimately stopped doing anything organized on his own land, though he welcomed more and more informal visitors each year. Was it just too difficult to do alone? Did it require too much money or time? Or did he lose faith that creating a school, however progressive, was the right way to educate?

I believe his thinking evolved early and was then reflected in his decisions about how he ultimately wanted to use his land. In a 1974 essay submitted for publication Bill wrote, "We assume education is a product of schooling when it is not." He went on to explain how he had come to believe that education should be community centered, not school centered. To develop a social conscience and the desire to influence their world for the better, children needed to learn from adults around them who are excited about doing this themselves; the community, not the school, needed to pass down wisdom about the making of a life and a living that had meaning.

Bill was far from a conventional educator; his preferred way of teaching involved traveling, building, cooking and eating together, even designing the course together. But after his experiences working as an educator in different institutions, he seemed to no longer believe in the separation of education and community, or in institutions themselves, however progressive. He felt most school environments to be too competitive, focused on encouraging and rewarding individual achievement rather than cooperation or solving problems for society at large. This translated after school to a focus on financial achievement, professional ambition, and competitive advantage for some at the expense of others. He also saw school as a world centered on the young, for whom opportunities to evolve and change were deep and extensive but where the skill to educate oneself all the way through elderhood to death was not taught, perhaps because of the cultural belief that the time to learn was finite, that old age wasn't a time of evolution but a time for rest (something Bill equated with stagnation).

Notions of retirement, or having a hobby to take up, or recreating in free time—so accepted by our culture—were all anathema to Bill. He believed in the ideals of collaboration, encouragement, apprentice-ship, and what he called the lifelong adventure of learning. He wanted to live in a place where all generations were learning from one another in the context of real life challenges and surrounded by the natural world and through that coming up with solutions for more cooperative and less consumptive ways to live.

In a letter to friends in which he encouraged them to come and form a community with him at his homestead, Bill wrote: "I think schools as we know them starve both kids and adults . . . I would like us to spend our lives living and not teaching. Learning every moment that we can—from the land, from one another, from visitors—from the world. In schools we spend so much time rushing around helping others to learn that we forget to grow—and thereby depriving the kids of the richest element in their environment—mature, growing people."

Bill did spend his life living, and learning. It was doing that with people in residence on his land, the way he dreamed of it for so long, that came so much harder to him.

Chapter Ten

FINDING ONESELF

—Peter—

In 1924 a thirty-nine-year-old American lawyer traveled by steamship to India to seek out Mahatma Gandhi. That man's name was Richard Gregg. He spent four years in India, seven months with Gandhi at his ashram at Sabarmati. As Gregg left the ashram, Gandhi encouraged him to bring his teaching of nonviolence back to the States, and to mark that occasion he gave Gregg a cutting of one of the pear trees from the courtyard of the ashram. Gregg brought that cutting and those ideas home with him. He kept both alive.

In 1935 Gregg published *The Power of Non-Violence*, the first book to explain nonviolence as an active form of political and social change.

Twenty years later Dr. Martin Luther King Jr. would cite the book as among the most influential of his life. Soon after returning to the States, Gregg met an unusual couple homesteading in Vermont. They were writers, political activists, maple sugar makers, homesteaders. They used their heads to write books and speeches, and they used their backs to create a self-reliant homestead according to their ideals on purposeful living. They were Helen and Scott Nearing, public intellectuals whose beliefs against the war, against child labor, against corporate power were new and confrontational enough to mainstream American culture to get them "red listed" as communists, so they moved from New York City to the hills of Vermont to escape the scrutiny and harassment and to begin a new experiment in living. Gregg saw they were real, he liked them, and he built by hand, as they did, a stone cottage on their homestead to be close to his new friends. Richard Gregg replanted the pear tree there because that's where it belonged. Years later, in 1954, Helen and Scott Nearing would flee Vermont to a more rural place in Maine and take with them a cutting of that pear tree and graft it to rootstock at their new homestead in Cape Rosier. That pear tree in its new location would prosper for forty years more, when Bill Coperthwaite would prune a limb from that tree, carve a spoon from it, and hand it to me with the encouragement that I could carve a spoon.

Most of that actually happened, although horticulturally speaking there are parts that are a stretch. I have a picture of Gregg and Gandhi in 1930 in front of the ashram. I know that Bill and Richard and Scott were great friends, across different eras, who shared stories and encouragement. Before she died, Helen Nearing told me a story of bringing cuttings of fruit trees with them from Vermont to Maine. But no one else, outside of Bill, has ever mentioned that Richard Gregg traveled home from India with a cutting of a pear tree. And no one, now, can confirm that the spoon I hold in my hand has its roots all the way back to the ashram at Sabarmati. Do stories always need to be true to have meaning and value?

At that moment I needed encouragement like I needed food. I wanted to apply myself to meaningful work that felt real and to ideas that were part of a long story of progressive change. I had a sense of history and knew that life didn't begin and end with me, but a college education had mostly positioned me for life, not prepared me for it. My first decade of work had mostly given me the privileges and relationships to "get ahead," but I felt hollow and without real skills to contribute to life. I was learning some of those skills as a young conservationist and learning to ask bigger questions that I hadn't been encouraged before to ask. Why does conservation matter, whom does it serve, is that fair or good for conservation? When Bill handed me that spoon sometime in 1995 in front of Helen Nearing's homestead and told me that story of Richard Gregg and Mahatma Gandhi, I was inspired. Literally, I took a breath in; I made a quiet and steadfast commitment to myself. I would do everything possible to contribute to that long story of positive change.

Of all the human forces of good and evil, encouragement may be the most powerful. It is the energy that runs from human to human to help us do better, to reach for something one cannot grasp at the moment. Gandhi encouraged Gregg. Gregg encouraged Coperthwaite. Sixty years later Bill Coperthwaite, who was about sixty-five at the time offered me, at thirty, encouragement with this story of the pear tree and of how we are connected in a lineage of service and relationship. That story pulled me toward the person I wanted to become.

Bill gave me that spoon and the encouragement

to make one myself, but I had no idea how. In the early days of my friendship with him and my relationship to Dickinsons Reach, our differences were more visible than our similarities, and all I could do was quietly observe. I didn't know how to enter that world fully. I could take pictures and ask questions and show appreciation, but I was not yet of it. Bill was waiting for the right moment to encourage me to walk through that next door.

One week a few of us had gathered to help him with a thinking project, which I could do, and one morning Bill grabbed his felling ax and two-man saw and we walked into his woods to take a birch. He loved birch for making spoons and bowls because of both its beauty, aging to a lovely light yellow, and its availability. He had lots of it. Had Bill had a different wood, say, the cherry that I have come to love on our farm, he would have become devoted to cherry, making a life out of cherry. But birch was of his place, and he became of birch.

We dropped that paper birch to the ground, sawed a portion into rounds, brought a few rounds into his workshop, used a froe to cleave out several ten-inch sections of that round, and held them, still cold and green with life, considering their transformation into spoons. I

could never improve upon the beauty and usefulness of a birch tree, but I learned that day that I can make something beautiful and useful myself. Bill taught us how to use the shaving horse; how to hold a straight knife; why a crooked knife, which he learned about from his travels among the northwest Indians, made it possible to carve without a bench with no more than

one's two hands. Bill put a section of birch in my hand and a knife in the other and taught me how to use both. This was my first lesson in how to make a vision become a reality.

It felt as though I was practicing magic: holding this rough block of wood in my hand, imagining it could become something useful and start removing wood to reveal the spoon. The sinewy wood quickly became bloody with my mistakes and then, in time, warm and smooth. I had never made anything with my hands before, and yet I knew instantly how different this was from buying things. I knew immediately that this wooden spoon was different from a metal spoon and infinitely more powerful than a plastic spoon. Learning how to carve a spoon was the encouragement I needed to reaffirm the artist inside me, to show a bit of my soul to the world, and, later, to leave a career in conservation and begin a life in conservation, to care for a forest and a family, to conceive of a retreat center nestled atop a hillside pasture, to forgo petroleum and turn to wood and sun. Decades later, having found at Knoll Farm my own tapestry of which to make a life, I can see that every radical and transformative thing I have done there was born out of my ability to carve that first spoon.

Learning how to manifest and create something from within myself helped me see how I could be more intentional with my own life and that if I could transform myself, then I might also be able to contribute to a change in society. I remember the day the meaning of carving spoons hit me: I was reading Gandhi's autobiography in Bill's shop, the book resting in my lap because my hands were sore and cut, and I came to the part where he describes asking his people in India to weave their own cloth, not because they needed more cloth but because they needed to imagine that they could be free of British rule.

I needed to imagine a life closer to the land. I needed to imagine an identity different from my parents. And then there were the harder things. I wanted to confront the hypocrisy in myself that sought change in others before demanding it of myself. I wanted to take on that part of me that talked up a storm while living in calm and comfort. I had real dreams for my life that I ran from, rather than leaned into. I sensed the narrowness of my perspectives and privileges, which most often put me and people who looked like me at the center of the action. And I had a powerful hunger to create a life in alliance with others that was a livelihood, as opposed to a lifestyle. I wanted to find out what was real inside me, what might truly be of my own making and how to offer that to myself and then others.

For years my fingers were covered in Band-Aids, blood, and blisters, and my shirts and pants were frayed with cuts in all the same places from the repeated motions of drawing a knife toward myself. Sometimes I felt that everything was getting cut up in this process of making spoons. And indeed it was; my old life born deep into one culture was slowly giving way to a new life within a maker culture. I was busy in the private process of freeing myself, which is what I might have called it back then, but actually of making room for what was most meaningful.

And if it was meaningful to me, I thought, maybe it would be meaningful to others. With that simple idea, at the first program we hosted at Knoll Farm, in 2002, bringing together loggers and wilderness advocates in the Northeast who were at odds with each other in painful and visible ways, I nervously set out to carve spoons together. Tell me exactly, they said, why we have come together to carve spoons and how this is meant to help us? Without answering that question directly, I pushed forward, and soon the value of working together before talking together was clear, and the question didn't need an answer. That was a decade and several thousand spoons ago.

What I had learned from Bill was to trust my experience in life, no matter how young and inexperienced I might have thought of myself, and to follow those instincts. Spoon carving quickly became the symbol of our work at Center for Whole Communities, an aspect of relationship building and transformation that felt real and honest to almost everyone. Around 2009, after we had taught more than a thousand

citizen leaders how to carve a wooden spoon at Knoll Farm, I was invited to be part of a social justice conference in North Carolina and asked to bring whatever offering I felt would be most valuable to the hundreds of leaders that would be there from around our country. I thought through my years of keynote addresses, workshops, spoken words, the single thing I've shared that has fostered the most change. I decided to bring my tools and teach them how to carve something real, simple, practical.

I have since carved many spoons and bowls, in many different places; the list of ones I've given away runs four pages long, and I've taught—I hope—many others to do the same, and the lessons keep coming. I have come to better understand who I am. For example, I will never be a brilliant craftsman, yet I can make a beautiful, useful bowl when I take my time. I am learning important lessons late in life, making mistakes and recovering from them, making ten thousand strokes of the knife to carve a meaningful life.

Wendell Berry writes in *Citizenship Papers*, "The rational mind is the mind of analysis, explanation, and manipulation, the sympathetic mind is the mind of our creatureliness. All that the sympathetic mind can do is maintain its difference, preserve its own integrity, and attempt to see the possibility of something better." Every day I felt Bill watching me and others to see the possibility of something better. Through that kind of encouragement Bill helped me value and honor my own sympathetic mind over my rational mind, and he helped me understand how being empathetic is more important than being right in creating change in myself and others.

One of Bill's great gifts to me is the idea of encouragement, how it builds both relationship and transformation, but also his actual encouragement, though in practice this was inconsistent for me. There were important times, as around the building of our yurt, when I did not feel encouraged by Bill. I wish I had had the presence and the strength to have spoken of this to him. I wish I could have stopped him at his desk under the big circus tent, during the workshop, and taken him on a long paddle and said how his jokes made me feel, why his apparent disregard for our vision for the yurt felt like it was breaking something between us, how confused I was by his talk of simplicity when I got sent to the hardware store every day for more supplies, how it felt to be treated like a boss-man or a client by a man who, I knew, had low regard for bosses and clients. I would have wanted to say it like this: You have discouraged me from some of the most important things you have taught me, and I still choose to build this yurt alongside you. I still honor you and believe this yurt creation to be a celebration of your life. Will you take that in and see me for who I am trying to be in front of you? But I didn't say that. At the moment I didn't have that wisdom or strength, and I mostly shut up and kept my feelings hidden to everyone, except probably Helen, because they were too deep even for me to understand in the moment. Had I been able to articulate how I felt and to speak directly and honestly in the midst of the yurt raising, and had he been rested and able to hear me, I believe Bill would have been sympathetic, shocked even at how I had been impacted. He could be gruff and impatient, and at times, even, he could be mean, and yet I believed he always wanted to be sympathetic. Sympathy and empathy are impulses toward wholeness and the motivations of relationship. Bill definitely judged, but in the long arch of his life I watched him lean toward encouragement and sympathy as the final and most important language of his being.

It's easy to turn one's back and walk away from anyone who challenges you or makes you uncomfortable or disregards you. This nation we have created is adept at creating walls, putting up gates and "No Trespassing" signs. There's the triple wall between this country and Mexico, and the eight-meter-high wall between Israel and Palestine, but there are also gated communities everywhere, even one directly next door to Bill's Dickinsons Reach. And all of these gates and walls and boundaries are ultimately about insulating oneself from challenges to one's way of life, comfort, or ways of thinking. And the result might be the protection of different forms of wealth, but it also results in the loss of relationship, the loss of human experience, and less and less chance to learn from others' perspectives. I learned from my friendship with Bill about the importance of walking across boundaries, what I call being an edge walker, to see the differences between me and others and being willing to disregard the walls, the gates, and those differences that keep us apart so that we might shake hands and be in some fragile relationship. There was much that was different between Bill and me that might have kept us apart, and there were many small

and large slights that could easily, some say wisely, have made us walk away from one another. But I didn't, and neither did Bill. Because of that commitment to be in relationship, through the disagreements and feelings of being let down, I grew. His life asks of me: How do I put down other boundaries to welcome something new in?

Bill did see the possibility of something better, not only for himself but for the larger society, if each of us could be encouraged to design and create our own original lives. To carve a spoon therefore is the first practical step in creating a better life, which is the only possible route to create a better society. Working with one's own hands is the core act of self-determination and self-actualization, which is the foundation of all social change. Of course, Gandhi could not have thrown off British rule if his people *only* weaved their own cloth and hadn't entered the streets, protested, and risked their lives. Focusing on personal transformation is not the shrinking of our political imagination, as some of the big thinkers insist, but the only realistic place for it to start.

Bill's life had much to say about beauty, that it's about the symmetry and balance of what we see, that it's about the substance or meaning of the object, and finally, beauty also arises from the manner in which the object is created. Things that are appealing at the surface but that lack integrity or substance are less beautiful. Things that are appealing in a finished form but that arise from an ugly or violent process are not beautiful. All sorrows are less with beauty and amplified with ugliness and violence.

I learned the most from what Bill created, the least from what he talked about, and as a result of that difference I've worked with great intention to model rather than teach, to express what I am for rather than what I am against. Bill felt that if you made the effort to walk down the long trail from town to his homestead there would be a very good chance that you would arrive one hour later at his round home filled with positive impressions about beauty, care, and intention. Thousands of people remember the yellow sawdust that Bill annually lined his trail with so that it would be beautiful and stand out against the green, brown, and white of the forest. He believed that if we are drawn to things because they are beautiful, we will be encouraged to make something in our own lives more beautiful to others. At Knoll Farm, rather than talk about the inequalities in our culture and the need for justice and a new relationship, I've found it more transformative to act than to talk, to practice a kind of radical hospitality—the opening of our home and our family life to strangers, and the setting of the table for all—that many who came to Knoll Farm found at first perplexing and then disarming, the making of a safe refuge for them. Rather than talk about the role of personal creativity in creating larger social change, we helped a group of strangers to become allies while carving their own wooden spoons.

Seek out direct human experiences, let yourself be drawn to beauty, create rather than critique, address violence within yourself, encourage others. These are Bill's lessons, which helped me to find myself, and the most important, yet unspoken, ingredient is intention. Intention, for me, is my ability to follow the direction I set, to avoid distractions, to enact what I believe in, to engage myself completely in the task at hand (while avoiding violence to myself or others, most importantly my family). I learned, too, that these positive attributes of intention have a near enemy, which is single-mindedness and rigidity. Without time for reflection and, in particular, without the sharing of perspective that comes from relationships, it's pretty darn easy to slide from persistence to rigidity. Sharing my life with Helen, making a partnership, making a family, living in any kind of close community for a sustained amount of time puts a whole new spin on intention, which is no longer about simply following one's path but reexamining that path almost every day for your sake and the sake of others, then arriving at what you want and need to do. Intention is my ability to be both reflective and persistent, to return to the work with new ideas, to not give up. And all of these skills and attributes add up to personal power.

When I listen to an eighty-three-year-old man launch into reciting a Kipling poem start to finish, or help him survey his land with two

hundred feet of old clothesline, or watch him hollow out a wooden bowl with a hand tool that he just made, I think of personal power. Bill was interested in a life that advances personal power, not diminishes it, and one that encourages you to participate in life, not merely observe it. I've heard friends and colleagues say that their smartphone makes them stronger people; I will admit to having this belief once or twice myself. And yet my own experience is that calculators helped me forget how to do math, cars helped me forget the joy of walking, listening to songs is easier for me than singing them, reading poetry has kept me from memorizing poetry, medicine has helped me forget how to heal myself, and safety belts have helped me put aside the absolute craziness of hurling myself down a hill at thirty miles per hour in a thin steel box. After a short while that technology is all I know. Bill didn't care about attracting attention to himself, he didn't use Twitter or

Facebook, he didn't rely on Kickstarter campaigns to fund his ideas, and he had zero concern about what his ranking position on Google might be. He didn't use a phone or a computer. These technologies were irrelevant to him not because he was opposed to them but because he was completely fulfilled without them. He refused to relinquish much of his personal power or his sense of enjoyment of life to any technology. Bill represents this living tradition of knowledge.

And when I say I have learned things from Bill and still get lost, this is what I mean: I use Facebook; I'm drawn to the heroic, single great idea of TED Talks; I strive for things that are more about me, truly, than about you and me. I believe that grace in life comes from how we hold and come to understand these contradictions. I recognize ignorance in myself, and I see willful and inherent ignorance in most of us. This is what returns me, in these moments of self-absorption, to questioning and even discounting the scale at which Bill chose to work. How can I merely work at the scale of personal and family and imme-diate community? Many times I have fallen for that seductive question that arises from money: how will you take this to scale? Don't I need a really good personal video or compelling new website that makes clear

my one great idea? What draws me to shout big ideas out to the world, except, perhaps, that it releases me momentarily from doing the really hard work of the many small acts of change?

What had less meaning for him was striving to operate at a scale much larger than himself and a small group of people; fake-ness: any creed that wasn't matched by its deed; words and sentiments spoken casually (which means most social situations); consistently exchanging one's time for money; living happily and uncritically within standardized conventions; and efforts to build up oneself at the expense of anyone else. He found meaningless the acceptance of living in unbeautiful ways that lack symmetry, proportion, focus, and honesty; most efforts to replace labor or thought with a technology; anything from the use of language to the use of a technology that was disrespectful of people or of nature. This, Bill felt strongly, was not only meaningless but a form of violence. Bill understood his own imperfection, and meaning came too from his lifelong pursuit to become kinder and gentler himself. He was a twentieth-century white man living alone out at the end of a trail, which means he could be rigid. He often lacked balance in his relations, and there were many things about himself he couldn't see. Around his grave no one said, "And he was a headstrong s.o.b.," but we all knew at times he could be.

One of Bill's strongest intentions, which I try to emulate in my own way, is his commitment to the pace and quality of his own life. He knew that one had to slow down to satisfy one's thirst, but don't for a second think he was slow; if that's what you wonder, just consider the amount of labor involved for a person of any age to live alone in a cold climate with wood heat and not use any power equipment or have a car closer than a thirty-minute walk. He loved a pace that allowed him to be present to the tides and the seasons and the visitor who walked in unexpected. It was a pace built around letters. His was a life where one writes letters every morning, walks the letters out twice a week to the post office, and waits for a reply that might come back two weeks later. That pace gave him time to work and to think about what was meaningful. If he allowed himself to be distracted by whatever was distracting me, say, if I called him with my distraction, then he would be giving up some of his meaning. Not having a telephone for those fifty-three years didn't stop him from maintaining deep relationships with hundreds and hundreds of people. It didn't keep him from traveling all over the world. It didn't prevent him from speaking on college campuses. And it didn't keep forty of us from dropping every-thing we were doing in our lives to be alongside his body to bury him. His life had all the benefits of meaningful relationship without ever having a telephone, a computer, a smartphone, or a Facebook account or tweeting what he was doing.

Bill was not rushed. He never answered the question, "How are you, Bill?" with "Very busy." To be very busy, to be overwhelmed was clear evidence to Bill that you had surrendered something important to someone else. And while Bill never had much money, living all of his life well below what our government calls the poverty line, he was rarely ever without a sense of abundance and possibility. I now under-stand better that "being busy" may really mean for many of us that we're actually feeling less meaning, that our lives are filled with things that aren't important to us. It's not so much that we're too busy but that our lives are stuffed with responsibilities and actions that don't have enough meaning. If your life was brimming over with meaning and purpose, I doubt you would say, "I'm too busy."

But isn't that purely a first-world problem, not shared by many people on this earth who do not control their own time? Is it really pos-sible for all human beings to have such control of their lives? Doesn't this plainly disregard the majority of people who live hand to mouth and who work in sweatshops because there's no alternative? Doesn't it disregard the reality of a young American being asked to work long hours in the journey to become a doctor, a lawyer, or a banker? Is Bill's approach to time just another version of what one might expect from a privileged white guy wanting to control everything? Or does it offer all of us an alternative example of life? Was Bill's consistent choice of time over money an example of liberation for all of us? You will be judge, and for me his most difficult teaching may be this: One cannot be intentional about a life without a new relationship to oneself. This time on earth is mine. It is not yours. This life is mine. With gratitude to my colleague, Eddie Merma, I see more clearly how this fierce intentionality is also fundamental to nurturing larger social change,

which was equally as important to Bill as personal growth. The reason the world needs you to be intentional about what's most meaningful is so that you can create more beauty and nonviolence in the world.

Change making requires courage. Courage requires patience. Patience requires time. An abundant sense of time requires self-discipline. Or said another way, change making requires an open heart. An open heart requires being relaxed and having a sense of grace. A sense of grace requires devotion. Devotion requires a disciplined focus on what's most meaningful to you.

Having an abundance of time and honoring that, not wasting it, requires a personal commitment to do the work that's most meaningful, and to leave all the rest on the floor. To say that one can only be self-disciplined and intentional out in the puckerbrush of Maine is to give up on oneself. One can be graceful, intentional, and self-disciplined in Calcutta, in Dubai, in Athens, and in Brooklyn, as easily as at the very end of the trail. The critic says that this only works for a person living at the margins, or for a person seeking change only at the smallest scale of oneself. Really? I wonder what other scale of change is really possible?

I didn't take Bill's lessons lightly or informally. I did the most and the best I could with what I understood. I have not stopped drawing the knife toward myself. And his death has taught me even more. During the last decade, Bill lived at the end of a 1.5-mile-long foot trail with no phone, no office hours, no program for change making, no board of directors, no philanthropy staff to raise money for those programs, no curriculum guide, no outreach, no strategic plan, no striving on his part that people would show up . . . but people did show up. Many people. By my rough calculations about 250 people showed up every year, or something like 2,500 people over a decade. Four hundred or

so of those people cared enough every year about that experience with Bill that they would buy a calendar from him to help support his work. It didn't take much more money to keep him going. And judging by all the calls and letters I received upon his death, his life was profoundly important far, far, far beyond my view.

During that same decade Helen and I and our staff and board awarded about fifteen hundred fellowships to attend leadership development programs at our farm and elsewhere around the country. That required that we have a paid staff of many, a faculty of twenty-two, a faculty retreat, a 150-page curriculum guide, a board of directors, an annual budget of $850,000, and that I leave our farm and family to get on an airplane about twenty-five times a year for ten years. And while these are not an apples-to-apples comparison and I am not a person prone to self-criticism, I cannot be the graceful human being I aspire to be without critically asking myself, what resulted from my strivings? What things could I have done differently to more simply allow our lives to radiate? What teaching, what speech, what program, what workshop is more important than how I live my daily bread?

I often think about the thin, steel cable that runs around both levels of our wooden yurt holding the opposing forces of all that weight into a form of architecture that is beautiful and open, tension made visible. To me it is a metaphor of the tension I work the hardest to make beautiful: the struggle between leading a meaningful life as an individual and a family and, on the other hand, doing work that speaks to the needs of society as a whole. In founding and nurturing Center for Whole Communities, so much of our creativity was poured into work that served others, and served the world, while draining away time I might have been able to give to my children, my wife, the arts of photography, writing, farming, neighborliness. I asked my family to give up their privacy, to have less of me, to answer to my dreams as well as to the questions and doubts of others. Hard as Bill's life was, his was filled with daily, tangible expressions of his creativity, something that mine quickly came to lose in fulfilling my sense of service. And yet

I'm unwilling and unable to say that my salvation is any more important than someone else's whom I do not even know. And so I wrestle with my life as an individual and my life within the community, always trying to strike a balance that feels hard to attain.

This is what I've learned from Bill: When my own life is done, my legacy might be a physical place, made sacred by care and attention, experienced together by people who can also find on that land their deepest courage to go forward and to create beauty, to love again in dark hours. When my life is done, I want to have created a safe harbor on the land for my family, and others, to find and speak their truths, to practice creativity and to use their imagination. I want to help others to believe in the land again, to believe in their own personal power. I can imagine living and gardening as an old man there at Dickinsons Reach. I can see Helen there alongside me, both of us stooped over and moving slowly. I can imagine Wren having her own yurt somewhere there on the land and Willow bringing her family to visit once a year because she loves us. I imagine it becoming a sacred place for our family long after I am gone.

One October afternoon about ten years ago Bill and I were out on Hickey Island on one of those rare fall gifts of a day that is calmer, sunnier, cooler than any of the summer days. We were there to collect a large oak beam that Bill had seen washed ashore months before. The beam, to be used at his homestead, was 12 inches in diameter, 14 feet long, soaked with salt water, and far heavier than the two of us could handle. We rolled the beam on small round logs from the middle of the island to the beach, pushed it on round stones down the beach to alongside our canoe, and then waited for the tide to rise. As we sat there taking in the day, Bill said to me, "I try to bite off just a little bit less than I can chew, and the meal is always a delight. If you always bite off more than you can chew, you're always going to feel pushed and uncomfortable. Doing a little bit less enables us to work more consistently and allows for time to breathe and observe. Freedom to act is an overwhelming opportunity; some fill it up with activity, some fill it up with experience."

Chapter Eleven

COMING TO REST

—Helen—

Everywhere being nowhere
Who can prove
One place more than another?
We come back emptied,
To nourish and resist
The words of coming to rest:
Birthplace, roofbeam, whitewash,
Flagstone, hearth
Like unstacked iron weights
Afloat among galaxies

— SEAMUS HEANEY

T he sky seems to mirror my interior state as the workshop unfolds—first bright, then obscured by rain and fog, and for the last few days brilliantly blue, the air crisp and invigorating. Geese stream over in ragged bands of twenty, seventy, a hundred or more, calling to one another without pause. Scott's family, my dear friend Rani and their son, Quinn, arrive to help. Most of us throw ourselves into shingling the seemingly endless curved layers of the lower roof, crouching on our toes until our feet and legs cramp, shaving each cedar shingle with a knife to taper it top to bottom so it will make the proper curve, then securing it with two nails, in just the right place to be hidden by the next layer up. Mike builds little shelves with angled legs and the point of the

nail on the bottom of each leg that we can stick to the roof to hold our piles of shingles.

That first night after the storm, Bill, too, seems to feel a lift. Under the cold clear air, the red sparks of the fire flying up to meet the stars, he starts to tell stories again. Bill loves a good story, and most of his yurt stories follow a pattern: Bill shows up to lead the workshop, nothing is set up, things are looking bleak, and through some twist of ingenuity and sheer will a motley crew of assembled volunteers builds something extraordinary.

He tells about showing up to build a yurt on the Florida coast, having been told that the footings were all poured and ready to go. He is walking around in the dark, checking it out, and realizes that some of the footings are as much as 6 inches higher than others. Then he sees that when his shoe comes against a cement footing the material crumbles away and leaves a pile of gray sand. The workshop is to start the next day, and Bill knows he will have to start the foundation over; it is complete junk. "So we went out in the woods with axes," Bill recalls, "and cut all the foundation posts out of cedar. Then we had to dig eight-foot holes in sand and erect these posts. This was the only yurt I ever built on stilts, with waves washing under it. It was an adventure."

For someone so intentional, Bill thrived on the unexpected. "If you put yourself off-balance," he once wrote, "you gain new perspective and movement." It reminds me of Bill's tree house, three stories of wooden boxes, not connected, suspended by wire cables and swinging sixty feet up in a spruce forest. The climb up is hand over hand on the broken lower limbs of a spruce, with some long reaches and precarious balancing along the way, and finally, the part that gives me the most thrill, a half turn and full leap of faith over to the lowest swaying box at one's back. Bill still went up there to spend the night sometimes, and always on his birthday.

As I listen to story after story I appreciate the heroic nature of them and laugh with everyone else. Ingenuity and intelligence, the ability to come up with solutions on a dime with little at hand, the willingness to take on a job that at first seemed impossible, the delight in giving others an experience of learning were all parts

of what made Bill original, and I loved him for those. But I also had more insight now into how all those people who had invited him to build a yurt as a workshop must feel, going in with little instruction or organization, not quite knowing how much they would be winging it along the way. All those people ended up with a "finished" product that would be perfectly acceptable for someone like Bill, who rationalized the winter wind coming through the cracks in the walls "as oxygen so your fire won't go out," or who could make funky handmade stoppers to hold in a window without lock or latch, who was happy to find an old wool coat to cut up for weather stripping around the door. "Finished" to Bill didn't necessarily mean weathertight.

Bill never found adequate ways to convey to people the many design decisions he made, because he lived with them, adjusted and tested them over so many years. Here was a man who slept for a while in a yurt without a floor in Alaska to test whether or not floors were necessary, who designed buildings for many years without windows partly because he felt people should mostly live outdoors, who cut his woodstove down to size with a hacksaw so that it worked better in his

space rather than find a different stove, who jacked his house up and put another story under it by himself.

It wasn't just that Bill had the time and copious ingenuity to make these decisions; he was also someone who had fewer needs for comfort. His is not a hospitable place. It is often gray, raw, bone chilling. But when you are there a while you realize that Bill didn't need much in his daily life. Dry socks, a sweater, a warm vest. Your clothes don't need to be clean. The water you wash with doesn't need to be hot. The breakfast bowls can each be wiped with a quarter-square of paper towel. The dishwater can be tossed from the window. You can go to sleep when it's dark and wake when it's light. You can put a bucket out by the door to collect the rain. Bill lived simply partly because his domestic wants were few and his ways spartan and partly because he had designed everything around him to be simple. A friend tells the story of how on her first visit he made up a bed for her in the downstairs of the Library Yurt, then went upstairs to his own room. He left her a little brass bell. "Ring it if you need anything at all, and I'll come down and tell you how you can do without it," Bill said. "Let's figure out how to do less with less," was another of his favorite things to say.

If Bill didn't often deliver a yurt that others would call complete, imagining that they would complete it over years on their own, what Bill *did* give everyone he designed a yurt for was beauty. Bill had a more refined sense of beauty and proportion than anyone I've ever known, and his yurts were the fullest manifestation of his vision, of his belief in the marriage of beauty and function and in the unequaled grace and comfort of indigenous architecture.

The most beautiful part of our yurt, to me, is the upper-story roof, which is the last piece we need to complete. It's constructed with four layers of long tapered triangles of cedar, bent backward to make an elegant curve from the eaves to the skylight. Technically, Bill says, we're building a curvilinear paraboloid roof, but how's that for scaring away amateur builders from attempting it? For a long time Bill's yurts had simple conical roofs, like the one on our first story, or they had a pleated roof where the boards met at right angles and created triangular windows at the eaves, like the Harvard yurt. But Bill loved the beauty of a roof that curved inward as it went up, rather like a vase or the lip of a Tibetan bowl. He noticed and loved that shape in objects, so he designed it into his yurts.

The outward curve also allowed for a steeper roof, with more of an opening for a skylight at the top so more light could spill in.

We bent the long, thin cedar boards that would form the roof the first day of the workshop by soaking them, then stringing them with wires, like a bow, and they lay on the lichen in the rain, the fibers in the wood expanding with the moisture and slowly taking a new form. To put them up, we built a scaffolding—really a tripod stage—from the second story and from that sent up four long poles from which we tied two steel rings, a large one at the center point of the roof and a smaller one at the top. We screwed each cedar board to the top of the triangle windows, then wrapped it with a wire to secure it against the metal ring about halfway up, and finally rested its top against the upper ring. This was precarious at first, then slowly got stiffer and easier as we created a cone, then got harder again as we tried to cram all eighty-one slender boards into the circle. They all met at the top to make a tight complete circle—the compression band essential to the roof's integrity—but there were large gaps between the boards at the bottom. So we put on a second layer, interlaid with the first, until we had a complete ceiling.

Bill, who perceived Elizabeth's emerging gifts as a carpenter, assigned her the building of a ring entirely made out of thick blocks of wood, a thing of great beauty and complexity that is to act as a spacer between this ceiling layer that we had just put up and the two roof layers that would go above them, with insulation in between. Saying at first that she had no idea what she was doing, with Bill's confidence in her—which amounted mostly to leaving her alone to figure it out—and some help from Michael and Margaret she went forward. This was a feeling I was also starting to know.

Before this workshop I had no faith in myself to build anything more complex than a square lambing stall, and now, having struggled through so many tasks and learned from my many mistakes, there was almost nothing I wouldn't at least try. Bill even called me "a builder" one day, which astonished me. I had a few more carpentry skills, it was true, but I think what I gained most was an absolute trust in myself to

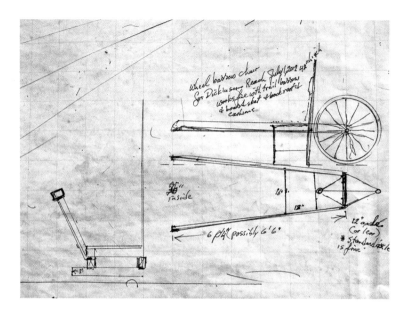

figure out something new. I realized that this must have been a skill that Bill learned early and honed over many years. Living alone into old age with so many practical problems to solve to make his life work, he had no choice but to be independent, inventive, and doggedly stubborn. It was that, or give up. I wouldn't say that he passed this gift on to me—I have always been independent and stubborn in my own way—but his trust in my ability to figure things out was pivotal, as if he saw something in me that was dusty, cleaned it off, and held it up to the light.

But Bill's encouragement of people, and his inconsistent use of it, had another side. Dan, who as much, if not more, than anyone else had carried Bill's yurt design torch forward in the world but was overlooked when Bill invited friends to his yurt design symposium, shared with me the tender question, "Why did he never consider me? What did he see in me, if he didn't see what I wanted him to see, what I valued in myself?"

Often I felt that Bill saw in us what was useful and meaningful to him, that he didn't see people whole. Or to put it another way, it was as if Bill cultivated his friendships through his love of ideas and desire to design projects, not the other way around. This could hurt, if one wanted to be seen and treated first and foremost as a friend. Bill was good at nurturing friendships over time and space—his letter writing was legendary—but not always was he the kind of friend who showed a willingness to be flexible, to compromise, to incorporate another's desires.

At his burial there was a poignant moment when three friends realized that Bill had written to each of them separately, assigning them some part of helping him with a new wheelbarrow design. The friend who made sculpture out of laminated materials was asked about glue, the friend who made boats was asked about Kevlar, and another who knew bicycles was asked about wheels. No one had the big picture except for Bill. They were all being put to use.

At the same time each of us cherished being asked anything by Bill, for he was one of those people whose attention one sought and desired. There was a way in which his constant questing and creating marked each of us close to him: if you had a good voice you were asked to lead the group singing after dinner, or if you were a literary friend you were asked to seek out the books on Bill's ever-changing list of out-of-print titles to add to his library. We all loved these invitations and the intimacy they contained, but on the other hand you couldn't easily take on a new role after that: to Bill you were always the singer or always the book friend, and so you felt both honored and unwholly seen at the same time. Learning to build made me feel more whole in Bill's world; our relationship took on new dimensions after that.

On the second to last day of the workshop our last major piece of work is to put the upper roof boards on, nailing their tops to this wooden ring. In many yurts Bill would use a wagon wheel or simple metal band for this top piece, or skip it all together if he didn't have any reason to add insulation. Bill insists on carrying the wooden ring up the

scaffolding himself and fitting it over the peak. He stands up through it, his white hair catching the sun, as if wearing as a skirt the entire elegant sweep of the roof below.

Bill spends the whole last day at the top of the yurt, balanced on the edge of the scaffolding, shirtless and hatless but with dark gray wool trousers, securing the final upper roof boards by trimming them to fit with his hatchet, cajoling and tugging them into place. This is where building one of Bill's yurts becomes much more art than science; nothing ever fits into the circle evenly or exactly, and a certain amount of fudging with hatchet or knife blade is necessary to get it all to fit neatly into the compression arch that is so important at the top of the building.

After lunch Bill doesn't even make the walk back into the woods for his nap but lies down on a giant pile of pine shavings on the floor and goes fast asleep as the rest of us tiptoe around. It's unbelievable how much we have done in thirteen days. I'm grateful that Peter is able to be present at last on the site, shingling, taking photos, because there's nothing else to forget now. What's forgotten is too late to retrieve, and what has been retrieved is all we need.

Peter has always been good at honoring: people and occasions. He is good at expressing his gratitude to a group, and he has anticipated the ceremony he'd like us to have. He and I gather everyone late that afternoon, just before our final meal together. We sit in the yurt, amid the shavings and tools, the insulation that will go in the walls and the windows yet to be made. It's far from

weathertight, but it's beautiful, stunningly so. The low afternoon light from across the water floods the room and creates soft curved shadows on the ceiling and patterns on the floor from the windows above. The second story is still open, so you can lean back and look up to the curved upper roof, delicately made, almost ethereal, with its bowl full of amber light spilling in from the skylight at the top and illuminating the wood. As Bill wrote in an article years ago, "the natural lighting of the yurt is its glory."

Peter and I get up and thank Bill, hug him, somewhat at a loss for words. I feel exhausted by the physical and emotional intensity of the last two weeks but on a high, too, and very grateful. When it's Bill's turn to speak he says that he is sorry that he hasn't been all that easy to work with, that he always wants to design something new and the new parts of this building only came together in the last couple of days. "So sorry if I've been tense," he says, clearly uncomfortable. "Now I'm just intense," he adds, and everyone laughs, a little awkwardly, knowing perhaps that there was much more to be said but also that this was enough.

Wren goes around the circle and hands out to each person a Veritas plumb bob in a cloth pouch. The brass objects have a nice heft in the palm. JoAnna comments that they represent to her what our time together felt like to her, finding your center. People share how much the experience meant to them, using words like "magical," "powerful," "unforgettable," "whole." I look at Peter and hope he is taking it all in.

Later, watching Bill walk away toward the shore with his simple bedroll under his arm, his back a little bent, I hope that he too has taken in what this has meant to everyone. I sense he is ready for it to be over, ready to have some time alone, to have a rest. Now I understand, when he tells his stories about yurt workshops he has done, what an incredible feat each one of them has been. He is spent, and it's not because he's eighty-one. It's because he has poured every ounce of his being into his creative process.

We don't see Bill again for several days. We say goodbye to everyone, one by one over the next day and a half. Taylor is the last workshop member to leave, and I paddle him across the pond with his enormous backpack so that he can take the trail out from Bill's to his car. Taylor has been barefoot since he arrived, so I don't think much of the fact that he is barefoot now, assuming he has shoes in his pack, if not for the hike out, then at least for the eight-hour drive back to Vermont.

When I return to the kitchen tent, looking sad now with its encrusted stove, its remains of dried beans and rice, and far too many dishes for the three of us to use, I see under the counter Taylor's shoes, curled up like discarded rinds. Beside them are a paperback novel and a pair of sunglasses. Everyone, it seems, has left behind something no longer needed.

The kitchen and dining tent feel empty and sad after so many meals and nights together by the fire, so Peter, Wren, and I head up the hill to take in a view of the yurt. From the outside the yurt appears small and close to the ground. Its proportions are so perfect to my eye it reminds me of a toy or small round box you could pick up and hold in your palm. Then inside, it appears larger than it is. The low outward sloping walls, the radial lines of the roof sweeping upward with perfect symmetry, the two stories of windows all the way around bringing in direct light as well as soft indirect light that glances off the lower roof all combine to give it a spaciousness that is, to use Bill's favorite word, "delightful."

While Wren collects her favorite spirals of pine shavings from the floor, Peter and I make a list of all the things left to do. We have

another ten days before it will be time to head back to the farm. Our list includes cutting all the windows, making a door, shingling the upper roof, burning the wood scraps, installing the woodstove, restacking the lumber, and packing up and cleaning up a monumental mess. It's all too daunting to contemplate, so we decide spontaneously to go into town, to do some desperately needed laundry, wash our matted hair, and sleep in a dry bed for a night.

As we head out from the point in our old green canoe it starts to rain, a sprinkle at first and then, part way down Johnson Point, a full summer-like downpour. The raindrops dance and slide on the surface of the sea

all around us, making perfect gleaming silver beads that stay intact on the surface before merging with the salty ocean—as if not wanting to leave the realm of the air. In all the rainstorms this is something I've never seen before, and it's magical, but it doesn't last; something about the quality and size and speed of the droplets or the particular flatness of the sea changes, the wind picks up, and it's just rain again.

While we're in town Peter arranges to have Josh, who was part of our original prep crew, and his friend Steve come back for several days to help us finish up. Most of our prep crew dispersed back to their homes a few weeks before, so it is a relief to have these two still in the area and able to help us. We know it won't be possible for us to do everything alone, so the next morning we hurry back to meet them with the canoe to ferry them across the pond from Bill's trail.

Our paddle back in is over luminous water, clear as green glass. We follow a loon for a while, trying to predict where it will emerge after diving into the deep. We are going back to push ourselves as hard as ever, and yet on the water I feel a lightness, a contentment, and a spaciousness that I haven't felt for weeks. Maybe it's the awareness that now I'll have more time alone in this place I love, that we know now that we are just days away from getting the yurt weatherproof and safe to leave, most of all that we are emerging from a journey that— like the yurt, imperfect and transcendent, trying and beautiful—will soon be ours to come to know and inhabit as we choose. Paddling up the reach to the rocky point of land is like every other time; there is no sign of our trail, or the yurt, or all the activity that has unfolded over these forty herculean days. Only leaving the water and knowing where to walk through the bushes and up the trail will reveal how much has really changed.

We begin another week of long days under gorgeous skies. Canada geese and snow geese fly over by the hundreds, more each day, each hour, and behind them comes the cold. Our drinking water is frozen solid in the morning, and the trails are slick with frost. Even at midday we have to stop every few minutes to blow on our hands. At night I

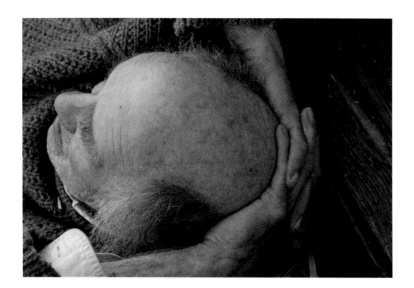

read *The Long Winter* to Wren, and Laura Ingalls Wilder's descriptions of running out of fuel and having to twist hay until her hands are raw to keep even a little warmth in their house where the snow blows under the door makes us feel cozy in comparison as we drift off to sleep in our down bags dressed in socks, hats, and two layers of clothes.

Then one morning, having barely paused for breath for days, we know tomorrow will be our final day. Josh and Steve have gone. Peter and I are in the yurt, and Wren is playing on the rocks with the goats when Danny Manchester calls, warning us that a hurricane is on its way up the coast and will bring rain and high winds in a matter of hours; he knows our plan was to cross by canoe, and he kindly offers to pick us up in his lobster boat and ferry us to Duck Cove the next morning. I can hear Peter talking on the step where he has been carving out a burl for the handle of the front door. I'm building the door, which I realize when I lay it out is shaped like the lid of a coffin, narrow at the bottom, wide at the shoulders and curved at the top. I'm ripping the boards lengthwise with a hand saw when I need to straighten up and stretch. Out the open windows I see Bill coming up the path. It is clear that he hasn't come to visit or relay a message; he has come to sit. He passes Peter, who is off the phone now, comes inside, nods, and takes in for a moment what I'm working on, then rests his back against the wall and slides slowly down to sit on the floor. Peter follows him in and offers him some coffee or tea, wanting to offer something, but Bill shakes his head no, thank you.

Bill leans against the wall with its perfect backrest angle and looks up to the ceiling and upper roof, taking in the graceful lines of his creation. I stop sawing. The silence in those long moments feels sacred, unbreakable, like the light itself filling the room and enveloping the three of us. I wonder what Bill is thinking; is he pleased with what he sees, or is he being critical or wishing he had done something different? Is he proud? Or is he thinking about time, about all the designs he has made and what might be left, at age eighty-one, to say?

In a conversation we had a month before he died, Bill shared with me his sadness that more people hadn't taken up the extended invitation that he had put out there through his workshops and writing and had most of all demonstrated through his way of life for sixty years: an invitation to put heads together and design a world with less consumerism, less exploitation, less poverty and war. "In the 1970s if you had asked me," he said, "I would have said that by my eighties we would have a world without exploitation. I really believed that." And then midthought, in a way that so often happened with Bill and that I loved, his mind danced to literature and he quoted Tolstoy's words on exploitation: "We're so concerned for the poor man who carries us across the river—we'll do anything for him except get off his back."

In that conversation—one of the last we had—Bill said that he thought he had always loved design so much because it was nonexploitative; anyone can design something, anyone can move toward doing something a better way. "Our society does not ask you to be a designer," he said, "and I think that's too bad. It's important to learn that you can design and shape your world." Dickinsons Reach was Bill's Great Design. It was also his Solace. As Dan said, "I believe Bill needed four hundred acres and four miles of coastline to hold his love and beliefs, which he felt were unrequited by the world."

After fifteen minutes or so Bill gets up from the yurt floor without a word and walks back down the path toward the mill pond and his wooden canoe, ready to paddle to the other side. Whatever judgment or blessing he may have reached was withheld. But strangely perhaps, the moment leaves me in peace, leaves me feeling resolved with Bill's current flowing deep beneath the surface. Amid the hurt, the conflict, the unspoken feelings, I cannot help but feel incredibly grateful to him for creating this place, for sharing his world, his work, all that he had the capacity to share. His presence with us in that round room of his creation with its amber shafts of light, its sawdust-gritty floor, its open door bringing the smell of salt wind from the ocean contained a kind of grace, a blessing, that I will always remember.

Chapter Twelve

A HANDMADE DEATH

—Peter—

I was still wrestling with what it means to craft a handmade life when Bill began to unfold his own handmade death. Five families received the same handwritten note; mine was dated September 28, 2005, asking us to join him at Dickinsons Reach for an important gathering to consider his remaining years and the future of his homestead. *"This is my artwork. This is my statement to the world. I need your help."*

When I got the note Bill had been homesteading at Dickinsons Reach for forty-five years. To put this in perspective, Thoreau's experiment in living in his cabin in the woods at Walden Pond lasted

215

two years, with weekly saunters to the Emersons' dining room table. Bill's consistency in how he lived, and what visibly resulted from five decades of healthy human relationship to the land, is the monumental accomplishment of his life. This was both a physical and an emotional accomplishment: One does not reject the dominant American way once and be done with it; it must be rejected day after day. Bill had to keep swimming against the current, a current that pushed every year harder and harder toward consumption, material accumulation, estrangement from nature, reliance on technologies, and violence in all of its forms.

His philosophy of democratic living is important, and his innovations in design have created and popularized a new form of architecture and given Western culture the word "yurt," but the stamina required to live by his values, his physical merger of deed and creed, is the thing that makes Bill's life so unusual. Many a rebel eventually conformed, if only out of sheer exhaustion. But not Bill. His experiment in living had already surpassed both Henry Thoreau's and Scott Nearing's for its integrity and durability, but not for their visibility. There were moments when Bill referred to himself flatly as "an old man alone out in the puckerbrush."

The biggest disappointment of his life wasn't a lack of visibility but the hard truth that no one else had joined him in his bold experiment. Thousands of people visited over the decades, and there were many conversations about a good friend who was rearranging their lives to soon move to Dickinsons Reach and to add their dreams and labors to his own. But it never happened. I engaged directly with Bill on a few of occasions of high hopes, helping him to think through how to make it work, but the conversations never moved beyond dreams. Lots of things scared people off: the remoteness of the place, the discipline required to live Bill's way, the truth that Bill might not tolerate different interpretations of how best to live there.

Forty years before we built our yurt there at the tide rip, Bill wrote a passionate letter to his friends Chuck and Laurel, inviting them and four others to join him in creating community at Dickinsons Reach.

They were all young, competent people starting out on their lives in their late twenties and early thirties, and Bill was writing to them one of the most important letters of his life: Please join me here, and let's try to make a better world together.

> *Those of us who have similar concerns need to create a community together if we are to have the lives we want for ourselves and our children. I think we need each other if we are to allow ourselves to grow in an optimal way . . . Most of the adults I know are stunted in their intellectual, moral and physical growth. Society just does not provide for that. I feel that for both ourselves and our children we must invest our material and mental wealth in a community—hopefully with the kind of people we admire and respect . . . I'd like to see us build a community here that would be a learning center for ourselves and for all who would come . . . It would be both a home base and an example of a way to live and learn . . . I would like us to spend our lives living not teaching. Learning every moment that we can—from the land, from one another, from visitors— from the world. . . . This is the longest letter I've written you (possibly the longest you will ever get from me) by far the most important I've written in a long time and one I've been waiting to write for years. It would be beautiful to build a community together.*

The six who received this letter in 1973 did not move to Dickinsons Reach. Half of them remained lifelong friends of Bill's, helping him with his dreams, allowing Bill to help raise their kids even, and yet they chose to unfold their own lives apart from his. All of the people to whom Bill wrote this letter believed in him, took him seriously, and loved him, yet none of them accepted his invitation. Perhaps they deeply valued Bill's story and knew there might be little space to share within that story, or perhaps they felt the need to test their hands at making their own unique lives.

Bill wanted a marriage and to share his homestead with a partner, and he did so briefly, marrying a woman named Harue, but the relationship didn't last. The student trips to Mexico and the years teaching at John Woolman School in California were shared with Harue, who wrote of Bill, "He was a mentor to me, as well, challenging me to have useful skills in the world. When we first met at Putney Graduate School, Bill was organizing a group to go down to Venezuela, but he wouldn't accept us because we couldn't 'do' anything, being academics. I learned after that to spin, weave, and homestead. He gave me my first double bitted axe and taught me survival skills which I appreciated . . ." Bill and Harue divorced, and Bill spoke of that chapter in his life only rarely.

On the night before we bought Knoll Farm in 2001, Bill drove the eight hours west to make me an offer to buy the tip of Proctors Point at any price I could afford. I was torn by Bill's determination; I was grateful to be included in his vision and felt a real commitment to

Proctors Point, but I was on fire to start something of our own at Knoll Farm. His dream was not my dream, but I agreed to the deal out of a longing to help both of us. It was a financial obligation that stretched me too much, and a few years later I had to stop making payments, write to Bill, and tell him I wanted out and wanted instead his support and enthusiasm for what we were doing at Knoll Farm.

The notion of a real community there at Dickinsons Reach, or even a family, was one of Bill's most powerful and conflicted longings. I witnessed that longing directly and poignantly each of the many nights when Bill pulled out and read from "the Willy Stories," a series of children's stories that he had written a few decades before when he was of the age to have had his own family there at Dickinsons Reach. They were stories of a young eight-year-old boy named Willy, and his unnamed mother and father, who homesteaded a wild stretch of the down east coast of Maine. Many of the adventures that Bill actually did have with the children of his friends, paddling out to islands, seeing whales, skinning porcupines, building things, scavenging for lumber, became immortalized as Willy Stories. And every time Bill brought these stories out to read, to entertain us, it felt like a ceremony acknowledging a love or a dream unrequited. It felt as if Bill was saying, "Maybe if you hear this story, you will be moved to bring your family here to stay and to make real what I have always dreamed about." Or perhaps they were simply reenactments without expectation of the things he found most exciting and beautiful about living there for fifty years. As his friend, I was more than sympathetic but still unable to help him make that part of his dream come true.

This was the unavoidable truth in 2005 when he wrote us that letter: Bill was seventy-five, living alone, in deteriorating health, and reconsidering his bold experiment in living. He was feeling mortal, that his time was shorter than ever before. High blood pressure made it difficult for him to walk, without frequent rests, from his homestead out to the main road. He had constructed twelve small hammocks in trees to give him resting spots so he could make the walk in or out. He had spoken with several of

us about a fear that he soon would not be able to live at Dickinsons Reach. A few friends quietly offered him our homes as his next destination.

He invited a group of us to join him on that cold fall week in 2005 to get serious about what might come next for him. I didn't know who would be there among the group. Over those decades of life-lived-in-place, many different individuals had come together in various ways to advance Bill's dreams. We knew each other vaguely or well, depending on the situation, often only crossing paths at Dickinsons Reach. Some, like us, knew Bill only in his later life; others were connected since their childhood; and others were connected to him through generations, their parents being students and colleagues of Bill's. But Bill was the hub and the reason that we knew one another. It was unclear exactly who among his many friends Bill would invite for this gathering, but I knew it would be a group important to him.

It had to have been a poignant visit for each of us, though we didn't yet have the relationship to one another to reveal this. We knew there were big questions on Bill's mind: How long could he stay there? What would happen to his work and his homestead after he left? And now Bill was indirectly asking us to consider his mortality. I could not imagine Dickinsons Reach without Bill, but he was requesting us to do that.

And he was asking us to help him have a productive old age. *"There's a beauty to life as long as you keep healthy. That's one of the things I can give you. Life is a great puzzle. Where are the eighty-year-olds on our campuses?"* We asked him and ourselves, how could we keep Bill's work going for another twenty years? And after his passing, how might we keep it alive in ourselves for another fifty years? What needed to change in my own life to carry forward some small piece of Bill's? Of all of Bill's friends, are we the right people to help him, and why? Are we committed to working together over the next decade and then much longer? Though there were so many questions and we talked about a great many things that first meeting, an intention was forming: Bill's lifework is important to each of us, and he needed our help to continue. And we felt a reciprocal need: We each needed Bill's teachings more than ever in our own lives. He asked us to consider this question: How does old age play out in contemporary society where the old are often shut away? How do we hold the fabric of Bill's life so that he might continue to enliven us?

We agreed to meet three months later, and Bill stunned us all then by announcing his desire to transfer his homestead and all the land he owned to this group of six, which would also include himself as an equal owner. And he said he hoped it could happen as fast as we could figure out how best to do it. He wanted us each to have a homestead site at Dickinsons Reach, and he hoped we would each build something there while he was alive to enjoy watching what we would create. Having spoken this powerful intention, he handed us envelopes bequeathing us Dickinsons Reach in his handwriting in the event he died before we could complete the legal work. And then he told us how and where he would like to be buried. In preparing to die, Bill was also preparing us to live.

A few months later we each received a letter from Bill asking us to each make a list of the ten things of his that we would most like after his death. I wrote back saying what I most wanted was time with him now. He and I agreed to do the trip together to Michoacán to search for copper and woodcraft.

Things began to move faster in a world where things hadn't changed for years. Our group of six families met over and over, each of us traveling great distances to meet, posing questions about what would need to shift for us, a group that hardly knew one another, to commit to Bill and to each other. What did Bill most need from us, and what did we need from each other? Could we afford to provide it? Would we be drawn to the place and to one another when Bill is no longer with us?

Slowly and steadily, I saw Bill's dream unfold as an entirely new teaching: How do we live and die today with intention? How do we ask for help, and how do we build community? I left our gatherings feeling more that this is a group of people I was willing to commit to, to speak truthfully to, to be vulnerable with, and with whom to take care of this great friend. But Bill was asking us something more: Will you also take care of what I have cared for?

These were enormous requests that Bill had made of us; if we answered yes to them, we would need to change our lives. I was not sure that I would be drawn to Dickinsons Reach after Bill died and that I could make such a commitment to this group that I hardly knew. For three years we met and wrestled with these questions, sensing what was right for ourselves and for Bill, working out the legal agreements to give us a structure. We found our ways individually, all but one of us, to answer yes. A group of us moved forward, those who could commit to supporting all of Bill's modest financial needs for the rest of his life so that he could focus on the work he felt was most important. We pledged to spend more time at Dickinsons Reach to learn from one another and to build homesteads and a community together. We committed to caring for his health and helping him to stay at his homestead for as long as possible. And if that were no longer possible, he would stay with one of us. We agreed to care for Dickinsons Reach and his lifework as best we could long into the future after he had died. And we wrote and signed a statement of our philosophy and intentions to provide reckoning: to help us remember our course when years later conditions might be murky and turbulent: *"We recognize what a gift it is to learn from one another in this way, and we pledge through the creation of this community to take full advantage of this opportunity to learn from and to help one another grow . . . the creation of this community is an intentional extension of Bill's life-long experiment in living."*

Helen and I were Bill's friends who came relatively late in his life and tested his word the most by accepting his gift of land, and actually building what we thought he most wanted: another presence there at Dickinsons Reach. But through that I learned that this thirst for community that drove Bill wasn't satisfied. Our presence there on his homestead, the new yurt he created, wasn't the heartbeat he most yearned for.

Perhaps we didn't fit perfectly into his dream, perhaps we weren't there enough, perhaps he liked community in idea more than in reality. This is what I know for sure: When our yurt was done and Bill rolled up his sleeping bag and went to his side of the pond, he returned to visit with us in our yurt just once in the two years we had together before he died. It happened about a week after the yurt raising when our family was moving fast, getting our new home and the lumber piles weathertight before a hurricane was forecast to come ashore. It was the calm before the storm: gorgeous, sunny, and blue. I was sitting on our front stairs carving an apple root collected at Knoll Farm to be the knob of our yurt's front door, which Helen was making on sawhorses just inside. I was marveling at and a bit jealous of what Helen had learned to do, when I glanced up the trail that leads from the tide rip to see Bill walking toward us. I had dreamed of this first neighborly visit. After the yurt raising was over I had even taken the old farm bell from Vermont and moved it across the tide rip to Bill's land so that he could easily walk to a spot on his shore and ring that bell for us to come get him in our canoe if he didn't want to paddle. I had thought those things would happen. But Bill wasn't visiting

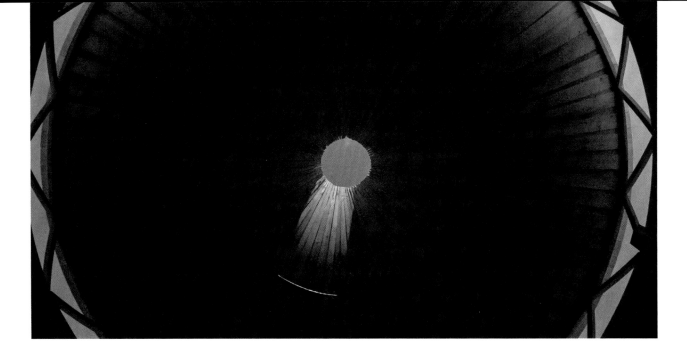

his neighbors so much as visiting his creation. I offered him tea and
sensed he didn't want to talk but to observe, and so we went about our
work in a relaxed silence. After some time he slowly creaked up from
sitting on the floor with his back against the sloped wall and gave each
of us a big hug before walking back down the trail in silence. He never
came back again as a neighbor. He did once or twice come through
with a group on a tour, and I heard he visited a few times to check on
the place when we were gone, but that was the only deep breath he
took with us in our home.

   I am drawn to lineage, to the inheritance of ideas, and to carriers
of wisdom, which is to say that I value respect. I believe that wisdom
is earned through long experience and that it is a gift to receive that
wisdom from others as well as to share it. And when one has worked
hard to earn the respect of someone else, and that respect has been
reciprocated, you have created a lineage with him or her. This lineage
is strong and helpful because it stretches back into the past as well as
long into the future; it creates community and relationship. It makes
our work, our ideas, endure. I had an intense experience of having
answered Bill's call, a call that he had put out for decades, having put
aside many of my own desires for how we would build at Herons Rip,

having surrendered to Bill's own way of doing it, and when it was over, he showed how ambivalent he was about our being there.

I've come to recognize, too, how there is often pain in being in service to wisdom carriers and having someone in your life who you feel is an elder deserving of respect. There is pain that arises from doing something that's not seen or reciprocated, a pain that arises from understanding how one person's wisdom is always incomplete, and there is also pain in understanding how the hardest questions can only be answered by oneself. I have honored Bill as a wisdom carrier for my life and for my family. Where we let each other down was hard to observe, for sure, and it was poignant and real. Sometimes, how he treated me made me feel an imposter to the qualities I most admired in myself, but it also helped me more fully occupy those qualities and make them more my own. Like Helen, who stepped up to build the bedrooms for Wren and Willow, in honoring Bill as an elder I had to figure out how to honor myself and step away from a need for his appreciation and respect.

What did it really mean for Bill to give us his land and homestead? What did that feel like to him? And what was the exchange between Bill and the place itself? What was the real debt between them? Bill became rooted there not just by what he built but also by loss and suffering, defeats, and grief. Though I could never know all the stories, I know there were both seeds and ashes for Bill in this land. I think of him, late in life, traveling the world—Siberia, China, Bhutan—and always returning here after long travels, entering the woods again, walking the trails, seeing his creations, taking his boots off, being home. How does a woman or a man hold up her or his end of the bargain to a place that has sustained and created them? Surely, part of the answer is to hold the place in one's heart and to do everything one can to ensure that it thrives without being hurt by other humans. That's a promise that Bill made and saw fulfilled.

And then it happened. The night of April 11, in his eightieth year, Bill had a heart attack. He was thousands of miles away from his homestead, in Assisi, Italy, getting ready to start construction of a yurt near Rome when he had chest pains bad enough that he allowed himself to be taken to a nearby hospital. The next day, all of us received a short e-mail, dictated to and sent out by Bill's friend Gay, suggesting he'd be back at work on the yurt by the end of the week, but at the end hinting at the reality: *"This is a treacherous path to be on with the end unknown, I love you all and thank you for making my life so rich."* Days later he was transported by ambulance to a medical center in Perugia for quadruple bypass heart surgery. Julie and Peter, among our community, were there within a few days.

At about the same time as I got the e-mail, I was walking up a familiar trail on our farm through a patch of old-growth maple I visit several times a week and found for the first time that a giant 250-year-old maple had crashed down in the night. I knew this would one day happen, but I was still stunned to see the violent fracture and splinters in the base, the giant tree on its side in the ferns, and the glaring opening in the canopy above. I could only stand there and stare. The ecology of that forest had shifted, just as the news from Italy had shifted our lives. I realized then, looking at our own land in Vermont, that if Bill lived I would do everything I could to learn from him, to be with him, to bring my family even closer to him. If Bill lived I would take all the modest savings I had and build a home for my family alongside his. I would make visible this friendship by building his dream into my dream. I would see what seeds we might plant together there on his home ground.

Bill survived, and months later made it back to the United States, traveling slowly across New England being driven by friends only as far as his need for rest would allow. Bill staged himself for weeks at Julie's house, a few hours south, practicing walking longer and longer each day so that he might return to his own place in the world, to his grand experiment in living. On June 15, 2010, he walked back into Dickinsons Reach.

It took a year of slow recovery, but eighteen months later he was atop the roof of our yurt working ten-hour days, designing the yurt in his head in the predawn darkness, sleeping outside among the bugs under a single tarp. The surgery had cleared out his plumbing, and Bill had come back stronger than I had ever seen him. He was thinner, his energy high, and his mind fast and sharp.

"The brain is like a well-honed axe. It works perfectly. I'm at the top of my game right now. But if the axe were a little bit dull, it won't work at all. I want to keep the edge as good as I can. Thinking is one of the great joys in my life right now, and poetry remains a big part of my life. What would life be like if I could no longer remember the poems?"

Shortly after closing in our yurt at the end of forty days of work, I gave Bill a ride into town to a doctor's appointment, and he confided to me that he wasn't sleeping great and that he suspected something to be wrong. There were more tests, and Julie and Peter got Bill to consult other doctors. The community gently gave support to Bill, finding him doctors and listening to their opinions, as the news unfolded over many months that he had cancer.

Bill approached the news as a challenge to be fully understood, then decisions to be made. He would do it his way. He'd skip the hormone therapy and follow the work of the best naturopaths to see if he could throw this beast through nontraditional medicine. Even this direction was extremely expensive, far more costly than Bill spent in an entire year, so Bill offered to build a yurt for his Chicago doctor in exchange for the treatments. The doctor agreed.

Around this time, when Bill was swallowing about seventy-five supplements a day, I visited him to help with a project surveying his land for a swap he hoped to do with a neighbor. It was October, and the sun was setting early in the afternoon. We started with lots of time to spare, but everything took longer than expected. We had a hard time finding boundaries. Bill was sure we were in the right place, but the landmarks weren't to be found. For this first time in my relationship with Bill, I saw him faltering, being confused, and taking bearings over and over, and second-guessing himself. He was disoriented. As the sun was setting and our job not half done, I suggested to Bill that we stop and head back home. He reluctantly agreed, and we looked at each other to say, which way is home? We had been in a thick forest of fir and spruce without any sense of where the sun was for more than three hours. It was easy to get turned around. Bill started off in one direction, but I had the compass and knew home was not that way. I called out, "Bill, follow me," and realized that I had never said those words before.

When we got home and settled in after some food, Bill told me a story as if to reveal to me some new truths about his life. A few months before, some friends had visited in a sailboat and had anchored in deep water out beyond the tide rips. They rowed in to visit Bill with their young son, who wanted to spend the night in the magical yurt. The parents returned to their boat. The next morning Bill paddled the boy back out to the sailboat, still at anchor in Moose Snare Cove. It was pea soup foggy, but a simple journey that Bill must have made a thousand times in all kinds of weather. Just keep the land to your left, and you'll be fine. Bill and the boy had some fun finding the sailboat in the fog by shouting out from canoe to boat, and they connected up fine. Bill stayed aboard for just a few minutes before announcing that he had work to do back home.

The route from the sailboat to the far shore to the tide rip that Bill would follow home was not much more than a mile. I can imagine Bill standing in the stern, the fog thick, and the ocean green and so calm Bill could have felt his way home by listening to his strokes echoing off the shore. But he never reached the shore. After fifteen minutes he realized something must be wrong, and he started to concentrate and look hard into the fog. He had no compass. Five more strokes, and he would certainly see the shore. No shore. A half hour more, no shore. Here was an eighty-two-year-old in a canoe lost somewhere in the fog in Little Kennebec Bay on a Monday morning. Surely he would hear a lobster boat or get some other indication of where he was. The map of this bay was part of his body, and he knew both shorelines intimately. All he had to do was find one of them, and he'd be fine. After thirty minutes of finding no shore, Bill realized he was somehow going in circles and threw out his stern line and watched it as he paddled to make sure he was going straight.

This helped, and within ten minutes he could hear the shore, then see it in and out of the fog. Okay, that had been a fun hour, and he rather enjoyed the intellectual challenge this had presented him, but now he really needed to get home, so he turned his canoe in the direction of home, with the shore on his right, and paddled to the tide rips. Just as he was relaxing into the list of things he wanted to do that morning, his mind triggered the feeling that something was wrong yet again, that he should have reached the tide rips.

Bill paddled for another thirty minutes before coming to a beach. He was by then completely disoriented. What the hell was a beach doing there? He felt he had to be just strokes away from his own tide rips when, in fact, he was three miles in the opposite direction, on the opposite shore near the mouth of the bay and the open ocean. Had he kept going, and likely missed Hickey Island, we would have never seen him again.

All of us were considering never seeing him again; we knew that it was inevitable. Every time I walked down Bill's trail last year, there was

a part of me that grew anxious and braced myself to find him not alive and was always overjoyed to be wrong, and to give him a big hug. Bill must have sensed those thoughts in us, too. We had all kinds of evidence that he was preparing for his death coming soon, finishing his yurt, signing various legal papers, and that seemed to relax him in a way that enhanced his health, made him stronger and more alive than we had seen him all year. He was vigorous and full of laughter and enthusiasm.

At our last gathering of the Dickinsons Reach community that Bill was part of, he asked what he could do for us. "I have a question," he said. "All of our conversations have been about me, but what I can do for you?" Julie asked Bill to visit her family more, and Dan suggested they travel up the Pacific Coast again, meeting all their carver friends. I offered that I was ready to begin work with him on two different book projects, one about all the different things from chairs to buildings that were "made by Bill," and there was the book about building our family yurt with him; was he ready to work with me on those?

We made plans to do all these things, and given his strength and vigor, we expected they would happen. He was planning another trip to Mexico, too, and had a big concentric yurt to start working on with Josh in the spring. He returned to a familiar theme that I had heard many times before but that I copied in my notebook for the first time: "Seeking and searching are everything right now for me. I have not given up the search. Don't stop searching yourselves."

Bill spoke about his own death. "I want it all to end as simply as possible and for those who come together to celebrate. I'm the richest person I know. There's not a book I can't find, not a tool I don't have, and all this fertile land dropped on me. I would like to be composted with a bush planted on me . . . something you can eat. Don't burn me. Now Scott [Nearing] wanted to be burned, but not me. If I had been braver, I would have burned up Scott there on the beach at Orrs Cove. I want to go back to nature in a hole in the ground. Put rocks on me, and if the ground is too frozen put me in a fairing and burn the boat and let me sink to the ocean floor."

Chapter Thirteen

THE LAST YURT

—Helen—

I want a lodge that is round like the day and
the sun and the path of the stars. I want a lodge
that is like the good things that have no end.

— HAL BORLAND

What Bill said was that he wanted to build a small studio yurt near his house, a single story, full of natural light, just big enough for a bed and a desk and a single chair. At first he described this building as a painting studio for the woman he loved—an artist by the name of Gay who lived in Italy and with whom he had spent a couple of winters, the last one recuperating at her house after his heart attack. Bill had hoped for many years that Gay would come to make a life with him in Maine. When that longed-for love faded in the last years of his life, he talked about the small yurt as a studio for guests or so that guests could use his house when they came and he could have his own space there among the maples. He even hinted at someone coming to live permanently in one of the dwellings, and that this place would "open up new possibilities." What he said is that he had always wanted to test out his design for a roof that was twisted from eaves to central ring—a "tortured plywood" roof.

What he didn't say was that he had fallen down the stairs of his big yurt one night when he was all alone. That he was scared of what a recent diagnosis of prostate cancer might do to his strength or any treatments might do to his balance. That he wanted to make a place where he could spend his last days, close to the site he had chosen to be buried. That he didn't want to have to leave home. Or be a burden to anyone. Or vulnerable. Or afraid.

That day in August the summer before Bill died, when I and four other women—Kim, Rani, Julie, and Sarah—helped him raise the tortured roof was the only time I've ever seen Bill look afraid. He was standing on a frail scaffolding in the center of the structure, and I was looking up at him from where I stood beneath the half-raised roof, one hand on part of the heavy plywood section immediately above my head and the other hand on a long pole that braced the part of the slab that was too high to reach. Next to me were Kim and Sarah doing the same thing with two other sections. One was balanced for now, precariously, on two poles that ran down to the ground. Rani was on the perimeter with hammer in hand, waiting for a signal to make it more secure. In his two large knuckley hands Bill was holding together the upper edge

of four sections of the roof—huge, heavy plywood slabs with metal brackets at top and bottom where they would be fastened into the metal rim of the skylight on one edge and the top of the walls at the other.

What made this roof unlike any that Bill had built before was the way the plywood had been twisted; each 4×6 plywood section of the roof met at right angles to the next at the rim of the building, making triangular windows all the way around. Then, as each section twisted 90 degrees, it flattened as it went up the roof, so that by the time it reached the skylight the slabs met in a flat plane. Bill had made many roofs where the boards met at right angles at the eaves, but he usually tapered the boards and laid them flat so that there was another, smaller triangle in a rim around the skylight. I loved that design myself, but Bill wanted to try something new, and although he had made paper models and worked hard on the design, the actual construction required some spontaneous mental brilliance. What he hadn't seemed to predict is how hard it would be to wrestle these huge, heavy sections into place at the upper edge, with nothing but their tension against one another to hold them up, and how disastrous it could be if one fell on one of us with our necks exposed a few feet below.

"Hold that thing up as if your life depends on it," he barked down at us, and he meant it. Little by little we worked our way around, holding the sections and trying to secure them by nailing into the metal brackets at the edge, then turning a bolt into a long metal bar at the top edge to marry each pair. It was cumbersome and wobbly, the plywood slabs stiff and slippery and, I worried, trying to spring back into their non-twisted state. The sections met at top and bottom but flexed out and left huge gaps in the middle of the roof. It seemed improbable. Maybe even impossible. Definitely not democratic. I wondered if Bill was losing it.

Like all the other buildings at Bill's homestead, this one had been a communal effort from the beginning. Tony and Becky, friends from Alaska who were visiting Bill for the first time, helped him dig the holes for the foundation, draining the water as they dug down through the stubborn gray clay. They had felled cedar trees and trimmed the branches from them, then cut them down to length and set the posts. Peter Lamb spent days with Bill, helping him work out a paper model of the roof to get it right and later made in his home forge the custom metal brackets that would hold the roof to the walls. Mike figured out what kind of metal would bend over the curves of the roof, Julie helped order it, and someone else paddled it in from Duck Cove. Peter and Dorn brought the plywood up to Tim's to make the prototype that became the roof.

Anyone who was up to visit got pulled in to help. Bill needed all of us for this one, that was clear; we were helping him build something where he would be less vulnerable, more prepared for what he saw coming. But these thoughts he kept mostly to himself.

When Bill's community gathered that August, the walls and floor were up. The roof was the next, and by far the hardest, step. The roof sections were stacked and lying on the dirt floor in Bill's woodshop, but they needed to be raised and fitted together like giant puzzle pieces. Bill talked about it casually at breakfast. Some folks wanted to paddle out to Hickey Island and make a day of exploring the coast. Bill was lining up volunteers for his roof raising, and it turned out to be a nice change of custom that the men went with the kids and the women tackled the building project with Bill. I had no idea it would turn out to be such a long, hot, epically challenging day.

To me this was an odd building all around. It looked less like a circular structure than any of his other buildings due to the fact that it was laid out in just eleven sections on a ten-foot base. Eleven? Why not the sacred geometric twelve? And its relatively small base with steep roof, no overhang, and wide skylight made it look like an awkward relative next to Bill's other buildings, whose remarkable grace was so much in their balance of proportion. On top of this he wanted to cover the plywood roof with bright red tin and the walls with horizontal lapstrake boards (one overlapping the next). The door was to be only four feet high, if that: a hobbit hole. The door could have perhaps been taller, except for the cable that had to run around the entire circumference at the top of the wall to hold it all together. So Bill had the idea that we would excavate some earth under the door so that you climbed up into it, the wall slanting outward above you, and were less likely to hit your head on the frame.

The oddity of this yurt propelled me into the world of design. I wanted to know how Bill designed, what went on in his head, why eleven sides, why such a departure in proportions, how did one possibly calculate the math required in a roof of tortured ply? Even our own yurt had been just a drawing to me, and although I felt at the end that I might have the skills to build another one, I had no idea how to design one. How would I calculate even the most basic parts, such as how many boards I would need for a circular roof made with two layers that overlapped more at one end than the other? If you actually sat down to design a wooden yurt, it wasn't as simple as you thought. They *looked* simple, but the eyes deceive.

The day after we managed to complete the roof, leaving the crazy oval-shaped gaps in between the panels to solve for another day, I asked Bill to sit down with me and explain how he thought about design. I wanted to know how his quest for simplicity and his love of design danced together, if there was a tension between them. It was hot, and Bill sat shirtless in his workshop across the table from me.

"Why eleven sides?" I began.

"Well, I started with twelve, but if it has twelve the roof angles are steeper than I wanted. We decided to flatten it out a bit."

"Why not just use smaller roof panels?" I asked.

"Well, I had this standard plywood and I wanted to use the full width to get big windows and the full length. I based the roof on the plywood, and the fact that I had a five-foot piece of glass I wanted to use up."

"So you designed this building around the materials, not the other way around?"

"Pretty much."

This, to me, said a lot about Bill. His mind bent toward the experimental, but he was also stubbornly practical. He embodied the Yankee sensibility of "if it ain't broke, don't change it," and "make use of what you have." He loved materials of all kinds—wood, metal, bone, leather, wool, even Kevlar and plastic and adhesives—and no doubt his quest after new designs could be bold and ambitious, but I heard him speak most fondly of the really simple yurts he did, the pole yurt of maple

236

saplings and birch bark coverings. Maybe if he had lived even longer he would have gone back to building nests out of found materials. Or who knows, maybe he would have us all hauling in steel beams and glass. I really don't know.

What I do know is that as Bill aged he wasn't calcifying or slowing down or becoming more predictable; he may have been building a place for a caretaker to live to help him get by in his dotage, but by God it was going to be a complicated structure that stretched the limits of what he thought he could do. It was a way that he could stay focused and creative in the face of a cancer diagnosis that was scaring the hell out of him. He didn't want to feel himself start to slip, and his doctor has said that some of the forms of treatment he was considering could do that, that he might feel depressed, or frail, or too tired to do much. The yurt challenged him mentally; he would forget what stage he was at and how to improvise next, given all the steps involved. And yet he persevered. This little building close to the ground, full of light, though not simple in a structural sense, represented to him a further move toward the simplification of his life, a way he could stay independent as long as possible on his beloved home ground.

In the last letter Bill wrote to me, a few days before his accident, he said that the red tin roof was up, the windows were screwed in, and that Margaret had come to help him paint the ceiling a beautiful light yellow. He spent a long time thinking about that color and asking people's opinions. On the inside of the walls he nailed a lovely red-grained maple that had been stored in his lumber shed for decades. And he wrote about trying to find a glass stove so he could watch the firelight. Another friend, Josh, would be bringing his family out after Thanksgiving to help him build and install the door.

The day before we put his body in the ground in the grove of maples, many of us found ourselves making a circle on the floor in Bill's last yurt, a Peruvian wool blanket he had tacked over the door swaying slightly in the cold winter wind. I took in the red-grained boards and the lemon-yellow ceiling, the circle of bare-branched trees tossing against the steely sky. I thought of Bill standing up there conducting us on that hot summer day just a few months before, conducting what would be his last composition. Then I realized that we needed to conduct the last; that the final piece of music, his requiem, was to be all of us carrying his body home.

All that day, as we dug the grave and finished the casket, prepared the boats and kept fires burning, people stopped in at the last yurt to visit, to pick up a tool and blunt an overhanging sharp edge of tin so no one passing would cut themselves, or put away some of the scraps and tools lying around. The children picked up all the ends of boards and made kindling for a fire near the grave; we cut a path around the building and into the woods for the casket to pass; someone made little leather washers for some of the screws around the windows to tighten them better against the wind. Everyone was caring for the last yurt as a way of caring for Bill. It felt good to put our hands on his tools, to do what he would have wanted, had he

been there, for us to do.

Later, after the ocean crossing with Bill's body, I saw as the casket was carried up the hill that others had sprinkled sawdust all along the new path to brighten the way. Our procession paid homage to his last creation before laying him down to rest. As we passed I was glad the door was still open to the wind and rain, a low door that requires bowing your head to enter, a door open to possibilities. Bill would have liked that.

EPILOGUE

—Peter—

S hortly after Scott Nearing died, his wife Helen had a visit from him in the form of a great blue heron. That October morning in 1983 a heron flew down into their homestead on Cape Rosier in Penobscot Bay and spent the better part of a day walking about the fruit trees and gardens alongside Helen before flying away.

We've had no such experience of Bill's returning to visit after his death, but in the last six months many people have chosen to tell me stories about the great blue heron. It turns out that most cultures within this bird's range have a similar fable about the heron. Some stories emphasize its vanity or its grace or its cunning, and all of them center on its solitary nature. One story explains in detail the sadness and tension the heron feels between the wisdom that arises from its solitary nature and the need to break that solitude in order to share the vision. Only the great blue heron, this fable goes, has the ability to go off into solitude and receive a vision, but it's a vision that must be carried out by the people. His sadness arises from knowing the importance of the vision he carries and the challenge of translating that wisdom for others.

In the moment of his death Bill was alone, but he has not been alone since, and there are many people translating the wisdom they received from him into their own lives. The community that he brought together, and many others who were close to him, fulfilled his wishes for how he would be buried. Some are continuing now to build community through yurt raisings, others are producing his annual calendar, and thinking about how his tools can be used to inspire and encourage others, and considering how to share more widely his ideas and unpublished papers. Many hundreds of people gathered in four separate celebrations of his life, reflecting the diversity of people and communities who drew inspiration from him. The five families who came to share

Dickinsons Reach with Bill took a pledge to care for that land and for Bill's lifework, and Helen and I will do our part to embody and honor that commitment. At Herons Rip, our homestead across the tidal pond from Bill's, we will be planting fruits trees this spring, and I am never far away from thoughts of what it will be like to grow old there.

About two months after we buried him, Helen and I got the news that the organization we founded and transitioned out of leadership of wouldn't be running programs at Knoll Farm for the first time in more than a decade. These two unmistakable messages were about the closing of a chapter in our lives and a demand of us both that we reconsider what matters most to us. The response from my own heart was intuitive: Let's invite everyone back who had come to Knoll Farm over the years, let's build a yurt together, and let's celebrate Bill's life through our own.

If the greatest gift that Helen Nearing gave me was the introduction to Bill Coperthwaite, then one great gift that Bill gave me was the introduction to Dan Neumeyer. Dan spent summers with Bill as a child, alone without his parents, and is now a designer and builder in the Pacific Northwest. For twenty years Dan and I have been friends through Bill, and now our friendship has no need of a bridge; it simply stands on its own. Dan answered my call and brought his son, Ravi, to live with us for a month to guide the creation of a small yurt atop one of the springs on our farm. We extended an invitation to every person across the country that had been to a program at our farm over the last dozen years; we would welcome them back, feed them, let them enjoy this place, and for those who were interested, we would build something new together.

The concentric yurt at Herons Rip was the last such yurt built with Bill, and this yurt at Knoll Farm was the first built without him. Almost seventy-five people came for a day or longer, some for a week, as we worked and lived together for two weeks shaping something inspired by Bill but far more than Bill. We envisioned a small, round building constructed over a one-hundred-year-old square foundation that housed our spring, where people could sit, face each other, look down into an open center in the floor, and consider water, the source of life. It would have Dan's own sense of beauty and grace, and we would build it in our own way. We'd use power tools but keep them restricted to the shop so that we could still hear the birds sing and have conversations as we created together. On the very first day, as we placed round stones from Bill's beach in Maine into our spring in Vermont, Dan said, "Don't be mistaken; we can't build this place just the way Bill did. We will do it our way with our skills."

Most of the people who picked up a saw or a hammer and joined us in building the Water Temple Yurt didn't know one another and had never used those tools before. They came from Brooklyn and Boston, from New York and New Hampshire and California. I realized as the days unfolded how this building project was a giant spoon that we had been carving: creating something beautiful together that none of us could do alone. Wendy Johnson, a friend from Muir Beach and Green Gulch Zen Center who had been one of our founding teachers and among the very first to come to Knoll Farm and Center for Whole Communities a decade before, returned on the last day of the yurt raising, which was also the night of the August full moon, to help us dedicate the moment and the building.

As Steve played his violin Wendy led us in a silent walk from the barn up through tall grasses to a delicate, round structure made of wood and intention. She asked us to circle it and to place our hands on the cedar shakes of the conical roof. Facing one another, this creation between us, as a full moon rose over the Northfield Range, I told everyone that it didn't matter that most gathered there had never met Bill. This experience was not about him. It was about us and what we do with all the things we have been taught in our lives. I asked everyone gathered in the moonlight to consider who have been their real teachers and mentors, and who looked to them today for help and guidance. What are the implications to oneself and to society when we honor our elders and teachers? How will we make space in our lives to help someone else, and to be helped in our own journey? What does it ask of each of us to be in relationship with someone different from oneself long enough to learn and grow from each other?

Bill's death has asked me to step more into my own life. In my grief the day after we buried him, I spent a full day photographing every inch of his home, his yurts, his summer kitchen, and his boathouse and, back at Knoll Farm in a creative frenzy of late nights and early mornings, produced a book of those images called *The Way It Was*, which I sent to all the families in the Dickinsons Reach community. Perhaps right then, just days after burying him, my intent through the photography was to make sure we knew how Bill had left his place so that we could do a better job of preserving it exactly as it was. Months later, having both grieved his death and celebrated his life, I see that book of images quite differently: If we had a record of the way it was, perhaps, we could let it all go.

While I want the four-story round home and his libraries and his tools, and the unmistakable smell of his sweat and cedar, to be there for a very long time for the sake of my children and others' children, so that Bill's presence on the land might continue to inspire them, what I want most now is the clarity and strength to take the wisdom he gave me and make it more real in my own life. I want to thank Bill and then gnaw my own bone. I want to offer encouragement to others. I do not want Dickinsons Reach to become a museum with things placed out of touch or under glass. Instead, I want to know how all of us, those in the Dickinsons Reach community and those just now finishing reading this book, will support one another's aspirations to walk with beauty and nonviolence, to make our own refuges for others, and to live with our own values front and center even with the inevitable contradictions that suggest we aren't perfect. It would be okay with me if, twenty-five years from now, at the end of a long 1.5-mile trail, there is only a bench and a plaque that says "Here, on this spot, lived an unusual man who changed the way a great many others live . . ."

This is the hardest part to write and to live up to: May they continue walking down the trail to come upon a new heartbeat, a homestead created by a young family there on the land, playing, working, loving one another, designing and making a better world. Let his round buildings return to the earth along with his body. Let us build new ones in our own way with the vision he shared, to be translated and shaped by many hands.

Acknowledgments

Sometimes the hardest part of telling a story is acknowledging to yourself that you have a story to tell, and we credit Bill with giving us encouragement to see that. It was difficult to step forward within the Dickinsons Reach community and to say, "We would like to tell a story about our relationship with Bill," because there are others who knew Bill longer, who could tell that story and probably tell it better. In telling our story we risk defining a story. We risk exposing other stories before their time. It was Bill who spoke up first to these concerns by saying, "If Peter and Helen are exposing anybody, they are exposing themselves." We hope this is true, that what this story reveals most is about ourselves and our relationship to a man who shaped our lives. We hope that by stepping forward to share our story, we might inspire others to tell theirs.

We want to give our thanks to that private group of individuals who have shared the closest holding and care of Bill's life and legacy, our fellow members of the Dickinsons Reach community and their families: Peter Lamb and Faith Harrington, Julie and Tom Henze, Dorn and Sarah Cox, and Dan Neumeyer and Elise Miller. Standing closely beside them is a wider circle of Bill's community who helped us tell this story, either by reading and commenting on the manuscript or by lending perspective on Bill's life, some of them having known him since he was a young man: JoAnna Allen, Rani Arbo, Sonni Chamberland, Laurel and Chuck Cox, Scott Kessel, Anne Panarese, John Saltmarsh, Michael Sacca and Elizabeth Billings, and Taz Squire.

This book has been significantly and positively influenced by a few colleagues who were kind enough to read a half-baked story early in our writing process. We are deeply indebted to Hank Lentfer, John Elder, Wendy Johnson, and Scott Russell Sanders, who gave us critical insights that we could not see and the encouragement to go further with our understanding of Bill and ourselves. Many other readers followed, including several who appear in the book and to whom we are grateful not just for their improvements and corrections but for their encouragement and graciousness in seeing a story told.

Every book is more than its words on the page, and the space it occupied in our lives, immediately following Bill's death, was protected and supported by friends and family. For giving us the space and quiet of their home for writing retreats, we give a deep bow of thanks to Megan Gadd and Nathan Wilson and to Joe and Carol Wishcamper. For moral support and for giving us time we needed away from work on the farm, we want to thank Eddie Merma and Coco O'Connor. To Willow and Wren, we are indebted for their patience, self-sufficient natures, belief, and love.

It is our good fortune that this book landed with Chelsea Green. Our editor, Brianne Goodspeed, guided it through the process with clarity, kindness, and a keen sense of story and nuance that has undoubtedly made this a stronger book. We are very grateful to her, to Margo Baldwin for believing in this project from the first, and to art director Pati Stone for her critical role in bringing the book into its final form.

Finally, the writing of this book was a journey. What a gift it was to make the long trek together from grief, loss, and hurt to the liberation of understanding and a deep sense of what will persist as real and strong from Bill's life and our own.

Chronology of a Life

September 19, 1930   William Sherman Coperthwaite is born in Monticello, Aroostook County, Maine.

1935   Bill moves to South Portland, Maine.

1949–1954   Bill attends and graduates from Bowdoin College.

1952–1953   Bill spends a year at the University of Innsbruck, Austria. Bill meets Lise Cérésole, Pierre's wife, at one of their work camps in Italy.

1954   Bill begins graduate work at Putney Graduate School.

1955   Bill has an appendectomy and a long hospital stay in Mexico. He sends "Dear Viv" letter to his sister, explaining his choice to be a contentious objector.

1956   Bill graduates from Putney Graduate School.

1956   "I went to Mexico with AFSC as a conscientious objector to do village development work."

1957–1958   Bill is teacher of elementary subjects at North Country School, New York State.

1958   Bill's father dies.

1958–1959   Bill is teacher of math and biology at Stockbridge School in Western Massachusetts.

1959 (Sept)–1960 (May)
Bill works for the Venezuelan government to produce "An Approach to Rural Community Development in Venezuela."

1959   Bill's house in Steuben, Maine, is sold to finance first purchase of Dickinsons Reach.

1960 (Nov. 25)   Bill buys the Mill Pond parcel of what becomes Dickinsons Reach.

1960–1961   Bill is "trying to get team together" to start a school at Dickinsons Reach.

1961   Bill builds A-frame with log base near Mill Pond as the first shelter at Dickinsons Reach.

1961–62/'62–'63   Bill teaches and builds yurts at The Meeting School in Rindge, New Hampshire. The students and Bill played with the yurt idea with sticks in the woods at The Meeting School.

1963 (Oct. 16)   Bill meets Helen and Scott Nearing for the first time.

1963–1964   Bill is a teacher of Spanish, crafts, and Mexico study trips at John Woolman School in Grass Valley, California. He and his students build the first pole yurt.

1964   Bill builds pole yurt at Dickinsons Reach.

1964   Bill builds center of first concentric yurt, his home until Library Yurt is built, later becomes Guest Yurt.

1964   In midsummer Bill takes a group of Woolman School students from California to Dickinsons Reach and back to California. They visit his contacts in Arizona, New Mexico, and Kentucky and visit Scott and Helen Nearing, Richard and Evelyn Gregg, Grand Manan Island, an organic dairy in Vermont, a Doukhobor community, Argenta Friends School, Paula Simmons, and a spinner near Puget Sound, then head back to Berkeley. While in Bucks Harbor, they build the center of the Guest Yurt at Dickinsons Reach.

1964   In fall and winter Bill studies at Museum of International Folk Art in Santa Fe.

1965   Bill builds lapstrake double-wall yurt with sod roof at Cox Farm in Plaistow, New Hampshire.

1965 (spring)–1966 (summer)

Bill takes trip to Scandinavia: Lapland, Finland, Norway. On this trip he first meets Wille Sundqvist.

1966 (fall)   Bill works in North Carolina for the federal government's War on Poverty and presents Project Mountain Sage, linking elderly and children for the North Carolina Fund.

1967   Nelson Proctor sells "Proctors Point" to Bill.

1967 (Jan–Aug)   Bill constructs a "barrel yurt" for Niilo Koponen, on Chena Ridge on the outskirts of Fairbanks. Bill and Laurel Cox drive down the Alcan Highway from Fairbanks in the early summer of 1967 to Lander, Wyoming, where they spend the month at the National Outdoor Leadership School with Paul Petzoldt. The trip goes into the Wind River Range and summits Gannet Peak.

1968–1971   Bill is at Harvard's Graduate School of Education; during this time he leads the building of a school campus of many yurts for the Study, Travel, Community School in New Hampshire. He builds the second concentric yurt in New Hampshire and a standard yurt at Cox Farm in Plaistow, New Hampshire. He also builds the Harvard Yurt.

1970 (fall)–1971 (spring)

Bill presents an Eskimo Traveling Museum, which was Bill's dissertation at Harvard, through many remote Native Alaskan communities.

1971   Bill receives doctorate in education from Harvard University.

1971 (fall)–1972 (spring)

Bill teaches at UMass Amherst and builds the first concentric yurt there on the campus.

1972   Bill earns $50,000 in sale of yurt plans from article in *Money's Worth*; he finances many of the buildings at Dickinsons Reach.

1973–1974   Bill lives for two months in the cliff dwellings of Cedar Mesa as a potential alternative homesteading site to Dickinsons Reach when Machias is threatened with a major port development project. He returns to Fairbanks, Alaska, to build yurts for the Friends community there.

February 28, 1975   Bill's mother, Lillian Coperthwaite, dies.

1975 (summer)   Bill builds the first West Virginia yurt, a fifty-four-foot tricentric yurt, at the Woodlands Mountain Institute.

1976   In his year in Japan Bill builds a yurt at the School for the Blind. Upon his return, he builds the first concentric yurt at Spruce Hill in the Adirondacks. Bill builds his Library Yurt with the help of Earlham College students.

1977   Bill and his team build yurts on an island in the Anacostia River in Washington DC for the Children's Park Project.

1982   Bill and his team build a yurt for Camp Jabberwocky on Martha's Vineyard for performance space.

1986   Bill goes to New York City to help train the first instructors of the NYC Outward Bound Center in craftsmanship.

1988   Bill builds a standard yurt for Helen Nearing at her Forest Farm on Cape Rosier, Maine.

1988–1992   Bill and his team teach five-day teacher in-service courses for Baltimore, Maryland, teachers.

1989   Bill builds three yurts in Assisi, Italy.

1990   Bill designs and builds Alma Ata, the first thirty-eight-foot free-span yurt at Woodlands Mountain Institute in West Virginia.

1993   Bill and Dan make trip to Siberia to study handcrafts. Peter and Bill meet at Forest Farm in July.

1999   Bill teaches at West Virginia Scholars program at Woodlands Mountain Institute.

2003   Maine Coast Heritage Trust buys conservation easement over Bill's land, protecting it for future generations and getting him necessary money for his elder years.

2003   PBS films *Colonial Village* film across Moose Snare Cove.

2004   Bill builds forty-foot-diameter bamboo yurt in Arunachal Pradesh, India.

2004 (June)   Bill makes a four-week trip to China to research crafts.

2005   Bill convenes the Dickinsons Reach community with idea of giving us his

land in exchange for our supporting his life and work over the rest of his life.

2007   Bill takes a trip to Michoacán, Mexico, to revisit his rural development work.

2007 (Sept)   Bill builds a concentric yurt in Michigan as a spiritual center.

2008   A corporation is signed among six families that creates the Dickinsons Reach community.

2008   Bill and his team build a concentric yurt in Celo, North Carolina, returning Bill to his 1966 War on Poverty sites; it helps fund his and Peter Lamb's Bhutan trip to study crafts.

2009 (Aug)   A new pole yurt is built by the land group to replace the 1963 pole yurt.

April 9, 2010   Bill suffers a heart attack in Assisi, Italy, and has major heart surgery in Italy.

June 15, 2010   Bill walks back into Dickinsons Reach.

2011 (May)   Bill returns to Spruce Knob and Franklin, West Virginia, for conference and reunion with Woodlands Mountain Institute staff.

2011   Bill gives all of his land to the Dickinsons Reach community, whose primary members are six families, including Bill.

2011   Peter and Helen build at Herons Rip, formerly Proctors Point, at Dickinsons Reach. Bill and JoAnna Allen do a six-week study trip to China.

2013 (spring)   Bill begins his Studio Yurt.

November 26, 2013   Bill dies in a car accident in Washington, Maine.

Image Notes

—Peter—

Frontispiece Early dawn in summer, bow pointed west across the pond to the tide rip and our homestead.

Preface This is a detail of a beautiful portrait made of Bill by Abbie Sewall in 1986, when Bill was 56. Bill's hands always looked much older than his face.

xii This hand-carved bowl made of willow and adorned with an Emily Dickinson quote was a gift to Bill from Wille Sundqvist, the famed Swedish master craftsman.

3 The morning before Bill's burial, Kenneth rests after putting the final touches on Bill's casket.

5 At the beach at Duck Cove, we wrap Bill in his favorite blanket and close the lid of his casket.

6 Rounding Johnsons Point with Bill, the sun comes out, and I look back to see Dan and Taz standing in the bow as Bill would have stood.

7 This picture of us paddling Bill home in the middle of the tidal pond was taken by Kenneth from high atop a spruce tree.

9 This image was taken in 1995 on an early visit to Dickinsons Reach. Bill loved to take visitors out onto the water before dawn to see and feel his home come alive.

14 On this particular occasion Bill was hunting porcupines and waiting for one to come down a tree so he could capture and make a meal of it.

15 Lunch Rock, which Bill and friends split by making a seam and freezing water in it, was then placed in the best spot in which to enjoy lunch. This is the place we come to when canoeing across Little Kennebec Bay that tells us we've made it home to Dickinsons Reach.

17 This image, found on a roll of film in a Leica camera with no self-timer, must have been taken by a ghost that wanted me to have a memory of the afternoon that I spent sitting beside the tree that killed Helen Nearing.

20 Late afternoon winter light is always the hardest to capture well but is so evocative to me of what Bill's experience there must have been like for long periods of every year.

22, top Wren is leaping for joy in the sunset on the beach at Hickey Island.

22, middle Bill's first-floor shop in the Library Yurt was often the gathering place where we made spoons and bowls, examined a new tool, or just sat and talked with visitors.

22, bottom Kindly setting up a warm place close by his woodstove, Bill gave Wren her first bath at Dickinsons Reach in a copper bowl made by the Nunzo brothers of Michoacán, Mexico.

24 Summer fog, Willow and Wren on the bridge to the summer kitchen and Mill Pond. Here Bill dammed the fresh water to create a place for the kids to bathe, wash off the tidal mud, and search for coins Bill tossed in.

25 Early morning winter light on Bill's desk on the second floor of his yurt. Here he loved to sit by the stove and catch up on correspondence.

26 Bill's cache yurt and a fine example of how he gardened a forest, selecting and encouraging even-aged maples to grow so that he would have the perfect woodlot in his nineties. Bill's stacking of wood was an ever-changing form of art on the land, something I never tired of photographing.

27 Always the conversation would turn to what was happening on the bay, and Bill would roll out his giant tabletop map of Dickinsons Reach covered with USGS maps, and we'd plan adventures out to islands, measure distances, talk through conservation efforts. Later, we'd eat dinner atop the map and the conversations would continue.

29 An image taken quickly of Bill's bare arm as he showed me something across on the tidal flats of Moose Snare Cove has become a visual symbol to me of his thirst.

30 An early morning view in February across Mill Pond from Bill's homestead to ours. The tide is rising and the ice breaking up.

32 Bill rarely lit campfires; perhaps he thought them a waste of good wood, and certainly they could be a danger in a dry summer, but on this night Bill allowed one down by his shore. It was Helen's first night at Dickinsons Reach, and I like to think Bill made the fire to welcome her.

33 Early morning in summer on Mill Pond. When I first met Bill we spent a great deal of time just like this: Bill standing in the stern of his twenty-foot canoe with me in the bow, turning occasionally to make an image of him.

34 Sawing wood on a cold winter morning was one of Bill's favorite activities. On this occasion we were cutting rounds of birch to make enough spoons for Bill to buy a car. He called that car his spoon car.

36 Late summer afternoon light always drew my full attention in Bill's yurt as so much beauty was revealed. Here Bill's collection of axes rests after a day of felling trees. Bill's summer washbasin is to the left.

39 This could easily be an image of Dickinsons Reach in the very early days of European settlement, perhaps 1809, just before the tide mill would have been built across the rip shown in the middle of this image. But it's actually a picture I made in 2003 with an old Rolleiflex medium-format camera of a movie set that was created on the Passamaquoddy land across from Proctors Point. Here the PBS series *Colonial Village*, which was an early "reality" television show about people living in precolonial times, was filmed. Ironically, the producers had no contact with Bill, who was living a real precolonial life just half a mile away. Bill gave the actors meals and conversation when they could no longer stand the "reality" that was being filmed. Our homestead, Herons Rip, is the forested land on the far shore.

42 There were times like this when we tried to leave, or enter, Mill Pond against the tide, which could only be done by getting out of the canoe and lining it through the rip by pulling the canoe against the tide. In this image the tide is about half out, and Bill can walk the shore. In another few hours the water would have dropped twelve feet, and lining the canoe would be treacherous.

44 Digging out the old well was one of the hardest and most fun jobs I've had so far in the creation of our homestead. Bill's encouragement that we could do it was the slimmest evidence I had that it could be done, and he was right.

45 JoAnna Allen, striking another iconic pose in the bow, as Bill paddles her and me through the tide rip as Mill Pond slowly empties of salt water. Herons Rip is the point to the right.

46 A fleeting image of Bill's canoe ready to set out on an adventure at 5:00 a.m. on an August morning. The fog was thick and the canoe barely visible, and I was able to make several different compositions before making this one, and then the fog lifted completely. This is a great example of how photography helped me to see and experience Bill's place; I've looked for this experience of light again and never found it.

49 Bill awakes from a nap out on Brothers Island, four miles out into the ocean from the mouth of Little Kennebec Bay. This was our first ocean crossing to that island, a trip that required very calm weather, good luck, and hours of strong paddling. In all my years with Bill he and I made it out to Brothers Island twice.

52 Summer on Mill Pond in the early morning; the tide rip is in the upper left of the image. Lobstermen and clammers time their passage through the tide rip so they can take advantage of the good fishing found in Mill Pond.

53 Bill's Fjord boat sits on the mud flats as Mill Pond drains of salt water. The tide rip and our homestead site are on the distant shore.

56 Scott reveling in Mill Pond in the late afternoon light. On this day two porpoises followed our canoes through the tide rip into Mill Pond and spent the day swimming alongside our boats.

60 Bill is explaining to Emily, Lindley, and Malena how to make one of his yurt outhouses. He gave us a sketch and a few hours of explanation, then off they went to our homestead to build one. This image is taken in Bill's shop in the late afternoon. The extended glass roofline is what inspired us to build the vestibule bedrooms for Willow and Wren in our yurt.

63, top The camp kitchen, recently cleared of thick alders, was not a pretty sight, especially as the ground froze hard in October.

63, middle The barge that Danny Manchester towed through Little Kennebec Bay and into Mill Pond with much of our building supplies can be seen just beyond Malena, Helen, Josh, and Lindley. Three barge loads brought in several tons of building materials, including the old woodstove from our Vermont farm. We built a cradle for it so the five of us could carry it the half mile to the yurt.

63, bottom Early morning fog at Grays Beach, about three miles south of Dickinsons Reach, as we load up the first barge with building materials. Tim Beal, our miller, and other suppliers dropped materials off on the beach at low tide when their trucks could get close to the barge. Later the high tide would lift the barge until Danny could pull it out into the bay with his lobster boat and up the coast to our landing site.

64 Wren and Quinn, both seven years old at the time of our yurt raising, contributed many important things to the life of our community; this sign is one example. When they weren't working right alongside us, they were off building their own forts, making trails, drawing, and collecting mussels.

66 The heaviest beams and posts were hauled up the steep hillside from the barge by rope, hands, and backs. It took six of us two full days of work to unload each barge and to move those materials from the water to the yurt site.

68 Josh, Lindley, and Malena are hauling one of the seventy-five foundation stones we collected in the bay, then moved to the yurt site.

69 Setting the foundation piers took more than a week of digging, hauling, fiddling, and then more fiddling.

73 Danny Manchester brings Helen, the goats, and some fresh vegetables to Herons Rip.

74 This image is one of my favorites, taken in Mill Pond as Bill is returning to his homestead just as Danny Manchester was arriving to help us. There was great respect between the lobstering community and Bill, though I was aware that they kept some distance from one another.

77 Bill's canoe and rowing Fjord high on the salt grass. This image suggests the power of the tides at Dickinsons Reach. Two hours before I made this image, we had all paddled across Mill Pond to Lower Moose Jaw Cove on a high tide. We pulled our boats as much as possible onto the shore, where they were quickly revealed by the dropping water. This life of constantly rising and falling water is why Bill ultimately chose canoes as his preferred way of getting around.

79 I found this anonymously posted sign one morning on the floor of our yurt and felt it said much truth about everything we were doing at the yurt raising.

80 Still life of Bill's desk taken in the spring of 2011, about six months before we began the yurt raising. Bill's sketches of our yurt are on the left, answered and unanswered correspondence with people from all over the country is neatly piled together.

83 Still life of Bill's desk as he left it the morning of his death. December morning light through the windows. In the middle of his desk is a letter from Julie inquiring about his health. My last letter to him is the Taos Pueblo note card, picture showing, in the upper left of his desk. Bill's to-do lists are visible in the lower left; one of them is a reminder to himself to bring his burial authorization form with him to be notarized that morning.

85 As the photographer, I have almost no pictures of me and Bill together. This one is from 1995, a few years into our friendship. We are reading a book together in the main room of the second floor of his home. In this room he cooked his meals on a woodstove, kept his desk and papers, sat with friends to talk and to read.

86 Early evening, 2005, at Knoll Farm during one of the retreats that brought together people working for the well being of nature and of people. More than seventy-five groups met over a decade on this spot, a place we call the story circle, and the light of the fast-approaching night balanced against the warmth of the lantern glow makes this an iconic image of that era of our work.

88 Beauty, art, story, dialogue, relationships were all things we tried to bring to the surface in our work at Knoll Farm, and this image, caught one morning in the windowsill of our farmhouse, says all that.

89 Hundreds of times I tried unsuccessfully to capture the meaning and beauty of that slender, wood-chip-covered trail that runs 1.5 miles from town into the heart of Dickinsons Reach. This image comes closest to conveying the feeling of following the yellow trail through the green woods to arrive finally at Bill's world. This was taken in May 2007.

90 These are the hands of an eighty-two-year-old man who made the tool that now carves the bowl. Bill's wood-shaving tool, simple as it is, reflects a decade of experimentation with crooked knives and gouges to arrive at the least costly, most accessible way for a person to make his or her own bowl. This image was taken in the winter of 2013.

91 Beach stones, later afternoon light, Point of Maine, 2013.

92 My favorite image of Bill striking his paddler pose. This image was taken at low tide in the very early morning of August 1995. A group of twelve of us were headed south through Little Kennebec Bay to Hickey Island, and somehow Bill ended up without anyone else in his canoe, affording me a rare chance to photograph him this way.

93, top Brothers Island, four miles off the Point of Maine, Englishman's Bay, in the autumn.

93, middle Paddling two canoes out to Brothers Island, August 1995. Bill often joked, "Whoever said not to stand in a boat didn't know how to paddle one." Bill stood as he paddled in part because it allowed him to see further out into the distance and partly because of the image it created. This image of two wooden canoes lashed together with all four paddlers standing most certainly caught the attention of anyone passing in a lobster boat.

93, bottom Cedars gardened by Bill above his bridge to the summer kitchen. March 2004.

94 Bill doing trail work in 2012, tossing stones out of the creek bed to build up his foot trail.

95 Bill gardening his woodlot in the fall of 2002.

97 Bill and I gathering discarded rope we found on Halifax Island, Englishman's Bay. Many essential features of Bill's homestead were gathered by combing beaches of the islands and coves in and beyond Little Kennebec Bay.

98 The spoon that's face down is the one Bill gave me that had been carved from the pear tree originating with Gandhi. The gold watch once belonged to Scott Nearing, who gave it to Bill, who gave it to me. Underneath is a list of the many hundreds of people—some friends, some I never met—who have received the gift of a spoon from me.

104 Peter and Helen on our wedding day at Knoll Farm. Photo by our friend Courtney Bent.

107 Bill resting between sessions on the cross saw. When he rested I could gulp for air and pick up my camera to make a picture or two before going back to work. Spring 2004.

110 Bill shares his sketches of the concentric yurt at Herons Rip that this group would build together over the next two weeks.

111 JoAnna Allen in 2004.

113 Helen and Scott's hands hard at work trying to figure out the right dimensions for the wall and ceiling for Wren and Willow's bedroom.

117 Bill proudly standing atop a 2009 rebuild of the pole yurt that was constructed on that spot in 1964. This is one of the very few images that Bill asked me to take and for which he posed. It felt important to him to be able to stand atop that structure at seventy-nine years old. It was also his way of proving to us the strength of that roof design.

119 Bill's 1970 Harvard doctoral dissertation glows in the late afternoon light of his library.

122 Bill reviews that day's construction challenges for the concentric yurt at Herons Rip.

123 Bill makes a variety of drawings of aspects of the yurt to help us create it on the ground.

126 The first day of building up from the foundation.

129 Two canoes lashed together with 2×2s was how we created a surface large enough to bring in additional materials after the barge had done its work. In this fashion we brought in lumber, a generator, stacks of insulation, and a few orders of ice cream on salt and ice. This is the way that Bill brought in almost all the materials to build his structures on his homestead.

130, top   Taylor, a great friend and chef we met at Knoll Farm, came to Maine to help us with the yurt raising and lifted our spirits with fire-roasted pizza.

130, bottom   A time exposure of the dining tent and kitchen as the September full moon rises over Dickinsons Reach.

131   Bill helping to get the mud out of a kid's ear who had joined him in running and playing on the mudflats, 1997.

133   In Santa Clara del Cobra, Michoacán, Mexico, in 2007, Bill tries to find the handmade culture that originally brought him to Mexico in the 1950s.

136   In Tacambaro, Mexico, Bill was always up first, often outside or at the window making notes on what he'd been learning and how to use that knowledge back at Dickinsons Reach.

139   Bill photographed on the summit of Mount Katahdin at age 26.

146   Bill wrapped in a serape and leaning against a wall somewhere in Michoacán, Mexico in 1954 when he was 30 years old.

147   This image was taken of Bill at the North Country School where he taught math and science in the late 1950s.

148   Dan Neumeyer, Elise Miller, and young Elias Henze rowing one of the Fjord boats out to Hickey Island, 2007.

153, top   Israel Hueta Garcia of Michoacán, Mexico, creates a batea in 30 minutes with one tool and lots of skill.

153, middle   Israel Hueta Garcia's outdoor workspace impresses Bill with its simplicity, functionality, and accessibility. You don't need money and fancy tools to make a beautiful bowl, just skill and determination.

153, bottom   Bill swaps stories and small gifts with Israel's family.

156   For the two weeks of our yurt-raising workshop Bill wore the same clothes: a button-down white shirt and gray flannel pants with his collapsible measuring stick in his back pocket.

157   Still life of that measuring stick hard at work helping Bill figure out the correct proportions and dimensions for the second floor of the yurt.

159   Helen's torn Carhartts and Scott's ability came to symbolize for me their fast-moving skill and determination in building Willow and Wren's rooms.

160   Bill is the first person shown pulling the metal cable in this 1974 image of a yurt raising. Bill subsequently figured out more clever and less labor intensive ways to tighten the cable that supports his yurts.

161   Bill atop the second floor begging for more ceiling boards to be passed up to him.

163   This is what the yurt looked like before we added the roof of the second floor. Each step of construction created something visually arresting that we then covered up.

164, top   Elizabeth, Helen, and Margaret work on creating the triangular windows for the second floor.

164, middle and bottom   The "design/build" nature of Bill's approach to building a yurt is best seen in these two images where Bill first sketched out what we could build for an entranceway to the yurt that would be both functional and beautiful. And then Peter Lamb led us in building it over the following two days.

167   In the end, hard rain engulfed us for only four of the thirteen days of the yurt raising, but it made our lives wet and cold and gave us very difficult conditions in which to work.

172   Wren didn't seem to mind the rain much, running from task to task. Here she saws wall boards under the guidance of JoAnna Allen.

175 Gardening the forest, felling trees, stacking split wood was such an art form for Bill that each place he worked became beautiful through his labors. I loved photographing these woodpiles so much I had to consciously restrict my diet over the years.

177 And some of that wood that he gardened he also shaped into spoons and bowls that took on characteristic forms that were as elegant as his yurts. Virtually any observer could readily identify one of Bill's spoons or bowls because its proportions and form were so intentionally and gracefully continued from occasion to occasion.

179 A favorite image of mine made in 2003 because it portrays my life with Bill: the carving knife he gave me and the old Leica camera with which I often photographed him. These objects were in the windowsill of our house at Knoll Farm.

180 Bill felling birch at Dickinsons Reach for spoons and bowls, 2008.

181 Bill uses a drawknife to trim a bunch of cedar shingles for the concentric yurt. Each shingle would need to be hand-trimmed into something like a long pizza slice to be nailed in place on a round roof.

183, top Courtney Bent took this image of me carving a serving spoon in my own shop at Knoll Farm.

183, middle Dusk in November at Lunch Rock in 2001. Dan and Bill enjoy a few slices of orange by the giant stone they helped to split with freezing water a decade or more before.

183, bottom Eventually I became skilled at making tools and carving bowls and spoons. This is a bowl that I made of Knoll Farm cherry while traveling through Guatemala. When I came to a village, I found a public tree under which

to carve and soon would be meeting people interested to know what I was making. In this fashion I met the folks who ran a school that the following year our daughter Wren would attend. Spoon carving became the way I connected with people and shared my soul.

186 These art forms called woodpiles were in a process of long-term transition. Eventually, two years before they would end up in Bill's stove, they would get moved into the bottom floor of his yurt. In this way he had a decade's worth of cut wood slowly moving toward his woodstove and being beautiful all along the way.

189 Among my last images of Bill, this one of his hands was taken while he worked on the yurt he completed for himself just before his death. When I reflect on all the portraits I made of Bill over two decades the few that reflect his soul most completely are the ones I made of his hands.

190 March 2010. Bill works at his desk in his Library Yurt.

193 Bill's mail, as he left it, stacked on his desk on November 26 and photographed there on November 30, 2013.

194 Bill beachcombing on Halifax Island, August 1995.

198 The bird's-eye view of our yurt before the second-floor roof was added. You can see the metal ring that would come to support that roof. Our friends are hard at work shingling the first-floor roof about fifteen feet below me as I stand atop the internal tower. This image was taken with a 10.5 wide-angle lens, which reveals my toes at the bottom.

199 The workshop was over, and we were racing to get the yurt weathertight. These were days

of rain and fog when we had to put on our warmest clothes, tie a safety rope around our waists, and just shingle until we dropped. Here, Helen, Scott, and Rani are working hard to finish shingling the second-floor roofline.

200   Bill telling stories and singing songs by the fire that we lit every night after dinner outside the kitchen tent. Some can be seen still carving or sanding their dinner plates, which means this must have been the first or second night of the yurt raising.

201, *left*   Elizabeth, Michael, and George work from the tower to bend the second-floor roofline into place. The two metal rings onto which the second-floor roofline was bent and secured are clearly visible.

201, *right*   A photographer, filmmaker, and builder, our friend Michael asks to have a board handed up to him for the second-floor roof.

202, *top*   Margaret stretches herself out while twenty feet up in the air. She's securing each of the second-floor ceiling boards to the metal ring with wire to keep the beautiful convex curve of the second-floor roofline.

202, *middle*   Casually up on the roof, Bill confers with Margaret and Isaac about the windows. Many projects were going on at once in this picture: shingling the first-floor roof, making the second-floor windows, and shaping the second-floor roof.

202, *bottom*   Helen's at the very top of the yurt, at a dangerously steep angle, that required a good grip with your toes and a safety rope, but the views from up there were spectacular. Without slippery rain, working on the roof shingling was a meditative practice punctuated by the call of birds and the light pounding of hammers.

204   Always designing and creating, Bill had wheelbarrows on his mind when he died. This plan was on his desk the morning he left, and he had just asked a number of friends to help him get different materials to build it over the winter.

205   Bill's errant white hair catches the last of the afternoon light as he puts in place the spacer between the second-floor ceiling and roof.

206   On a drenching cold afternoon during the yurt raising, Bill took his regular afternoon nap in this decidedly public spot, the floor of the construction site. He swept up a big pile of shavings and went to bed.

207   The roof is now on the second floor, and the entrance vestibule is up over the front door, creating yet another new experience of light. This image was taken from the kids' bedrooms that Helen and Scott had worked so hard to create.

209   The main structure of our yurt is complete, and the girls' bedrooms are going up in the left of the picture. Helen and Scott built the floor, then the walls, then connected the rooflines.

210   The weather turned cold quickly, and sandals and shorts were traded almost overnight for rubber boots and down jackets. Here Helen is starting on our door. The scope of work to be done to make our yurt weathertight before returning home was overwhelming.

212   The morning that Bill came by and visited us, sitting against the wall and taking in his creation, will not be forgotten.

213   This long exposure taken during the clear night before a hurricane arrived on the coast will long be one of my favorites. We had moved out of our tent and settled into our new home for just a few days before the weather and the calendar required that we head back to Vermont.

215 One of Bill's favorite sweaters, knitted for him by a friend and then "improved" by him by adding the straps at the hands and the waist where the sweater had begun to unravel. The straps were traditional Mongolian yurt bands that Bill repurposed to keep his sweater going. Though I took this picture while Bill was still alive, it speaks to me most clearly of his passing.

218 Bill tours another young brother and sister through his magical homestead, this time in 1996, walking the bridge over the stream toward his home. Mill Pond at half tide is visible beyond them. Three generations of kids came to know Bill in his place, though none were his own children.

220 In the summer of 2010 Bill managed to walk back into his homestead just three months after a heart attack and major surgery. There were times when we saw him weak and disoriented, and times when he was atop a roof banging nails. After twenty years of photographing Bill in his place, pictures like this were hard for me to make, yet I knew they were also part of Bill's reality of growing old and seeking the help of his community.

221 Taz and Maria, dear old friends of Bill's. Taz grew up spending a great deal of time with Bill and often worked alongside him on yurt workshops and at his homestead as an adult.

224 The view of our second-floor ceiling at moonrise, October 2011, the evening before we headed home.

229 My notebook and carving from the last meeting of the Dickinsons Reach Community that Bill participated in. At this meeting, he told us about how he would like to die and to be buried.

232 Bill's desk and main room in May 2013. On his desk is the prototype of the roof that he would put on his last yurt six months later.

235 Bill and Helen talk yurt design in Bill's shop on a hot August afternoon.

236 This day in August 2013 I took a series of images, my last of Bill, as he walked past his creations. The quality of the day, the casualness of his walk, the way he leaned into Helen or carried his tools made me think he was content with this great life he had lived.

238 This concluding image by Michael Sacca was taken one winter morning when Bill was visiting Michael in Tunbridge, Vermont. They were engaged in conversation and Michael had his large camera (a Mamiya 7 which makes 2¼″ × 3¼″ negatives) nearby in the hope of making a portrait. I'm glad he did make that portrait, as we cherish this last image of a pensive, warm Bill Coperthwaite.

Time-Lapse Photographs
of Yurt Raising

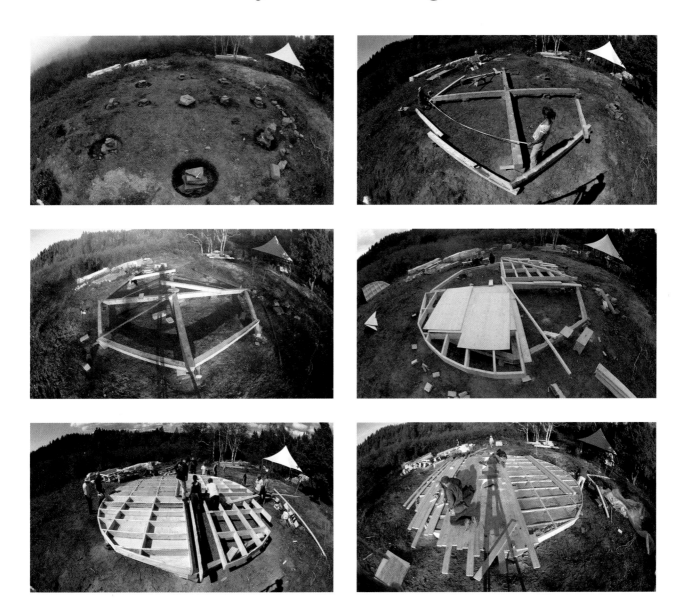

About the Authors

Andrew Dillon Bustin

Peter has become a leader for the American conservation movement by creating a life in conservation as a photographer, writer, and storyteller about the relationship between people and place. For the last fifteen years, Peter has focused his energies on bringing together and strengthening the worlds of conservation and social justice and offering those professions his experience with story, facilitation, and relationship to nature. He is the coeditor of *Our Land, Ourselves*, author of *The Great Remembering* and *What Is a Whole Community*, and coauthor of *Coming to Land in a Troubled World*. He collaborated with Bill Coperthwaite as the photographer for *A Handmade Life*. You can learn more about him at www.peterforbes.org.

Helen's life as an educator, farmer, and writer follows a career in book publishing, where she was an acquiring editor for W. W. Norton and the publisher of their Countryman Press imprint. She is the editor of *Dead Reckoning: Tales of the Great Explorers 1800–1900* and many other titles. She and Peter Forbes are married and live at Knoll Farm in Vermont. Helen runs their organic family farm, mentors beginning farmers, and homeschools their youngest daughter, while continuing her writing life. You can learn more about Knoll Farm at www.knollfarm.org.

A Handmade Life describes Bill Coperthwaite's ongoing experiments with hand tools, hand-grown and gathered food, and handmade shelter, clothing, and furnishings out into the world to challenge and inspire. His writing is both philosophical and practical, exploring themes of beauty, work, education, and design while giving instruction on the hand-crafting of the necessities of life: house, tools, clothing, and furniture. Richly illustrated with luminous color photographs by Peter Forbes, the book is a moving and inspirational testament to a new/old way of life. Chelsea Green, 2007.